Luminos is the Open Access monograph publishing program from UC Press. Luminos provides a framework for preserving and reinvigorating monograph publishing for the future and increases the reach and visibility of important scholarly work. Titles published in the UC Press Luminos model are published with the same high standards for selection, peer review, production, and marketing as those in our traditional program. www.luminosoa.org

Circulations

Circulations

*Modernist Imaginaries of Colonialism
and Decolonization in Papua New Guinea*

Courtney Handman

UNIVERSITY OF CALIFORNIA PRESS

University of California Press
Oakland, California

Suggested citation: Handman, C. *Circulations: Modernist Imaginaries of Colonialism and Decolonization in Papua New Guinea*. Oakland: University of California Press, 2025. DOI: https://doi.org/10.1525/luminos.231

Library of Congress Cataloging-in-Publication Data

Names: Handman, Courtney
Title: Circulations : modernist imaginaries of colonialism and decolonization in Papua New Guinea / Courtney Handman.
Description: Oakland, California : University of California Press, [2025] | Includes bibliographical references and index.
Identifiers: LCCN 2024043570 | ISBN 9780520416000 (paperback) | ISBN 9780520416017 (ebook)
Subjects: LCSH: Communication—Papua New Guinea. | Papua New Guinea—Colonial influence.
Classification: LCC P92.P33 H36 2025 | DDC 302.209953—dc23/eng/20241230

LC record available at https://lccn.loc.gov/2024043570

GPSR Authorized Representative: Easy Access System Europe, Mustamäe tee 50, 10621 Tallinn, Estonia, gpsr.requests@easproject.com

34   33   32   31   30   29   28   27   26   25
10   9   8   7   6   5   4   3   2   1

For my mother

CONTENTS

MAPS

FIGURES

Coming to the end of this project, it has been a pleasure to try to think through all of the people who have influenced my thinking and writing on it. The list of folks here is undoubtedly incomplete, just as my thanks are necessarily inadequate for acknowledging how much intellectual inspiration and guidance they have given me.

Some of my initial thinking about this book began while I was teaching at Reed College. In addition to many students, I thank especially Paul Silverstein and Sarah Wagner-McCoy for conversations that helped to shape this project at the start. I began the primary research for this book only after coming to the Department of Anthropology at the University of Texas at Austin. Many colleagues here and in other departments on campus have made this a welcoming and intellectually stimulating place to work. I want to especially thank Kamran Ali, Craig Campbell, Jason Cons, Tony Di Fiore, John Hartigan, Elizabeth Keating, Ward Keeler, Erin Lentz, Becca Lewis, Maria Sidorkina, Jacob Stewart-Halevy, Pauline Strong, and Tony Webster. In addition, a number of people who started as graduate students have, over the years, become colleagues from whom I have learned so much, especially Krishantha Fedricks, Alex Kreger, Deina Rabie, Morgan Siewert, Nora Tyeklar, and Aniruddhan Vasudevan. I also thank the students from the Media and Circulation graduate seminars; I looked forward every week to their insights and excitement.

Some very kind people read drafts of one or more chapters and gave extremely helpful feedback on them, including Ilana Gershon, Alex Golub, Jessica Greenberg, Rob Moore, Sarah Muir, Alejandro Paz, James Slotta, Rupert Stasch, Matt Tomlinson, and Sarah Wagner-McCoy. A well-timed and incredibly rewarding writing retreat with Jessica Greenberg was essential to getting this book into the final shape that it took.

I have been inspired and enlightened by many friends and colleagues, sometimes with a brief but brilliant comment and sometimes with patient hours-long conversations. Without being able to account for every chat or email exchange I've had over the past few years, I want to particularly thank David Akin, Barbara Anderson, Rachel Apone, John Barker, Jon Bialecki, Rob Blunt, Jocelyn Chua, Lily Chumley, Lise Dobrin, Peter Dwyer, Ayala Fader, Christiane Falck, Luke Fleming, Sue Gal, Niloofar Haeri, Nick Harkness, Jordan Haug, Angie Heo, Jacob Hickman, Robin Hide, Ingie Hovland, Dan Jorgensen, Hillary Kaell, Webb Keane, Derrick Lemons, Lauren Leve, Michael Lucey, Tanya Luhrmann, Fraser Macdonald, Paul Manning, Debra McDougall, Francesca Merlan, Townes Middleton, Daniel Midena, Rob Moore, Costas Nakassis, Minna Opas, John Durham Peters, Josh Reno, Joel Robbins, Alan Rumsey, China Scherz, Bambi Schieffelin, Ryan Schram, Tori Stead, Greg Thompson, Matt Tomlinson, Dave Troolin, Christine Winter, Rihan Yeh, and Chip Zuckerman. It was my great privilege to work with Michael Silverstein as a graduate student, and his thinking remains foundational to all the work that I do.

Some of the most important conversations I've had about this project happened when I was invited to speak about my work at UC Berkeley, UC San Diego, the University of Chicago, Cambridge University, the University of Melbourne, Australian National University, Brigham Young University, and, at the University of Texas at Austin, the Department of Religious Studies and the SALSA conference. I thank the organizers of these events and especially the audiences, who not only suffered through early versions of the chapters that appear here but provided excellent feedback on them.

Research for this project involved a number of trips to various archives: the Archives of the Evangelical Lutheran Church in America, the Archives of the Evangelical Lutheran Church of Papua New Guinea, the National Archives of Australia, and the National Archives of Papua New Guinea. Countless archivists put up with my endless records requests with great patience. I thank them for their invaluable help. I also thank Teena Gementiza, who photographed many files at the National Archives of Australia after I had returned to the US.

While this research did not directly involve ethnographic work with communities in the Waria Valley, friends and interlocutors there remain important influences on how I understand Papua New Guinea's colonial history and postcolonial present. I would particularly like to thank Jehu Ttopoqogo, who did so much for us when my husband and I lived in Titio village. I also thank Dzaro Ahe and Dansu Khara, Steven Ttopoqogo, and Hoopusu Gomai. The late Rev. Mumure Ttopoqogo was an extraordinary person, and his loss is keenly felt.

Funding for research trips to archives in Australia and Papua New Guinea came from a Humanities Research Award, from the Department of Anthropology, and from the Edward A. Clark Center for Australian and New Zealand Studies, all at the University of Texas. I thank Rhonda Evans, director of the Clark Center, for her support. A grant from the College of Liberal Arts made it possible to

ACKNOWLEDGMENTS xiii

publish this book open access, and I thank Associate Dean Rob Crosnoe for this subvention funding.

I want to thank our intrepid Department of Anthropology chair, Kamran Ali, for additional support for the subvention and for making meetings with one's chair far more intellectually engaging and funny than they had any business being. In the Anthropology office, Thomas Fawcett's work as a source of administrative knowledge, music recommendations, and good vibes is much appreciated. At the University of California Press, Kate Marshall and Chad Attenborough have been a joy to work with. From initial conversations, to soliciting incredibly helpful reviews of the manuscript, to the later stages of bringing the book to production, I could not imagine a more seamless process.

This book would not have been finished without some important moments of setting it aside in favor of more recuperative experiences. Karen Christensen and Rhea Nelson helped me keep things in perspective and reminded me what it was like to be a struggling student.

I want to thank my family for their unflagging support, from the earliest days of graduate school to the present. I would never have stuck with it all without the encouragement from my mother, Judy Smith, to whom this book is dedicated. I wish my father, Ken Handman, were still here so I could celebrate this project with him. I am fortunate to have more parents than most, and I thank Drew Smith, Alana Handman, and Karen Slotta for their love and support. Chris Handman and the rest of the CHEB clan always provide welcome respite and just the right amount of wackiness.

Finally, it is my great joy to share my life with Adele Slotta and James Slotta. Although I am hereby forbidding her from becoming an anthropologist herself, Adele's questions and observations about the world as she grows into being a thoughtful, curious young adult have been inspiring. James Slotta is a true partner in all respects. This book would not exist without all of the fun, exhilarating, demanding, and occasionally mildly aggravating conversations we have had together. I cannot thank you enough.

. . .

Several of the chapters take material from earlier publications. Portions of chapter 1 appear in "The Spatiotemporal Transformations of Lutheran Airplanes," *Signs and Society* 7(1): 68–95. Chapter 2 is a revised version of "Languages without Subjects: On the Interior(s) of Colonial New Guinea," *HAU Journal of Ethnographic Theory* 7(1): 207–28. A small amount of material in chapters 2 and 3 is from "Language at the Limits of the Human," *Comparative Studies in Society and History* 65(4): 726–50. Chapter 4 takes some sections from "Ritual, Media, and the Here-and-Now of Decolonization," in *The Oxford Handbook of Ritual Language*, edited by David Tavárez. Parts of chapter 6 come from "Defying Predictions: Global Bureaucracy and the Art of Not Making Guesses about the Future of New Guinea," *Oceania* 94(2).

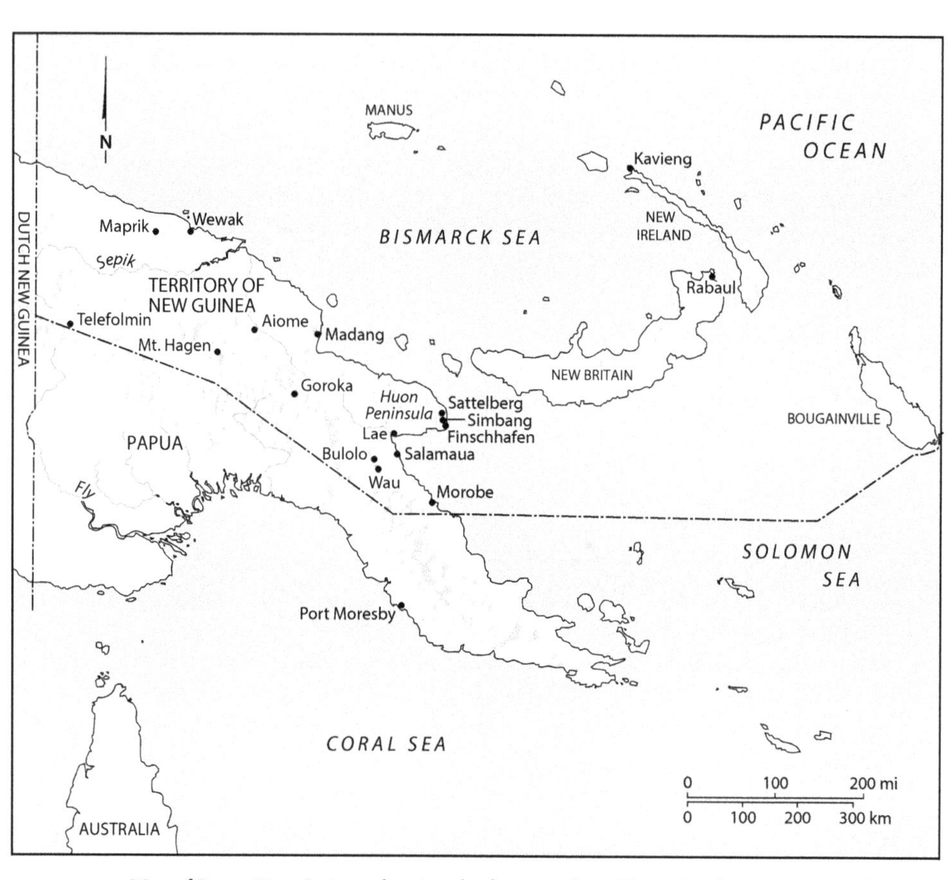

MAP 1. Map of Papua New Guinea, showing the former colonial boundary between Papua, the Territory of New Guinea, and Dutch New Guinea. (Map by Bill Nelson)

Introduction

Like many other books about Papua New Guinea, this book starts by pointing out two important features: Papua New Guinea is very mountainous, and it is the most linguistically diverse place in the world. Unlike many other books that treat these two features as determining causes of material conditions there, this book looks at how these mountains and languages became the primary icons of an overarching colonial and decolonial fixation on problems of communication—problems of getting people, talk, and material goods moving across Papua New Guinea's social and geographic space. In order to understand how mountain peaks and dialect chains became so central to the story of Papua New Guinea's past and future, we need to understand the modernist imaginaries of circulation that colonizers and decolonizers brought to the country.

An excerpt from a patrol report written at the tail end of the colonial era gives some flavor of the obsession with circulation.[1] In the months leading up to Papua New Guinea's 1972 self-government (before official independence in 1975), an Australian patrol officer named Robin Barclay was tasked with going on a special patrol to establish formal government contact with a few communities in the remote areas around the Nomad Station in Papua. After a long and difficult walk through rough, mountainous territory, during which he managed to find just forty people who had not previously been recorded on any earlier census rolls, Barclay was in a philosophical mood. He included several appendices to his report, one of which offered sardonic cautions to any officer attempting the kind of patrol he had just undertaken:

In this Year of Grace, if one were to subject the Territory to the most rigid microscopic scrutiny, paying special attention to the most remote corners, one may, if favoured by fortune, find some inaccessible small valley where perhaps 20 or 30 people may eke out a precarious existence totally oblivious, you feel certain, of the Administration. If you are assured by the most thorough research that they remain in their pristine state, then you may be moved to contemplate a journey there. Sent on your way by the stirring marching music of massed bands, backed by the rousing cheers of assembled throngs, you may endure weeks of unspeakable hardship and determinedly overcome insurmountable obstacles, buoyed along by visions of the shining goal. At last, after the most heart-rending suffering, you arrive, and as you make tremulous enquiry you will very likely find that the Government had passed this way 10 or 20 years ago, and you will find to your unbounded dismay that the group was then known by another name. But if, perchance, you discover to your delighted surprise that no one has yet visited here, you may be very smartly pulled up when they proudly produce Exhibit 'A', a man whose curiosity had moved him to visit a Patrol in some neighboring area, and he will regale you in great detail with tales of what the Government is, and what it does, and you will find his assessments surprisingly accurate. But if you survive these two great stumbling-blocks unscathed, you must be cautious and not give way to transports of joy just yet, because now you are to be dealt the coup-de-grace: the final ego-shattering blow. As you prematurely launch yourself into impassioned speech you will observe a look of polite boredom settle over their faces. Some obnoxiously officious person from over the hill when trading his tomahawks and knives here has ticked them off for their repugnant practices and unsavoury habits: the pervasive effects of the ubiquitous Government have already regulated their lives in absentia and they have heard it all before.[2]

The fantasies of isolation that Barclay skewers in this quote were an abiding preoccupation of colonial agents across Papua New Guinea. He captures both the romance of remoteness that was part of the lore of colonial history there and the reality of circulations happening beyond the view or control of the government. Massed bands and cheering crowds rarely, if ever, gathered to see a patrol officer tramp off into the remote bush, yet his sarcastic invocation of them points to the ways that administration agents thought of patrols as both extremely difficult and extremely important. It is, then, an "ego-shattering blow" to realize that after a long slog, the colonial officer has come not to a "pristine" community free of outside influence, but instead to a place that had experienced government-once-removed in the form of bossy neighbors happily scolding their trading partners through their repetition of administration lines about sanitation or health. Rather than being the communicative primitives of modernist imagination, they are bored. "They have heard it all before."

What makes this commentary so compelling is not just that it thematizes the colonial obsession with the difficulty of traveling to and communicating with remote communities living in mountainous territory, each speaking a different language. It also highlights the corresponding colonial paranoia that communication might not be so difficult for others, Papua New Guineans in particular. The colonial desire to be the heroic savior of isolated communities meant that patrol officers created problems of circulation even where they did not exist. That is, colonial concerns about circulation did not mitigate so much as intensify experiences of remoteness, up to and including forcing underlings to go on months-long patrols in search of the last few people who could be compelled to collaborate in a drama of "first contact." Patrol Officer Barclay's commentary indicates that colonizer concerns about circulation were not inevitable or necessary, but rather were the outcome of people taking particularly modernist assumptions about circulation with them to the colonies.

This book is an account of how modernist assumptions about circulation have profoundly structured both colonialism and decolonization. Not only did colonizers in places like Papua New Guinea spend a lot of their time dealing with problems of circulation, but they seemed to spend much of the rest of their time talking with one another about those problems. Newspaper articles, patrol reports, missionary memoirs, United Nations (UN) resolutions, and any number of other documents are filled with comments about how there were too many mountains and too many languages in Papua New Guinea to make modern communications possible. Papua New Guinea became defined by an imaginary of circulatory primitivity, a sense of primitivity that is based on the incapacity to move people, goods, or talk easily.

But it was not just the colonizers who thought so. Even those invested in the rapid decolonization of Papua New Guinea, particularly the anticolonial members of the UN Trusteeship Council, likewise thought that its circulatory primitivity fundamentally defined it. Moreover, both colonizer and decolonizer argued that this could be overcome only through the management of communication infrastructures, bureaucratic information flows, and the introduction of English. And yet the development of such channels tended to produce a greater sense of fragmentation. Decolonizers and colonizers were caught up in a paradox of connection, in which an increase in channels only made what seemed like communicative blockages stand out in greater relief.

More broadly, this book is an attempt to use questions of communicative circulation as a lens on colonialism and decolonization, bringing into the same framework infrastructure, information flows, and language. The chapters are concerned with how different people and institutions tried to create communicative channels across what appeared to them to be incredible barriers. By channels, I mean institutionally and culturally codified means of enabling communication, including things like radio networks, bureaucratic forms, and lingua francas. Communicative channels are material, cultural, and linguistic formations, but they are reducible neither to the material technologies of communication networks nor to the cultural enactments of linguistic interaction. This twin attention to infrastructure and language means, on the one hand, that I emphasize linguistic issues to a greater extent than studies of infrastructure usually do, but that, on the other hand, I situate language in terms of a broader framework of communicative technologies in a way that scholars of language-in-use rarely do. In contrast to studies that are framed in terms of interaction, my focus on communicative channels of circulation emphasizes the historical, cultural, and ideological formations that precede interaction. What forces came together such that Patrol Officer Barclay had to go on a long and lonely patrol in search of a few unregistered soon-to-be Papua New Guinean citizens?

MODERNITY AND CIRCULATION IN PAPUA NEW GUINEA

As a small nation-state in the Pacific Islands region that encountered European empires relatively late, Papua New Guinea may seem to be an outlier in histories of colonialism and decolonization. However, the particular conditions there offer an exceptionally clear example of the central role of the modernist imaginaries of circulation in these processes. First and foremost, Papua New Guinea has a set of features that people saw as "natural" barriers that make channel formation difficult. The second largest island in the world, New Guinea (which today is split between Papua New Guinea and Indonesian West Papua) has a massive central cordillera with peaks over forty-five hundred meters high and imposing coastal mountain ranges reaching almost as tall (see map 1 and figure 1). Papua New Guinea is also the most linguistically diverse place in the world: not only are there about eight hundred languages spoken there, but the median number of speakers of these languages is twelve hundred people (Kik et al. 2021). The sheer number and height of the mountains, paired with the extraordinary number of languages, have led to endless commentary on fragmentation and immobility. This was, as already noted, the colonial perspective that led to an obsession with circulation.

Second, aspects of Papua New Guinea's history make the continuities between the colonial and decolonization eras particularly visible. With respect to the colonial era, the concern with blocked circulation can be seen in part as a reflection of the fragmentation and incoherence of the colonial state. Papua New Guinea was in fact two colonies—Papua in the southeast and New Guinea in the northeast—that were, at different points in the twentieth century, colonized by, administered on behalf of, or occupied by the UK, Germany, Australia, Japan, the League of Nations, and the UN. Within these two territories, five major Christian missions acted as powerful states-within-states (joined later by scores of smaller missions). The Lutheran missions in the Territory of New Guinea, which I discuss in the first part of this book, are an excellent example. They had their own road, shipping, aviation, and radio networks; their own printing presses and distribution centers for Bibles, hymnals, and newsletters; their own schools, hospitals, and economic aid organizations. Yet these networks and systems were only ever partly and poorly integrated into the colonial administration, a fact that caused endless problems for both the missions and the administration in the years leading

FIGURE 1. An example of the kind of forested and mountainous terrain that covers much of Papua New Guinea: the Waria River Valley, Morobe Province, looking southwest toward the western end of the Owen Stanley Range. (Photo by author)

to independence. The circulation of information, people, and goods around Papua and New Guinea was often made difficult by the many institutional and bureaucratic blockages created by constantly fluctuating forms of colonial control.

In the years after World War II, when the newly formed UN Trusteeship Council oversaw Australia's administration of the Territory of New Guinea, this problem only became exacerbated. The Trusteeship Council, and especially the anticolonial delegations on it, pushed for Papua New Guinea's independence early in the 1950s, before many of the local independence movements themselves got going. In other words, the most explicit demands for decolonization initially appeared as top-down demands from a global bureaucracy. Although many of the famous stories of postwar decolonization across the Global South assume a bottom-up, unifying nationalism acting as a catalyst for independence, Papua New Guinea's history gives us a different perspective on anticolonialism and decolonization. Particularly in the 1950s, when Papua New Guineans' critical stance toward the colonial administration could look more like a set of religious events than political mobilizations, some of the most recognizable forms of decolonization for people outside of Papua New Guinea were organized by the channels of international bureaucratic communication. Indeed, because Papua New Guineans' critical stances were not necessarily recognized as political demands, groups like the Trusteeship Council felt that they needed to bureaucratically manage decolonization themselves.

Finally, Papua New Guinea offers an important vantage point for thinking about the formation of communicative channels because of the prominent role that Tok Pisin, the English-based lingua franca, has played in its colonial and decolonial history. If anything ever seemed like a potential solution to the communicative problems of Papua New Guinea, it was Tok Pisin. As a pidgin language, Tok Pisin's origins can be traced to the period from 1867 to 1914, when roughly two hundred thousand Pacific Islanders were "blackbirded" into indentured labor (Firth 1976) to work on plantations across the Pacific.[3] The men from the Territory of New Guinea who were coerced into labor contracts in German Samoa and in coastal New Guinea first helped develop and spread Tok Pisin (Mühlhäusler 1978), and it became the default language of the colonial state in German New Guinea (later, the Territory of New Guinea).[4] Here would seem to be the answer to the colonizer's prayers for communicative ease in the most linguistically diverse part of the world.

Yet antipathy to Tok Pisin was widespread. With few exceptions, administrators, missionaries, and even the anticolonial delegates from the UN all wanted to see Tok Pisin disappear. Tok Pisin was a language born of circulation—in particular, the circulation of laborers—yet it seemed to put to the test the idea that circulation itself was modernizing or healthy. It became instead a sign of the ways in which circulation could be disruptive, disorganized, and insufficiently transformative.

While I discuss events from as early as the 1920s and as late as the 1960s in this book, most of my discussion clusters around the 1950s, when questions of circulation were particularly pronounced. I focus primarily on what was known as the Territory of New Guinea (in contrast to Papua to its south), where both the Lutheran missions and the UN were active. Starting with the continual emphasis on mountains and languages as what seemed to be circulatory blockages, the chapters to come focus on how the colonial multiplication of communication media made the emphasis on remoteness greater rather than smaller: teleradios, airplanes, and lingua francas made the place seem all the more disconnected and fragmented. Yet Australian administrators, foreign missionaries, and international observers kept coming back to the idea that managing the problem of circulation might be the way to fix the colonial problem, leading to Trusteeship Council attempts to take over information flow, and in some ways to take over *through* information flow. This fixation on circulation produced a concurrent concern with the threat of free-moving information beyond either colonial or decolonial restriction. This meant attending to both colonizers' fears of "native" telepathy and their Cold War fears of encroaching Asian communism.

Across all these different concerns, Tok Pisin stood in as the image of circulation gone wrong, and as possible proof that solving the circulation issue would not be the magic bullet so many hoped for. Throughout this book, I move between analyses of communicative infrastructures and the discourses about them on the one hand, and the attempts to eradicate Tok Pisin on the other. The various ways in which Tok Pisin was made into a deficient language tell a story of how linguistic channels that allow information to flow can get figured instead as linguistic boundaries. The ways in which colonizers and decolonizers came to condemn Tok Pisin equally (but for different reasons) are important components of the constant effort to make Papua New Guinea into a space of circulatory primitivity that could be technocratically overcome.

Many scholars who have looked at Papua New Guinea's political independence hoping to find the classic story of nationalist mobilization leading to decolonization have tended to be disappointed. In place of that story, two narratives have been dominant: either that the colonial experience was so brief and diffuse—at least in contrast to the extreme violence and lengthy history of colonial disruption in parts of Africa, for example—that an anticolonial movement could not form; or that Australia never really stopped being the colonial ruler. That is, either Papua New Guinea was never fully colonized or it never fully stopped being colonized (Golub and Handman 2024). Both narratives frustratingly put the emphasis and agency almost exclusively on Australia's actions.

There are two ways to try to reframe the discussion. The first is to focus greater attention on the projects of decolonization that Papua New Guineans engaged in, both during the final years of official colonial rule and in contemporary moments of navigating the relationship both citizens and the state have to Australia. A number of scholars are developing this critical historiographic response to the dominant narratives of Papua New Guinea's colonization, highlighting how much work Papua New Guineans were doing to critique, reform, or end their colonial experience, even if they were doing so using genres of speech and action that differed from those of canonical political movements (see, e.g., Gammage 1975, Waiko 1996, Gardner and Waters 2013, Shilliam 2015, Banivanua Mar 2016, Stead 2019, Dobrin and Golub 2020, Martin 2021a, Martin 2021b, Swan 2020, Smith 2021, Golub 2024, Wu 2024).

A second way to reframe the discussion is to critically analyze the conditions under which the idea of Papua New Guinea's decolonization became unthinkable and, consequently, the conditions under which the Australia-focused narratives could become so dominant in popular and scholarly conversations. What made the decolonial or critical responses to Australia so hard for colonizers and even anticolonial allies to recognize? I argue that the imaginaries of modernist circulation played an important role in why colonial actors and anticolonial allies did not recognize Papua New Guineans as political agents. Because this book is focused primarily on these modernist imaginaries and the ways they organized the kinds of colonial and decolonial perspectives that administrators, missionaries, and UN delegates had, it is also primarily focused on those administrators, missionaries, and delegates, and less on Papua New Guineans themselves. I look to the growing scholarship that is telling those narratives, while also suggesting that even a bilateral focus on Australians and Papua New Guineans might not be sufficient, as Guha (2003) and others have observed. A broader orientation to the then emerging institutions of the postwar global order can contribute to the reconceptualization of Papua New Guinea's decolonial history.

In the rest of this introduction, I discuss circulation from several perspectives. I first look at the place that circulation has in theories of modernity in broad terms, before discussing circulation's role in colonialism and decolonization. I then look at how different scholars have discussed circulation in terms of what I am characterizing as communicative infrastructures, encompassing both technosocial infrastructures and languages.

MODERNITY AND CIRCULATION

In the contemporary United States, where I am based, circulation is often discussed in the particular sense of information flow or the information economy. Both scholars and participants in public discourse define places and times by the ways in which information flows within them, from Cold War cultures of secrecy to the Information Age to the current concerns about misinformation. Characterizing places and times in terms of information flows has also meant characterizing the kinds of transformations that could or should happen there: information should spread more widely, more carefully, more quickly. It means characterizing the kinds of fixes that policymakers focus on: developing better telecommunication networks, creating institutional repositories or authoritative information, or even just opening up roads. In other words, information flow is a particular perspective to take when looking at a place. But this is just one instantiation of a broader modernist project that equates circulation with different forms of progress.

As Wolfgang Schivelbusch (1980) discussed in his account of how passengers experienced railroad travel in the nineteenth-century United States, the modernist bourgeois concept of circulation assumed that the flow of goods, information, or people is a moral and economic positive. The jump into modernity was theorized as a jump into mobility (Simmel 1997). Modernity is supposed to involve the capacity to not be held back by tradition or connection to the past, so much so that literal and figurative movement is, in itself, salutary and freeing: modernist ideas about circulation assume "that communication, exchange, motion bring to humanity enlightenment and progress, and that isolation and disconnection are the obstacles to be overcome" (Schivelbusch 1980: 197). Circulation is health.

The primary institutions of modernity—markets, publics, and nations, to name just a few—normatively (but do not actually) depend on the free circulation of goods and information (see Mattelart 2000, Day 2001). In each of these cases, information flow is understood to be either the natural state of things ("truth will out") or, if not natural, then at least what ought to exist in order to create flourishing communities. The hackers who leak state secrets, for example, or the transhumanists who want to upload their minds to the cloud both work under the assumption that information should move without friction or obstruction (Hayles 1999: 13). Contemporary concerns about misinformation or disinformation notwithstanding, the modernist assumption has been that more information flow is better: people would in general be better citizens, capitalists, scientists, or psychological subjects with more talk and more information, with fewer paywalls and more open access.

For theorists of modernity's main institutions, such as Adam Smith (1970 [1776]), Jürgen Habermas (1989), Max Weber (1978), and Benedict Anderson (1991), the organized flow of things and language in many ways constituted the institutions themselves. The invisible hand of the market, as Smith describes it, flexes its guiding powers only when sellers know where their goods are wanted and when buyers know where prices are lowest. In this model, markets and prices themselves are incredibly powerful means for rapidly and easily communicating information (Hayek 1945). Flows of information produce divisions of labor, as markets require an organized array of knowledge, goods, and people in communicative contact. Even in market ideologies that assume that the circulation of goods may need to be regulated or channeled in particular ways, that is because of a sense that goods, like truth, want to be free to move.

Modernist imaginaries of circulation are about not just the salutary role of the flow of talk or goods across space and time, but also the ways in which this horizontal flow creates hierarchically greater totalities. This sense of communication producing a social whole might be clearest in Habermas's story of the bourgeois public in liberal democracy or Anderson's story of the imagined national community under print capitalism. The communicative imaginaries of publics and nations involve not only co-occurring moments of interaction among geographically discrete groups of people, but a sense that some higher-order entity emerges out of—by flowing through—these local events. For Anderson, this included not just the rituals of newspaper and novel reading that could offer a sense of simultaneity in homogeneous, empty time, but also the "creole pilgrimages" that state functionaries undertook as they moved through bureaucratic structures (I return to this below). Circulation, either directed or undirected, hierarchically organizes itself into these larger-scale institutions.

Colonial moderns took these background assumptions, about modernity being characterized by freely flowing information and goods, with them to the peripheries in which they worked, hoping to usher in modernity by inducing circulation. Not only were places where information did not or could not flow freely considered non-modern because of this lack of information flow, but colonial attention fixated on the obstacles to movement as an almost separate plane of primitivity to worry about. To take one example, a 1955 broadcast on Radio Australia's Overseas Broadcasting Service introduced Papua New Guineans as fundamentally disconnected and possibly incapable of integrating into any larger polity: "The indigenous population is divided into thousands of small politically independent groups, differing in language, conditions of life and development. Before coming under control they fight constantly with one another."[5] I argue that this was an ideology of *circulatory primitivity* above and beyond particular Western horror or fascination at supposedly primitive cultural practices. While circulatory primitivity and cultural primitivity interacted in the colonial imagination, most of the anthropological attention to colonialism has emphasized the realm of cultural primitivity: the exotic stories about and condemnatory talk of cannibalism, headhunting, naked bodies, or Stone Age tools (for Papua New Guinea, see Dixon 2001, Stella 2007; for West Papua, see Rutherford 2018, Stasch 2015, Stasch 2019; see also Lutz and Collins 1993, among many others).

What came across so clearly to colonial actors in Papua New Guinea was not just the sense that it was filled with culturally primitive people, but the sense that there were barriers to communicative circulation that seemed almost insuperable. Rather than being sedentary because they were culturally primitive, colonials saw Papua New Guineans as primitive because they did not seem to be mobile or even desire mobility. Yet as Erik Harms and colleagues (2014) discuss, mobility, primitivity, and remoteness are overlapping categories of modernity.

It is important to pause here to emphasize how mistaken these colonial actors were, both broadly about the connection between modernity and circulation and specifically in terms of Papua New Guinean communities. Anthropological theory throughout the twentieth century focused on gift exchange, in part, not only to demonstrate that circulation existed in what were then called "traditional" societies, but to show that these forms of circulation were foundational to the structures of all social life (Lévi-Strauss 2016 [1949]). The resulting division between traditional "gift societies" and capitalist "commodity societies" maintained, in certain ways, the modernist idea that regimes of circulation could be the basis for a "great divide" model of historical transformation, even though one of the most important and early contributions to exchange theory argues otherwise.

Marcel Mauss's (1990 [1925]) foundational study of the gift was predicated on the idea that the obligations to give, receive, and reciprocate are the bases for *all* forms of social recognition, "modern" or "traditional." Although his discussion of the *hau* of the gift has received the most commentary, I've always found his account of the Ts'msyan [Tsimshian] myth about Little Otter especially important (Mauss 1990 [1925]: 40–41). As he recounts it, a Ts'msyan chief has a grandson who can take the form of an otter. The chief invites his fellow chiefs from all the other communities to a feast and gives them gifts. Telling the guests about his grandson, he says that he should not be hunted if he is seen in otter form in the ocean. But the chief has neglected to invite one leader, who, in his ignorance, later hunts and kills Little Otter. Here, the capacity to be a living person is based quite literally on the circulation of information. Rituals of recognition create personhood through circulation.

In contrast to the colonial imaginary of Papua New Guinean immobility, fragmentation, and stagnation, anthropological research on exchange networks in

Melanesia showed that people have long been incredibly multilingual and mobile, interacting with neighboring as well as quite distant communities on a regular basis (e.g., Strathern 1971, Swadling 1996, Malinowski 2002 [1922]). This research has also shown that communities were and are dynamically borrowing from one another (Harrison 1993), with local people defining themselves in fluid relational networks (Strathern 1988). Motuans traveled along the south coast for *hiri* trading voyages, while communities in the *kula* exchange network sailed in the open ocean to visit trading partners. For almost all Papua New Guineans, and especially for men, multilingualism was the norm because of the dense set of interactions that people had with both neighboring and more far-flung communities on a regular basis (Sankoff 1977). And even if one wanted, for some reason, to exclude these forms of mobility from consideration, the colonial administrations were themselves responsible for an incredible mobility in the form of temporary labor migrations (Firth 1976, Fitzpatrick 1980, Hess 1983, Jolly 1987, Stead and Altman 2019), although I will show in later chapters how this mobility was made invisible, especially by Lutheran missionaries. Papua New Guineans had always been, and during the colonial period continued to be, mobile (see Hayano 1990, Beer and Church 2019, Dwyer and Minnegal 2023). And yet, this does not change the extent to which the imaginary of circulatory primitivity was a consequential part of the colonial history and even of Papua New Guineans' contemporary conceptualization of modernity as an era of potential and actual movement (e.g., Lawrence 1964, Burridge 1995 [1960], Wardlow 2006, Silverman 2013, Lipset 2014, Handman 2017b).

To return to Schivelbusch, whether circulation is bureaucratically channeled or self-organizing, productive of broader institutions or the outcome of them, it is one of the foundations of modernist ideologies of progress. It was seen as something to be cultivated or unleashed in different contexts to produce healthy societies and subjects. Yet as much as modernist theories suggested that more circulation was better or healthier, one of the recurring themes in the chapters to come is that once people started to recognize something as circulation in Papua New Guinea, they tended also to consider it suspect or illicit. If there was a unified modernist lens on Papua New Guinea that figured it as a space of circulatory primitivity, then the contradictions across different colonial projects always seemed to produce concerns that whatever circulation had begun needed to be controlled or contained.

FRAGMENTATION AND COLONIZATION

In the colonial era, both the number of languages that indigenous people spoke and the ruggedness of the mountains that covered large parts of the island of New Guinea contributed to a sense that it was extremely difficult for administrators and missionaries to physically move across the landscape or get much done in the way of governance or "progress," however conceived. They often referred to this problem as an issue of fragmentation. Yet fragmentation presupposes a totalizing whole—within which circulation is relatively unproblematic—that has come undone. Nevertheless, colonial anxieties about Papua New Guinea's fragmentation focused on the fact that no such totality had previously existed or seemed possible. One of the concerns was that Papua New Guinea could not scale up (Carr and Lempert 2016) into a greater unit, but was instead destined to remain a series of disconnected outposts of colonial control.

Colonialism is itself a kind of circulatory project to link periphery and metropole and bring what colonizers see as primitive fragments into modern relationship with one another. James Carey (1989) has discussed the telegraph as a technologically novel separation of communication and transportation: signals could move without the movement of people. As Carey notes, this facilitated, among other things, the shift from direct colonial control to telegraphically mediated empire—an "encephalated" form of long-distance management of far-flung outposts. John Ogborn (2007), Zoë Laidlaw (2005), and Bhavani Raman (2012) have looked at the development of novel genres of writing that were needed to allow for colonial control at a distance, just as Joanne Yates (1993) has done for the development of command and control management structures in nineteenth-century American business after the development of the national railroad network. What these different accounts of management at a distance assume is that the far-flung outposts of empire or industry are reachable, however slowly or dangerously. The question was *how* to connect different nodes in a network, not whether connections could be made at all. But the colonial obsession with Papua New Guinea's mountains and languages always kept the more basic question of accessibility on the front burner. For the colonial administrator or missionary, the question was whether the mountains and languages of Papua New Guinea would allow it to become something more than a fragmented collection of discrete, highly localized, highly remote (Ardener 1987) communities. As Sasha Newell writes about remoteness, it is more "a lack of connectivity rather than distance per se [that] produces such an unfocused arena" (in Harms et al. 2014: 367). Could these communities add up to anything more than the sum of their communicatively isolated parts?

For the Lutheran missionaries that I discuss in the first two chapters, there was a constant concern about the fragmentation of their work, which to them seemed to be a natural hazard of the geographic and linguistic features of colonial Papua New Guinea. Some of this concern is apparent even in the complex organization of the various Lutheran missionary societies. The Neuendettelsau Mission in what was then German New Guinea was begun by Johannes Flierl in 1886 when he started to work in the Finschhafen area of the Huon Peninsula. A few years later, the Rhenish Mission started work near Madang, but it was never as successful as the Neuendettelsau Mission either in maintaining the health of its missionaries or in increasing the number of Lutheran converts. After World War I, during which Australia took control of New Guinea from Germany, more Australian and American Lutherans joined the missions, especially because some of the original German missionaries were not granted visas to return to New Guinea.[6] After

World War II, this trend only intensified. As Winter (2012) discusses, and as I return to in later chapters, the organizational splits between the original Rhenish and Neuendettelsau missions plus the uneven incorporation of Australian and American Lutherans continued to fragment the work by, for example, codifying different church lingua francas. Yet there were many other ways in which the missionaries experienced this fragmentation.

The many mountains and languages kept the missionaries settled into particular areas and feeling isolated and remote. While the colonial administration was often in tension with the missions, its officials were nevertheless glad to be able to offload some of the problems of administration onto the many new missions that entered Papua New Guinea after World War II. If no one organization could adequately cover the territories of Papua and New Guinea as a whole because of a lack of mobility, then various mission organizations could help cover as many discrete sections of the territories as possible. But in this sense, the concern with fragmentation only created problems of further fragmentation later on, as when the administration in its later stages was faced with the problem of trying to bring order to an unruly diversity of mission education systems.[7] With so many missions controlling a different but isolated patch of country, all those relatively autonomous kingdoms could not easily be aligned in the run-up to independence.

Fragmentation is one of the oldest colonial tropes used to describe the Pacific, and Melanesia in particular. From early in the history of European engagements with people in the Pacific, the relative size and uniformity of some communities as opposed to others has put the people of Papua New Guinea at the bottom of an evolutionary and civilizational scale. For example, the French navigator Jules-Sébastien-César Dumont d'Urville (2003 [1832]), partitioning the Pacific into different cultural areas, placed the people he called Polynesians in a separate category from those he called Melanesians, for multiple reasons—the most important of which were the former's relatively lighter skin color, the size and hierarchical organization of their political communities, and the uniformity of their language (Dumont d'Urville assumed that all Polynesians spoke the same language). He found Melanesians lacking in all three categories, having darker skin, tiny polities, and endless variation in their languages.

Although he did not mention language in relation to his belief in the legitimacy of European colonization, it is clear that standardized French was, for Dumont d'Urville, a mark of supremacy and civilization. Fellow French speaker Ferdinand de Saussure would make this link explicitly several decades later: "Left to its own devices, a language has only dialects, which do not overlap. Thus it is destined to infinitesimal subdivision. But as a civilization in the process of development increases communication, a kind of tacit convention emerges which is of interest to the nation as a whole" (quoted in Joseph 2000: 153). Because nineteenth-century philologists thought that writing, as a more "civilized" mode of circulation, stopped linguistic diversification to the extent that "language diversity was . . . a sign of primitiveness in and of itself" (Fleming n.d.: 12). In this mode of thinking, civilized people necessarily have larger linguistic communities that enable easy movement and circulation.

European colonizers assumed that the fragmentation they saw existed independently of their political control. Yet fragmentation and its concomitant problems of circulation were in many ways the effects of colonial control. The many different administrations and organizations produced discrete, sometimes contradictory networks of connection as they tried to get people in different institutional positions to move themselves, their goods, or their talk across the island. Colonizers assumed that more circulation was better, and yet when faced with the conflicts among their different projects, they kept qualifying what kind of circulation would actually produce modernity: a unified language, but not Tok Pisin; a Christian mobility, but not if it meant that Lutherans had easy access to the territory; connection to the "outside," but not communist influence.

Colonial groups differed in their ideas about when and how circulation was a problem. To give a brief example, Christian missionaries like the Lutherans tended to be more concerned with trying to cultivate some unification of all the fragments. As a practical concern, they wanted to create a set of communicative infrastructures—roads, radios, airplanes, and the European and Papua New Guinean missionaries who would travel on them. In another sense, however, the unification that the missionaries ultimately aspired to would happen in heaven, far from the transportation issues that plagued the Territory of New Guinea.

The administration shared the Lutherans' more practical concerns, particularly in terms of the development of communication and transportation infrastructures. They needed ways of getting raw resources, market commodities, and their own people in and out of the rural areas. However, there were also moments when they were happy to let these Papua New Guinean fragments stay disconnected, especially if they saw this as a way to oppose anticolonial aspirations. In 1959, when the Trusteeship Council was putting more intense pressure on the administration to speed up decolonization, some administrators paused from talking about the language problem or the lack of roads to lament the passing of a circulatory form of innocence: "It is no longer possible to look forward to the New Guinea of the future as consisting of separate and isolated communities of peasants happily enjoying their own culture and speaking their own particular languages under the paternalistic protection of the Australian Commonwealth."[8]

As I discuss more in the next section, the moves toward decolonization did not involve a move away from the problem of circulation, but just a change in the kinds of circulations at issue. Rather than a problem of moving people, things, and talk across the island, the UN-initiated attempts at decolonization were figured as bureaucratic problems of managing the upward and downward flows of information through which anticolonial actors tried to produce local projects of decolonial politics. The 1950s movement from the colonial to the decolonial era of Papua New Guinea was a movement from the infrastructural problems of moving people, things, and talk across "remote" and "primitive" spaces to the bureaucratic problems of trying to manage information in order to elicit from local people an emerging sense of their position in a holistic territorial space working toward self-determination.

CIRCULATION AND DECOLONIZATION

While discussions of the bureaucratic colonial or postcolonial state are common at this point (e.g., Laidlaw 2005, Ogborn 2007, Heatherington 2012, Hull 2012, Raman 2012), the same is not true of bureaucracy's role in decolonization. Decolonization stories have tended to focus on the emergence of national identities and subsequent political movements for independence. At the same time, because colonial states have become so associated with bureaucratic orders, bureaucracy itself has been characterized as a colonizing technology. Yet bureaucracy is not limited to colonial or postcolonial states, and it is important to see the kind of roles that bureaucracy has played in a wider range of stories about decolonization. In particular, the important role of postwar global bureaucratic orders like the UN has yet to be fully analyzed, a gap that is perhaps itself a product of the hegemonic role of nation-states in the postwar decolonized world that the UN helped create.

Scholars of decolonization and the postcolonial world have long been critical of the nation-state form and the promises that came with nationalist struggles for independence (e.g., Chatterjee 1986; for the Pacific in particular, see Hau'ofa 1994, Banivanua Mar 2016). Critiques of decolonization focus on how the nation-state form was too entangled with the colonial order to have ever offered colonized peoples a chance at real self-determination. In response to the growing chorus of criticisms of the nation-state, some scholars are looking to the decolonization era to unearth the sometimes forgotten models and experiments of decolonization that lost out to the hegemony of the nation-state (Scott 2004, Wilder 2009, Imlay 2013; see also Trentman 1999, Collins 2013). While these models and experiments largely failed in the sense that nation-states became the preeminent goal for anticolonial political movements, they offer a different view of the aspirations that colonized peoples had for a postcolonial order and for models of self-determination. This book contributes to this project by examining the ways in which global anticolonial bureaucracies tried to usher in independence movements through the demand for and control over information flows.

Adom Getachew (2019) argues that an important but so far overlooked aspect of decolonization is the extent to which national self-determination was not an end in itself, but rather a way of cultivating an anticolonial international order. In places that are at the storied center of decolonization—India, Ghana, Egypt, Indonesia—the development of both a nationalist movement and an international order went hand in hand, as national independence led to prominent roles at the

Bandung Conference or the UN for Nehru, Nkrumah, Nasser, or Sukarno. Yet not every former colony's history follows that trajectory.

For those not quite at the vanguard of decolonization, the timings of national and international engagement could be quite disconnected. The empowered new nations within the UN, especially in particular sections of it like the Fourth Committee on Non-Self-Governing Peoples and the Trusteeship Council, tried to bring colonized peoples into the UN bureaucratic order first, with an eventual goal of self-determination through a nationalist project coming later, sometimes much later. This meant that decolonization in these cases was a matter of developing an informational infrastructure that might eventually lead to nationalist movements for self-determination.

As I will show later, anticolonial delegates of the UN were often disappointed by the lack of political demonstration for independence in colonial Papua New Guinea. In fact, the seeming absence of organized political movements for some kind of independence or autonomy was seen in negative terms by both the anticolonial factions of the UN and the UN delegates from the major colonial empires. For the anticolonial delegates, what appeared to be a lack of political consciousness in colonial Papua New Guinea threatened the idea that all colonized people naturally want to be free from colonialism (see Imlay 2013: 1110). For the colonial empires, the apparent "backwardness" of people and conditions in colonial Papua New Guinea put to the test the idea that colonialism was able to "uplift" colonized peoples. In that sense, Papua New Guinea played against both of the dominant narratives at work in the Trusteeship Council.

Much of the information that Australians sent upward to the Trusteeship Council was concerned with the capacities of Papua New Guineans to communicate with various others. That is, not only was information flow an issue, but much of the information that flowed (especially upward) was about information flows. The Trusteeship Council shared with colonial Australians the sense that political and civilizational advancement depended on the ways that information could or should flow across boundaries, whether these were linguistic, geographic, or ethnic. For the council's members, if the Australians were not creating a form of mass society in which communication happened across boundaries, and with the UN, then the Australians were not advancing Papua New Guineans at all.

In the postwar era, Australians used a sense of circulatory primitivity—the incapacity for information to circulate—as an excuse for their failures of colonial administration and as the defining characteristic of New Guinea as a colonized space in which the colonial circulation of people, things, and talk had to be organized by infrastructural forms like radio networks and roads. The Trusteeship Council likewise saw circulatory primitivity as the defining characteristic of Papua New Guinea, but they envisioned their supervisory capacity as one in which they would demand information as a spur to decolonization in and of itself.

They would decolonize through the creation of a new mode of circulation: publicity about their work to the people of Papua New Guinea and requests for documents about Papua New Guinea from Australia.

The 1950s was an important period for the Trusteeship Council. Particularly after the 1955 Bandung Conference, the new nations acted as an important voting bloc in UN bodies and especially on the Trusteeship Council. In contrast to the ascendant power of these anticolonial nations, diplomatic cables and other documents in Australian archives show civil servants and politicians in the Department of Territories and External Affairs resisting as strongly as possible all calls for speedy timelines toward independence or self-government for dependent territories. By 1960, though, it was clear that the balance of power in the UN had shifted toward decolonization (Hudson 1970). This was especially true after the General Assembly's 1960 Declaration on the Granting of Independence to Colonial Countries and Peoples.

The centrality of circulation as the problematic running through colonial and decolonial discourse can be exemplified briefly in a comment from an Australian administrator in 1961. Especially after the 1960 declaration against colonialism, Australians figured the United Nations as the central node in a politically dangerous communicative network too widespread in scope and too radical in content for Australia's administration of Papua New Guinea: "The Administration . . . recognized that in the near future there would arise the demagogue, the man who gathered a couple of hundred people around him and started a national movement. His next step would be to get into communication with the United Nations and send his report to those people who advocated a different system from ours."[9]

Even though decolonization did not happen for Papua New Guinea until 1975, I focus on the 1950s in part 2 of this book because it was a transitional decade. By 1950, UN institutions were up and running, even if certain protocols and procedures took a bit more time to become finalized. After 1960, the demand for a speedy end to colonialism had become so unified and strong among the noncolonial powers that several of the Trusteeship Council administering authorities stepped back from their positions of resisting timetables for attainment of independence. Thus, the 1950s was when the contentious relationship between administering authorities and the anticolonials was most intense, when the outcome was not yet foreseeable. And in the emerging Cold War order, the rising power of socialist and communist movements and the insurgencies in places like Kenya and Algeria contributed to the sense that the global colonial order was getting destabilized. During this period, Australia made its strongest case for the ways in which circulatory primitivity was the fundamental problem in the colonization and infrastructural development of Papua New Guinea. Likewise, it was in this period that the anticolonials on the Trusteeship Council made the strongest case that bureaucratic information flows would be the backbone of decolonization.

Questions of circulation were at the center of two competing visions of the political future of Papua New Guinea and other dependent territories.

CIRCULATION AND COMMUNICATIVE INFRASTRUCTURES

In this book, when I say that I am looking at circulation, I mean that I am examining the communicative pathways, or channels, that are central to particular cultural or sociopolitical orders. What counts as a communicative pathway in a given context? What sociopolitical orders are those pathways tied to? What do the participants in those pathways think their networked connections add up to? What work is required to maintain that form? What infrastructural forms are required to establish the communicative pathways? Circulation in this sense is a concern shared by both analyst and participant. In fact, most communities have some kind of interest in defining what counts as a legitimate mode of passing on messages and what does not (Gershon 2019).

Theories of circulation from linguistic anthropology have been vitally important to understanding interactional events as the particular spaces in which circulation happens. This work has primarily looked at how stretches of text or types of discourse are made to seem semiotically repeatable across contexts (Bauman and Briggs 1990, Silverstein and Urban 1996). More broadly, this line of inquiry about circulation has established the fundamental role of cultural knowledge in any successful event of circulation. Semiotic processes of repeating or reproducing instances of types of cultural knowledge, such as genres, are successful only to the extent that they are accepted by audiences who also have access to these forms of cultural knowledge (Gal 2018, Gal and Irvine 2019).

While interaction and interactional orders are central to circulation, the analysis of interactional events of circulation can sometimes assume the very thing that an emphasis on circulation makes visible: the nature of the connection or pathway linking people to one another. That is, analyses of interaction do not necessarily problematize communicative connections, since these are often already established by the time of the interaction. People examine how interactions differ based on the affordances of the different media, but the question of how communicative connections are made can be bracketed because the successful event of interaction is the rationale for the analysis to begin with. Without an interaction, there would be nothing to analyze.

But in both colonial and contemporary Papua New Guinea, there are consistent concerns about the very possibility of communication—of the ability for an interaction to happen—whether because of worries about the many mountains and languages or because the infrastructures of communication seem to always be on the verge of breaking down. Collectively, Papua New Guinea came to be seen by colonizers and decolonizers—whether Australian, Papua New Guinean, or other—as a space that was organized by this deep distrust about whether communication as such had happened or could happen. Following in the footsteps of linguistic anthropologists who have examined the problems of the "phatic function" of language (Nozawa 2015, Slotta 2015, Zuckerman 2016), I focus on circulation as a broader question of the different channels that form the communicative networks that precede interaction and make it possible (Lemon 2013, Edwards 2018, Manning 2021, Tomlinson 2024; see also Nakassis 2016).

The formation of sociotechnical communicative connections includes looking at the channels that people construct, the work they do to keep these channels open or closed, information that circulates through these networks and channels, and the ways that people use and talk about them as the bases for political projects of building different polities. These are the hard and soft infrastructures that Brian Larkin (2008) highlighted. I focus on some of the different networks of communication that connected colonial organizations across Papua New Guinea, and on the ways that Tok Pisin speakers and Tok Pisin commenters participated in these networks. Tok Pisin and Tok Pisin speakers were allowed to be part of some of them, but were excluded from others. The modes of circulation helped to create the sociological and cultural contours of space in Papua New Guinea, making some places feel remote and others near, some traditional and others modern.

As Benjamin Lee and Edward LiPuma (2002) argue, "cultures of circulation" require attention to particular languages and language use, but also to the institutional and discursive basis on which communication within that regime happens. Cultures of circulation involve not just the circulation of talk or goods, but the self-reflexive discussion of that circulation (Warner 2002). One of the most influential examples of a culture of circulation that Lee and LiPuma discuss is the nationalist imaginary that Benedict Anderson theorized and that countless others have commented on, criticized, or used as a model. The capacity for mass media like newspapers to create a kind of typicality of national life, along with the so-called creole pilgrimages that state functionaries took in Latin American colonies, were the foundations of national imaginaries. These national imaginaries could be fed, under print capitalism, through the daily reassurances that readers of a newspaper all existed together in the same homogeneous empty time of the secular nation. Other authors have borrowed from this template to examine different impacts of mass media on the formation of national identities.

In linguistic anthropology, works focused on language and nationalism, and on the language of national mass media forms like newspapers, radio, and television, have been staples of the discipline for the past twenty years. Much of this important research has looked at the ways in which languages are transformed in the process of becoming the languages of mass media—creating a top-and-center standard variety that relegates all other variants to the status of regional or sociological particularities (e.g., Fishman 1968, Woolard 1989, Blommaert and Verschueren 1995, Jaffe 1999, Silverstein 1999, Heller 2006). Work in this area has also made important contributions in terms of highlighting the frequent forms of exclusion that speakers of minoritized or indigenous languages experience from the national mass media and the language of the nation-state (e.g., Davis 2018, Shulist 2018, Smalls 2018, Rosa 2019).

But note how much of this literature took a story that was fundamentally about circulation in Anderson's version and turned it into a story about register formation—that is to say, a story about linguistic types. By focusing on registers instead of on the channels through which those registers traveled, the emphasis in language and nationalism literature was on a speaker's ability to speak in ways appropriate to a context of using a national language or on a speaker's feelings of inadequacy in those contexts. That is, the literature told stories of indexical successes and failures that typified given communities within the nation-state, often varying by race, class, gender, ethnicity, or age.

My goal in this project is to return to the emphasis on circulation that was so integral to Anderson's original work. Rather than focusing on the mass media of nationalism like newspapers or radio, I want to return to something like those creole pilgrimages that in Anderson's story helped produce a sense of simultaneity and sharedness in the nation-state space through the actual movement of people and information across a territory. I cannot say whether it was the most consequential element of Latin American nationalisms and revolutions in the 1800s. But an emphasis on this aspect of Anderson's argument does at least have the benefit of turning attention back to the consequences of specific pieces of information, or specific kinds of people, moving back and forth across a particular territory. It allows us to talk in more concrete terms about how organizations shape and are shaped by the ways in which information flows through them. In other words, this is less about speaker or hearer indexicality than about the structure and infrastructure of organizations and social groups.

Several forms of mass media emerged in the colonial period of Papua New Guinea, including newspapers and newsletters in church lingua francas or in Tok Pisin (see Mackay 1976, Sinclair 1984, Schram 2022). I want to add to this conversation by looking at the formative role that narrowcast channels of communication had in the colonial period of Papua New Guinea's history, and especially during its early history of decolonization. As much as Tok Pisin and English-language newspapers started to give shape to a national identity, the process of decolonization was helped along through point-to-point communications between different agencies and bureaucracies that often happened well outside of the emerging public sphere. That is, colonization and decolonization happened in important ways through narrowcast communication.

These narrowcast channels, and the conversations about the capacity for communication that happened on them, organized the shape of decolonization in 1950s Papua New Guinea. Rather than a project of rationalist discourse as in a Habermasian public, or a project of nationalist spread, the colonial and decolonial regime of circulation was a project of creating a defragmented bureaucratic hierarchy, one that would eventually become the basis for a higher-order identity as either a territory of Australia or an independent nation-state of its own.

LANGUAGE AND CIRCULATION

I have talked at points about Tok Pisin and English functioning as pathways, which requires special comment. While airplanes and teleradios became the technological components of the colonial networks in Papua New Guinea that garnered a lot of attention, Tok Pisin and English became the primary linguistic components of those networks. In some of these chapters, we see instances in which Tok Pisin is figured by colonial administrators and others in something like channel-ish terms. In Roman Jakobson's (1960) discussion of the functions of language, he delineated the elements of the speech event as speaker, hearer, context, message, code, and what he called contact (what in other places sometimes gets called channel). We might think about why code and contact, or code and channel, sometimes seem to merge for speakers, or why Tok Pisin or global English seems to itself be a channel. Linguistic anthropologists wouldn't want to erase the distinction, for many reasons; but it is interesting to work through the ways in which speakers or observers themselves see code and contact or code and channel as collapsible into each other at certain moments (see also Edwards 2018, Lemon 2018, Rabie 2022).

Colonial administrators and local people were often concerned with the transmission of particular pieces of information at important historical moments. This was sometimes out of a sense of paranoia about laborers organizing against the colonizers. Was a signal passed? Had word been sent? The sense in which a code like Tok Pisin comes to be seen as a channel, as a basis for interaction and the passing of knowledge, is foregrounded in this kind of historical perspective on information transmission. Just as colonial administrators and patrol officers struggled to walk through mountainous regions and coerce Papua New Guineans to maintain walking paths, they also struggled to construct the linguistic basis for their passing on of information. Colonials pit English and Tok Pisin against each other as languages that would create different networks of relations, different sets of channels to different people and nations. In part, languages looked like channels because circulation was the perspective that administrators and other colonial or decolonial actors focused on when they tried to imagine Papua New Guinea's future.

To linguists and linguistic anthropologists, this may sound too much like the language-as-conduit metaphor (Reddy 1979), which presupposes a speaker who has a nonlinguistic form of thought that they deposit into language, speaking the thought in its temporary languaged form and then waiting for it to be decoded by a hearer. What is undoubtedly an impoverished and incorrect model of language and its relation to thought might turn out to be a somewhat more useful model of how people see language in its relation to circulatory networks—that is, in relation to the environment, sociotechnical formations, and political networks. In this Papua New Guinean context, we see language and pathways together figured as channels of knowledge, as channels of other languages, or as channels of political relations. Here the focus for speakers and analysts is on a process of circulation or movement, and on establishing the ways that language, environment, and sociotechnical formations offer affordances for it.

The problems of communication in frontier zones are particularly apt to conjoin channel and code. When Euro-American speakers are unsure they can communicate at all, medium and language merge. Stories of impromptu sign languages or hand gestures in the history of European colonization—or the sometimes bizarre experiments in media formation that have featured in attempts to contact intelligent life elsewhere in the universe (Oberhaus 2019)—point to how frontier communications often prompt participants to switch to a different kind of communicative channel, from oral to manual in this case. Colonial paranoia about the ability of the colonized to communicate telepathically offers an example of this concern that the otherness of the other involves a change in not just language but medium—a formation of new and different *kinds* of channels. Frontier zones such as European colonies are particularly known for efforts at making these connections across differences, where those differences are recognized in ways that link contact and code in a broader problem of mediation (Peters 1999, Guillory 2010).

When we focus on circulation by tracking how communicative interactions link people in historical networks, the differences between code and contact start to dissolve. A person's ability to participate in a chain of linked interactions may depend as much, say, on whether they have access to a two-way radio as on whether they speak English. Both may be necessary in order to be a link in that chain. The technologically focused administrators, bureaucrats, and diplomats who were trying to colonize and decolonize Papua New Guinea tended to think in these sorts of terms that examined language as a component of a broader technological setup that could either inhibit or facilitate the passing of messages. Like mountains that blocked the construction of roads or blocked certain kinds of radio waves, the languages of Papua New Guinea were seen in terms of their infrastructural possibilities or inhibitions. Rather than separating language out as a unique semiotic modality, I discuss languages like English and Tok Pisin in conjunction with mountains or radios because of the varied forms of communication they allow for.

OUTLINE OF CHAPTERS

The six chapters that follow are split into two parts. In part 1, I look at the ways in which colonial Papua New Guinea was figured as a space of circulatory primitivity. I focus here primarily on the work of the Lutheran missionaries in the Territory of New Guinea because of the outsized role they played in the colonization of the region and because of their extraordinary emphasis on creating communicative networks. The Lutheran missions built roads, radio communication networks, aviation networks, and shipping companies, in addition to engaging in the linguistic and educational network-building that is associated with creating a religious community—translating and printing texts, teaching lingua francas, organizing synod gatherings. The colonial administration opted out of at least some of these projects and, in so doing, left it to the Lutherans to create some of the circulatory features of the colony. In chapter 1, I focus on the forms of remoteness that were intensified rather than eradicated with the creation of Lutheran radio and aviation networks that connected their mission stations. In chapter 2, I focus on the Lutheran attitudes toward Tok Pisin, and how the language was treated "merely" as infrastructural rather than cultural. In doing so, they excluded Tok Pisin from being a potential language of evangelism, a code that could act as the communicative channel between souls and God. In both chapters, we see that as much as different infrastructural improvements seem to make the accessibility of Papua New Guinea greater, the Lutherans retain a sense of the ultimate remoteness of the people they are trying to reach.

While this story of Lutheran concerns with accessibility and remoteness is focused on the ways in which colonial Papua New Guinea seemed impassable to colonizers, this sensibility was always paired with an equivalent paranoia that Papua New Guinea was in fact extraordinarily porous for some, including local Papua New Guineans and the external other of mid-century Australian society—Asian communists. In chapter 3, I examine the surprisingly robust discourses about Papua New Guinean and Pacific Islander telepathy, and how colonizers spent a good deal of time worrying that laborers were telepathically communicating. Although Tok Pisin is mentioned explicitly in these contexts only on certain occasions, telepathy discourses and Tok Pisin discourses share the broader concern with communication outside of the colonizers' control. To this list is added the threat of deceitful communists, who Australians worried were always on the cusp of some kind of invasion into Australian territory, whether from neighboring Indonesia or the more distant Soviet Union or mainland China. In terms of the larger argument about Tok Pisin's role in Papua New Guinea's history, we can see how the ability for Tok Pisin to take on the collapsed code- and channel-like features of telepathy becomes the basis for suspicion about it. Colonizers worried about their own inability to transcend distance as well as Papua New Guineans' ability to do so with ease.

Part 2 turns to the role of the UN Trusteeship Council in the decolonization of Papua New Guinea. The colonial-era response to the problem of circulation was to create communication infrastructures that ironically regimented and reinforced distances. By contrast, the top-down projects of bureaucratic decolonization tried to cultivate global connections. I focus in particular on the council's demand that information flow in certain directions as itself a project of decolonization. In chapter 4, I provide an introduction to the Trusteeship Council, a bureaucratic organization that has not received much attention in anthropological accounts of decolonization in the Pacific or elsewhere (but see Hudson 1970, Downs 1980, Mazower 2009, Denoon 2012). Here I focus especially on the structures of bureaucratic information flow that organized the council's work.

In chapter 5, I examine the council's demand that Australia "eradicate" Tok Pisin. As much as it was concerned with the circulation of information as a mode of development, the council decided that the only language in which such circulation might conceivably happen needed to be killed. Answering the question of why the council would make this demand, given all their professed concern with circulation, is the question that initially motivated the research for this book. As I argue in chapter 5, the Trusteeship Council, including the most anticolonial delegates on it, demanded Tok Pisin's eradication because it did not create the right kind of communicative networks, whether tied to colonial metropoles or to a global anticolonial struggle. English would allow for a better connection to the UN and other centers of decolonial activity, connections that would ideally provide the proper basis for cultivating a local decolonial consciousness.

In chapter 6, I look at how Australia and the Trusteeship Council came into conflict over the council's demands for different kinds of information in annual reports, including especially "timetables for the attainment of Independence," a term that was so alarming for Australian bureaucrats that they would only euphemistically talk about it as the issue of "attainment." Australia dodged demands for timetables by claiming that they were impossible given the different forms of fragmentation that governed Papua New Guinea, and used biannual Trusteeship Council visiting missions as chances to demonstrate this fragmentation in a bureaucratically organized way. Questions of sovereign control and oversight were negotiated through the bureaucratic management of the problem of fragmentation. As with the critiques of Tok Pisin, the UN and Australian actors struggled to structure the right kind of information flows and, in doing so, struggled to carve out different futures for Papua New Guinea.

. . .

Before moving on, two clarifications are in order. First, I want to emphasize that there *are* lots of mountains and very many languages, and it *was* (and continues to be) difficult for people to move around in colonial and postcolonial Papua New Guinea. Infrastructures are often at a point of breakdown, if they exist at all, and communication is hindered at times by the number of languages spoken. My argument is not that circulation was in fact easy and that the colonizers were simply mistaken in seeing things otherwise, but that the focus on circulation in the history of Papua New Guinea is not simply a natural fact of the size of the mountains and the number of languages spoken. Circulation became an obsession in the way that it did because colonizers' modernist imaginaries were the lens through which they saw all those imposing mountain ranges and complex speech communities. They developed a colonial culture of circulation in their encounters with the mountains and languages, one that extended into the process of decolonization as well.

Second, circulation was not the only thing that colonizers worried over. Like academics, colonizers seemed to never be at a loss for things to complain about, and the underfunded, understaffed administration gave them many opportunities to grumble. But problems of circulation were part and parcel of the complaints about the lack of funds and personnel. Many of the proposed solutions to problems of circulation never got past the proposal stage because no money or men could be found to develop the ideas further. This was true whether those proposals involved relatively mundane projects of road building or more outlandish attempts to cut across the problems of mountains and languages. Neither the administration file on the idea of building aerial ropeways into the mountains nor the file on the idea of teaching Ogden and Richards's Basic English (or other international auxiliary languages) was particularly thick, because trying to implement such projects was typically considered impossible.[10]

Beyond taking an anthropological look at a moment in twentieth-century Papua New Guinea history, the aim of this book is to show how colonialism is a culture of circulation, much as others have argued that nationalism, liberal democracy, and capitalism are, at their core, social formations of circulation. Seeing colonialism in this way also underlines the key role of circulation in decolonization and in the UN-led global order that resulted from it after World War II. As I briefly discuss in the book's conclusion, this history of communicative orders continues to have effects on Papua New Guinea to this day, and attention to the ongoing history of colonial cultures of circulation can be an important part of reconsidering contemporary projects of decolonization as well.

. . .

Finally, a note on terminology: I use a number of terms throughout this text that are, strictly speaking, anachronistic. Papua New Guinea as a country uniting the territories of Papua and New Guinea did not come into being until 1975. Before that, its inhabitants were usually referred to as either Papuans or New Guineans. Most of my discussions center on the Territory of New Guinea in the 1950s, when it was officially the Trust Territory of New Guinea, administered by Australia on behalf of the UN. I use the contemporary terms *Papua New Guinea* and *Papua New Guinean*, although it should always be clear from the context that I am talking about the colonial era. I also use the name *Tok Pisin* to refer to the varieties of English spoken mostly in the Territory of New Guinea. Up through the 1950s, this name was almost never used, with most people instead talking about *Pidgin, Pidgin English, pidgin,* or sometimes *Neo-Melanesian* (a neologism coined by the linguist Robert A. Hall Jr.).

When I quote from historical texts, I do not change the terms used. Outside of direct quotations, I tend to use the contemporary versions of these terms because they suffer less from the colonial overtones of their predecessors, particularly for Papua New Guinean readers. And yet, as many have noted, *Papua* is a Malay term for "frizzy hair" while *New Guinea* refers to the fact that early sailors thought that local people looked similar to the inhabitants of the Guinea coast of Africa. *Tok Pisin* is just the term for "pidgin language" in Tok Pisin, and to that extent maintains a link to its origins as what was then considered just a simplistic or garbled form of imperial English. In that sense, there is no way to bracket the racial and colonial overtones of any of these names.

PART ONE

Infrastructures of Colonial Distance

Remote Networks

*Airplanes, Radios, and the Making of Communicative
Distance in Lutheran New Guinea*

In 1955, Carl Spehr, the radio engineer for the Lutheran Mission in the Territory of
New Guinea, was optimistic about the new network of two-way radio stations for
Christian missionaries. An Australian group called the Christian Radio Missionary Fellowship (CRMF), based in Sydney, was organizing many of the Protestant
missions in the Territory of New Guinea into one very large radio network that
would allow missionaries to coordinate aviation needs, order supplies from their
storehouses, or call in for emergency medical evacuation or advice. There was even
a hope that missionaries could occasionally chat with one another more casually.
According to the minutes of the 1955 annual conference of Lutheran missionaries,
"Mr. Spehr expressed the hope that it may be possible to use our radio sets for
routine transmission, such as discussions between missionaries, etc."[1] For Spehr
and the others who helped put it together, not only would this network make life
safer and easier in terms of the practical difficulties of living in remote areas, but
the radios might even make missionaries feel connected to one another.

By 1968, a little over a decade later, things had taken a turn for the worse. The
network was well established, linking several hundred stations and serving a dozen
different Protestant missions.[2] The missionaries were using the radios not only
to facilitate aviation and request supplies, but also to chat with one another—
frequently, informally, and sometimes scandalously. So much so that the new
radio engineer, George Groat, devoted much of his annual report to the Lutheran
conference that year to complaining about how out of control the missionaries had
become on the network. He warned them:

> Uncomplimentary remarks, argumentative transmissions, etc., shall not be tolerated
> by any stations. A Christian business-like attitude shall be the order of the day. If
> it can't be said in Christian love and in a Christian manner, then don't say it.

> Going over into another mission's time with persistent regularity is extremely rude and un-Christian-like behaviour. We have what we have by the Grace of God . . . . let us not abuse it.[3] (all ellipses in original)

By 1970, things were so bad that Groat threatened to shut down the radio operations for Lutheran stations that were still not cooperating with his requests and with administration regulations. His report includes a desperate "Please do not embarrass us."[4] Only fifteen years separated Spehr's hope that the missionaries might use the new radios to occasionally chat with one another and Groat's plaintive cries that his garrulous Christian servants needed to show some basic decorum and restraint.

The missionary radio network had taken years to get approved by the Australian colonial government. It took another decade to build the network up with hundreds of expensive two-way radio sets (supplemented with a huge amount of surplus material left in Papua New Guinea by the US Army at the end of World War II). And throughout its operation, the missionaries had to fight endless pressure from the administration's Department of Posts and Telegraphs to shut the network down. The question that motivates this chapter comes from the fact that after working for years to set up and then maintain the radio network, one of the most frequent things missionary leaders kept saying to their rank-and-file evangelists was "Don't use the network so much!" After pouring all that time and money into creating a complicated system that was technologically capable of both person-to-person conversation and broadcasting, why did keeping people from using it become so important?

While radios and aviation systems (which I will discuss in the first half of the chapter) are both communication technologies that are usually thought of as eradicating a sense of distance, the Lutheran missionaries who established these networks often did so in ways that exacerbated and even enforced their experiences of remoteness, isolation, and fragmentation. Solving the problem of that fragmented existence became a fundamental orienting goal of the mission. And yet, whenever people started to think that this problem was getting solved—that people, things, and talk were able to move freely around the colony—it seemed to put the autonomy and even the existence of the mission at risk.

DISTANCE AND COMMUNICATION

A wide range of communication historians and theorists have discussed the ways that telephony, telegraphy, and radio seemed to transform users' experiences of distance (Carey 1989, Kittler 1999, Peters 1999), to change the very sense of what distance could be. The eradication of physical distance by the telegraph seemed to be so absolute that it sparked projects trying to eradicate metaphysical distance between the living and the dead. In séances and other rituals of the emerging spiritualist movement at the end of the nineteenth century, female mediums used "the spiritual telegraph" to contact those "on the other side." Spirits signaled yes or no by making knocks or raps like the clicks of a telegraph, or the Ouija board helped coax spirits to spell their communications out letter by letter, as in Morse code.

But as various authors have discussed (Bolter and Grusin 1999, Peters 1999, Gershon 2010), experiences of immediacy or of the eradication of distance are notoriously unstable. David Bolter and Richard Grusin (1999) explain that experiences of immediacy are not cultivated by the communicative technology alone, but rather by the ways that users compare and contrast one medium of interaction with another. The use of a telegraph can feel immediate when compared with using the postal service to mail a letter, but it can feel highly mediated and distancing when compared with a telephone call. Making a related point, Ilana Gershon (2010) talks about how users of these media bring with them different and constantly changing media ideologies that affect how they think about what kinds of interactions should take place through what kinds of media.

John Durham Peters (1999), too, notes that immediacy or the eradication of distance is not a feature of the technology itself so much as a way that people conceptualize what communication is or should be. He emphasizes the ways that immediacy and distance are necessarily paired against one another, meaning that the same medium produces both presence and its opposite. Wherever there is a medium that promises to bridge the distance between speaking selves, the corresponding worries that it will only produce chasms instead are never far behind. This is not a story of technology so much as a story of communicative ideologies. Concerns about self and subjectivity were channeled into worries about media long before the telegraph, but the development of different communicative media since the middle of the nineteenth century has intensified the oscillation between experiences of distance and immediacy among speaking subjects. To extend Peters's argument beyond those individual subjects, these kinds of oscillations between experiences of distance and immediacy helped produce the circulatory imaginary of the colonial space as a whole. Colonial actors saw Papua New Guinea as a space of radical distance, and yet fears that Papua New Guineans might be too accessible were never far behind (a point I will come back to in chapter 3).

In colonial Papua New Guinea, the Lutheran missions stitched together large communicative infrastructural systems that at various times promised, if not to eradicate the distance between all those isolated mission outposts, then at least to lessen it. Like the Lutheran medical aid networks that Britt Halvorson (2018) analyzes, these infrastructural formations were central spaces for defining and experiencing missionary Christianity. First with their aviation network and later with their radio network, Lutheran missionaries had moments of being able to create those communicative bridges across the mountaintops. Yet whenever that distance seemed on the way to being eradicated, the autonomy of the mission came into question. If the interior spaces of colonial Papua New Guinea could be connected, then the rationale for the mission's relative freedom from administration oversight started to fall apart.

Australian administrators for the Territory of New Guinea were trying to do colonialism on the cheap and ended up outsourcing much of the process of colonization to Lutherans, Catholics, and Seventh-day Adventists. But these were just the three largest missions. After World War II, dozens of mission groups entered the Territory of New Guinea and participated in what the administration hoped would be a civilizing project. Required by the terms of the UN trusteeship agreement to allow different religious groups to enter the territory, the Australian administration did not initially insist that the different systems established by these missions be integrated with one another or with the territorial administration. The endlessly varying educational systems, evangelistic techniques, health care regimes, and economic aid systems were tolerable only because it seemed like the integration of the colony into a single system was part of a future that was so far off that it didn't need to be taken into consideration. In that sense, both the missions and the administration had a stake in maintaining the frame that things could not circulate in Papua New Guinea.

In other words, fragmentation and distance were colonial policy. Not in the sense of a divide-and-conquer attitude to keep Papua New Guineans from organizing—the idea of such complex political activity was almost unthinkable. Rather, fragmentation and distance were colonial policy in the sense that these were the alibis for the administration's laissez-faire attitude toward the missions. The administration's oversight of the missions was relatively light, in part, because of the sense that they were working in remote spaces. This meant, though, that Lutheran networks could not actually be allowed to eradicate distances in the way that many thought was the inevitable outcome of telecommunication infrastructures.

This chapter looks at Lutheran airplanes and radios as interconnected networks that created the sense of remoteness (Ardener 1987) that missionaries used to describe their work to themselves and others, to organize it into a structural hierarchy, and to relate to the colonial administration. In the first half of the chapter, I examine the development of the Lutheran aviation system, how the Lutherans talked about the project, and the ways that the aviation network helped them imagine the colony and its Christian converts as part of different spatiotemporal orders (Munn 1977, 1986). Yet the aviation network became central to the accusations against the mission as a whole and against particular German-citizen missionaries during World War II. The idea of the colony being too easily accessed, by airplane in this case, fed into Australian fears of Nazi activity in Papua New Guinea. The rationale for interning most of the members of the Lutheran missions during the war was based in part on this sense that they not only had created a state within a state, but had made the region too navigable.

The production of proximity destabilized the relationship between the mission and the administration.

The same dynamic recurred in the postwar years. The development of a Protestant missionary radio network was heralded within the Lutheran missions (the network's dominant members) as allowing an extraordinary experience of communicative proximity with other missionaries. And yet the mission and radio network leaders were aware that their autonomy from administrative regulation was possible only to the extent that proximity could never be fully realized. The founding imaginary of Papua New Guinea as a colonial space of circulatory primitivity—in which people, things, and talk could not circulate—was not eradicated by the introduction of various communicative networks. Rather, circulatory primitivity organized not only how these infrastructures were implemented, but also how the different missions related to one another and to the administration.

LUTHERANS IN PAPUA NEW GUINEA

In the late nineteenth century, the German Lutheran missionary Johannes Flierl was working at a mission station on the Cape York Peninsula at the northeastern tip of Australia, but he was hoping to find a way into New Guinea to work with "a totally untouched heathen people, not yet trampled on, oppressed and pushed aside by white settlers" as he thought Aboriginal Australians had been (quoted in Wagner 1986: 35). However, unlike some other missions in the Pacific that were able to begin operations before colonial governance began (see Barker 2008), the Lutherans were not able to begin work in New Guinea until after the division of New Guinea island during the Berlin conference of colonial powers in 1884. While the western half of New Guinea island had already been claimed by the Dutch, the eastern half of the island was split between the British, who took the southeastern part as British Papua, and the Germans, who took the northeastern part as Kaiser-Wilhelmsland, or German New Guinea (see map 1). After two years of waiting for permission from the German New Guinea Company, Flierl established the first mission station of the Neuendettelsau Mission Society at Simbang in 1886, not far from what was then the headquarters of the German territory at Finschhafen, both on the Huon Peninsula. The following year, a different German Lutheran group, the Rhenish Mission, established a base near Madang. The German administration gave the Lutheran mission license to missionize from Madang east to the border with British Papua, while they gave German Catholic missions the territory from Madang west to the border with Dutch New Guinea. Although these comity agreements kept denominational hostilities relatively quiet, Lutherans who worked at the edges of their mission territory constantly complained about "flock stealing" by the Catholics (Handman 2019a).

At the start of World War I, Australia took possession of German New Guinea, and in the years following the war, Australian and American Lutherans started to join the missionary effort. The initial Lutheran mission stations were largely coastal outposts, on the Huon Peninsula and on nearby islands. One early exception was the Lutheran work further inland along the Waria River Valley, from its mouth at Morobe station up to Kipu and Garaina (see Handman 2015). It was not until the start of the 1930s that gold-prospecting expeditions went into the mountainous central cordillera of New Guinea and Australians realized that there was a large population living up there in vast highland valleys. And it was not until the mid-1930s that the administration allowed missions to enter this part of the country, as I will discuss below.

The Lutheran missionaries were fractured along various lines. Missionaries were members of different organizations and had different nationalities: the Neuendettelsau and Rhenish missions from Germany and the Australian and American Lutheran missions. They supported the use and promulgation of different mission lingua francas, including Kâte, Jabem, and Gedaged. They supported different missionary practices—advocated by Flierl or by Christian Keyßer, another German Lutheran missonary—that approached local culture in different ways. And as Hitler began to take over Europe, they supported different sides of the emerging conflict, given that some of the German Lutherans were Nazi Party members or sympathizers (for a rich history of the German Lutherans in colonial Papua New Guinea, see Winter 2012). During the war, the Lutheran missionaries were placed in internment camps, and most of the German nationals were not allowed to return after the war ended. The postwar years were dominated by increasing numbers of American Lutheran missionaries, including especially the longtime superintendent of the mission, John Kuder, who worked closely with his wife, Louise.

The Lutheran mission organization was a vast collection of ministers, teachers, doctors, printers, transportation managers, and many others, but much of the day-to-day work of the mission in the rural areas was done by Papua New Guinean men and their wives who had converted to Lutheranism. These "native evangelists" became missionaries to other communities in which the Lutheran mission was just starting to work. With a constant shortage of European missionaries to staff all the different areas that Lutherans hoped to enter, native evangelists did much of the pioneering work of establishing mission outposts in newly approached communities. The native evangelists ran and taught Lutheran primary schools, led weekly church services, and identified and prepared candidates for baptism. They were also responsible for teaching local people the church lingua franca used in the area.[5] On their twice-yearly visits, the European missionaries would check on schools, baptize and give communion to those who were official church members, and try to solve any church-related problems the native evangelists were having. But unless living near the mission station at which the European missionary lived, a local Papua New Guinean church member would rarely see the missionary, much less his wife and children.

While map 2 gives the impression of a dense Lutheran presence by 1960, especially on the Huon Peninsula, in fact the Lutheran missionaries were scattered

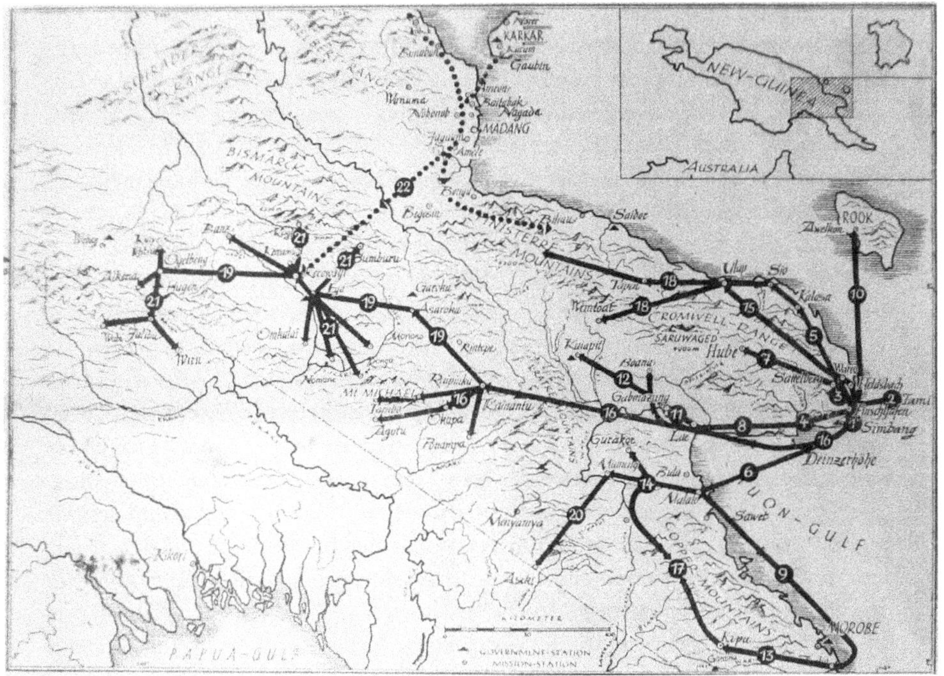

MAP 2. Map showing where Lutheran missionaries worked in the Territory of New Guinea. Black lines show the movements of missionaries with the Neuendettelsau Mission, starting on the Huon Peninsula and moving south and inland into the Highlands region. Dotted lines show the movements of the Rhenish (later, the American Lutheran) Mission. Numbers show a rough chronology of the Lutherans' movements. For a more detailed view of this map, see https://sites. google.com/view/courtney-handman/home. (*Lutheran Herald* vol. 41, no. 16, August 26, 1961; Lutheran Archives of Australia, Periodical Collection)

widely across distant stations. Even if missionaries were living at geographically proximate stations, they were isolated in their individual roles, learning different languages and responding to different cultural practices. Missionaries tried to learn the local language spoken in their region, reporting back on their ethnographic, missiological, and linguistic findings in annual meetings. Overcoming these distances became an important practical and even spiritual project of the mission.

THE INFRASTRUCTURES OF CHRISTIAN MOVEMENT

When Johannes Flierl and his Neuendettelsau Mission compatriots started working in New Guinea, the missionaries encountered a landscape that seemed impenetrable for a number of reasons. They were starting to realize that not only was it a densely forested and mountainous tropical island, but it was linguistically extremely diverse. Immediately, problems of communication and circulation—in both the linguistic and transport senses—became overriding technical concerns.

More than that, movement itself became the dominant framing of morality and transformation. If circulation was the figure of freedom and health in modernist discourses of European progress broadly (Schivelbusch 1980), circulation was the figure of Christian freedom and progress for missionaries specifically. Lutheran missionary texts depict non-Christians as immobile, stuck in defensive geographic positions, in contrast to the missionaries' own urge for movement and evangelistic expansion.

Because it makes such a tight connection between the process of circulation and value transformation, I use Nancy Munn's (1977) "The Spatiotemporal Transformations of Gawa Canoes" as a model for analyzing how the Lutheran missionaries created value through movement and how value transformations structured different qualities of movement in space and time. The value transformation I am talking about in this case is the transformation of souls, from unsaved into saved, and the movement I am talking about is the capacity to cut across, through, or over the dense rainforest that covers New Guinea island. For many of the missionaries in the Lutheran missions, movement was itself a practice and sign of Christianity, because for them heathens were trapped in states of fear and darkness that made movement impossible. In order to go from darkened heathendom to the free movement of salvation, Lutherans created a set of Christian technologies of circulation and transportation. Just as Mary Taylor Huber (1988) talked about the ways that ships structured the nearby Catholic missions, I argue that when the Lutherans decided in the late 1920s to use aviation in their evangelism and forgo walking along mountain paths into the New Guinea highlands, they had to make those airplanes vehicles for godly bodies able to ascend, eventually, to heaven.

In a manuscript titled "The Secular Involvement," which largely covers Lutheran infrastructural improvements in the Territory of New Guinea, the equation of movement and Christianity, of movement *as* Christianity, is highlighted clearly. Prior to missionization, Papua New Guineans lived their lives governed by fear: "The very first missionaries who came to New Guinea could not do much in improving the bush tracks. The people were not interested to communicate with outsiders. They were fearful of enemies from every side. In the mountain areas people built their villages on ridges which were hard to reach and easy to defend."[6]

The missionaries were deeply mistaken about the movements of local people in precolonial and colonial eras. Papua New Guinea has long been a site of intense circulation of people and goods in long-distance exchange networks (for a small sample of classic texts on this topic, see Strathern 1971, Munn 1986, Swadling 1996, Tuzin 1997, Malinowski 2002 [1922]). Entire communities were in some cases highly mobile (Hallpike 1977), while in others men were consistently engaged in long-distance travel for hunting (Healey 1990). By not recognizing the kind of precolonial mobility that Papua New Guinean people engaged in, Lutherans thought of movement across the territory as a novel sign of growing Christian faith. After conversion, the impenetrable jungle opens up into communicative pathways:

> The new-won freedom from fear had encouraged these young christians [*sic*] to build "roads on which the 'miti' ['Gospel' in Kâte] could travel" as they expressed it. As time went on similar developments could be noticed in other areas. As the Gospel took possession of the minds of the people their old fears and hatreds disappeared. No longer felt they imprisoned in their tribal area. Now they began to move about.[7]

Not only was movement equated with Christian salvation, but the speed and quality of movement seemed to matter too. From the Lutheran missionary perspective, there was a quickening pulse of Christian life that went along with an expanded road network:

> Everywhere the missionaries encouraged the building of roads or at least paths suitable for travelling by horse. Along the coast local canoes could be used. But when the work spread inland it meant building suitable lines of communication. With the introduction of steel such as axes, knives and shovels work went ahead at great speed. As the influence of Christianity grew, the desire of the people to connect up with the pulsating life of the outside world grew at the same time.[8]

The intense concentration on infrastructure stemmed from the Lutherans' ongoing problems with transportation and circulation in what they thought of as a rugged and isolating territory. As large as the Lutheran Missions were, the missionaries themselves more often thought of them as forming discrete pockets of Christian influence rather than as a unified region of evenly spread Lutheranism. Each missionary was an island, an outpost of colonial Christianity that lacked the communicative linkages that various media—roads or radios or languages—could offer.

AVIATION FOR SOULS

The attention to the qualities of movement increased when the mission started using airplanes in 1935. A number of different qualities of travel, and the subsequent conversions that were attributed to that travel, became overt topics of discussion for missionaries and other colonial actors. Of greatest importance was the fact that airplanes were obviously quicker than horses, canoes, boats, or walking humans. The radical change in travel times that the airplanes afforded made it possible for the mission to expand into the recently opened highlands. Without the use of airplanes, a missionary and dozens of local people working as carriers would need three weeks to walk from the north coast town of Lae to the highlands. With the use of an airplane, they could make the same trip—bringing even more cargo—in about an hour.[9] The Lutherans were at the forefront of creating a novel form of modernist circulation in the remote highland areas.

A second characteristic of airplane travel, in addition to speed, was the sense of lightness, both as the opposite of heaviness and as the opposite of darkness. Airplanes used in Lutheran evangelism flew above the steep mountain walls and rainforests. Not only were the planes associated with the sun-filled heavens, but also, importantly, they were above the muck of the rainforest roads that had been so painstakingly built over the years: "The time was ripe to leave the muddy and leech infested mountain paths and to use wings."[10] Slow, muddy paths were transformed into fast, sunlit airplanes capable of creating more and better Christians.

The original pioneer Lutheran missionary to Papua New Guinea, Johannes Flierl, first brought up the possibility of using airplanes in evangelism with his assembled missionaries during their annual conference in 1928. Flierl emphasized the speed and smoothness of air travel. More than that, the very idea of air travel seemed to play with time, turning an old man young again:

> The reverend pioneer of our mission, Senior J[ohannes] Flierl, had one evening set apart for the discussion of his proposal that the time was ripe for the installation of a mission aeroplane. How young he seemed that evening, how easily his mind accommodated itself to the age of modern technical progress and its terms! It was very humorous, when he described to us the great ease of travel in the air, where there were no spoon-drains and no watertables,[11] where the traffic police could not watch you, and where no dogs could run into your wheels, and where you need not be in constant fear of a pedestrian appearing around the corner. But we soon learnt that our old leader was very serious and was quite convinced of the necessity of an aeroplane for the proper development of our work in New Guinea.[12]

Flierl was making an argument for aviation as a mode of transportation free of any kind of restriction, whether geological (the spoon-drains and water tables), governmental (the traffic police), or social (the dogs and children).

Flierl's imagination of aviation was deeply mistaken, of course. Management and understanding of geology, civil administration, and social relations are all required for regular air traffic. Once the mission started depending on its airplane, new stations were built in areas adjacent to government airstrips or on level enough sections of land on which airstrips could be constructed.[13] Missionaries had to ask congregations to help clear and level ground for airstrips. They had to constantly maintain, and the Department of Civil Aviation had to constantly inspect, the airstrips in order to ensure proper drainage for their continuing "aerodrome" licenses. Nevertheless, it is clear from this account that Flierl spoke of aviation as a space of great freedom of movement, almost entirely untethered from the ground and the earthly concerns that one has to take notice of while moving upon it. It took seven years from this initial inspiration from Sr. Flierl to get to the first "aeroplane" delivered on February 19, 1935: an all-metal Junkers F 13 christened the *Papua* and flown by a World War I German ace, Fritz Loose.[14]

Airplanes transformed the space-time of evangelism in ways that seem not to have been true of canoes, boats, axes, knives, or shovels. Even in a place that was derided for not being in the Iron Age, it was air travel more than steel axes that created a set of questions about the temporality of Christian evangelism in a colonial context. The extent to which aviation and missionization are celebrated parts of Papua New Guinea's history is evident from a series of stamps that were

FIGURE 2. The Lutherans' Junkers F 13 airplane is memorialized on a 1972 postage stamp, one in a series of four stamps commemorating the fiftieth anniversary of aviation in Papua New Guinea. (Alamy)

produced by the Department of Posts and Telegraphs, one of which memorializes the historic role of the *Papua* (see figure 2). One reason that airplanes, and the *Papua* in particular, play such an outsized role in colonial narratives has to do with the fact that this was a novel form of transportation for the European missionaries as well as for the local people. Although airplanes had been used in World War I as a military technology, civil aviation was still in its infancy when Flierl first proposed using an airplane for evangelism.

Lutherans were able to change their concept of what the mission could be when they started using airplanes in their work.[15] This became particularly important as the Lutherans in the early 1930s were starting a fierce competition with the Roman Catholic and Seventh-day Adventist missions for converts in the highlands of Papua New Guinea, an area that white colonizers had only recently encountered and that seemed to have a population of perhaps half a million. Eventually termed the "gold rush for souls," the competition among different missions in the 1930s for access to the highland populations was intense (see Handman 2019a). In the earlier-missionized coastal areas of Papua New Guinea, colonial administrators had helped define missionary spheres of influence—rough boundaries dividing up colonial spaces among various missions. However, the colonial administration had decided to change tactics when they opened up the highlands for missionaries. They refused to create spheres of influence, and in fact hoped to spark missionary competition. The goal was to pacify and civilize the highlanders as quickly as possible. Using a kind of market logic, the colonial administration hoped that close competition rather than regional monopolies would spur the missions to work at a more rapid pace. Since the missions provided many of the services that are usually associated with states—schools, medical outposts, economic opportunities—the pace of mission work was considered especially important to any plans for "civilization."

Although administrators, planters, and mineral prospectors at the time laughed at the technological one-upmanship and literal sprints to new territories involved in the Lutheran-Catholic competition for the highlands, the missions were playing by the administration's rules when they engaged in this heated race for congregants. And both missions took the challenge seriously.[16] For the Lutherans, the race to the highlands was a crucial part of their capacity to reimagine their mission on a much wider scale: not just a regional mission for the Huon Peninsula, the Lutherans could envision extending across the Territory of New Guinea and keeping pace with the Catholics. And while Flierl pitched the aviation program to his fellow missionaries in terms of light, fast freedom of movement, former missionaries then in Germany were encouraging Flierl to start using airplanes because of the rumor that Catholics would soon start doing so. In an annual report for 1927, Flierl writes, "I received two letters from Bro. Keysser, written at the beginning of August, with the news that an airline company was being formed for all Catholic missions in the world, including New Guinea which would place aircraft at the disposal of the Mission. . . . Keysser complained in his letter that 'always and everywhere the Catholics are ahead of the Protestants.'"[17] The Board of Foreign Missions of the American Lutheran Church also considered the Catholic competition the crucial reason for supporting the purchase of a plane: "From various sources, we are told that the Catholics are going to missionize with planes in [Papua New Guinea]. That would give them a big lead over us."[18]

THE INFRASTRUCTURAL NETWORKS
OF LUTHERAN MISSIONS

The use of airplanes in the Lutheran missions' work meant they needed to add another layer to their already vast and complex transportation-communication network. In particular, the advent of "aviation for souls" required the purchase of what were then called teleradios.[19] These were two-way radios, able to both receive and send transmissions, akin to extremely large walkie-talkies. Initially they were powered by someone—usually a Papua New Guinean servant—pedaling a bicycle-like generator device. The Papua New Guinea administration installed teleradio sets in regional centers starting in 1933 (Sinclair 1984: 94). By 1936, colonial officers were using the "portable" hundred-pound sets in their work in the remote parts of Papua New Guinea, while businessmen at far-flung plantations used radios to connect to the nearest town.

Newspaper reports from the time describe the revolution brought on by these radios as they reduced the feeling of isolation and increased a sense of measurable distance from somewhere, at least from somewhere that was within the four-hundred-mile range of the radio. Contemporary accounts emphasize the ways that teleradios allowed people in remote spaces to be located at a particular spot, rather than just "in the wilds." Newspaper articles detail the many ways that people in need were able to be located by ship or by airplane because they had a teleradio set: injured people could be picked up and patrols in remote Papua New Guinea could radio in for more supplies.[20] Teleradios meant that one was not simply lost.

In 1935, it was still quite novel to have radios in airplanes, and civil aviation in Australia and Papua New Guinea was just starting to use them regularly. Australian newspapers reported on the great progress made in 1937: *almost* every major "aerodrome" in the capital cities now had a radio, and all passenger-carrying planes did. In 1937, after the *Papua* started flying regular runs into the highlands, the Lutheran Mission was granted licenses for two teleradio transceiver sets, one at the Lae-area airstrip where the *Papua* was housed and one at the original Finschhafen headquarters of the mission. An unpublished manuscript notes that "the daily transmissions would include the flight plans of the Mission aeroplane 'Papua.' All missionaries concerned, for instance in the highlands, would listen in case their station was concerned." The highland missionaries could only receive, not transmit, messages. "Twice a week positions were given of the aeroplanes of Carpenters Airline which flew from Australia to Rabaul. . . . The radio service was greatly appreciated by all people concerned, the missionaries as well as other persons profiting from it."[21]

Locating oneself—as well as the planes—was an important part of how the radios transformed the space and time in which missionization took place. Missionaries listening in for flight schedules could align their watches and clocks to standard time, since the Lutherans would broadcast from Lae or Finschhafen at specific times of day.[22] Planes traveling overhead were not just somewhere in space, but locatable in relation to the ground through radio transmissions broadcasting their position. Flierl thought of airplanes as allowing one a radical freedom of movement, yet the infrastructural innovation of radio-enabled airplanes was to allow the planes to be located in regimentable time and navigable space, rather than just in a vast, unbroken expanse.

In his memoir, missionary Wilhelm Bergmann writes about the weeks when the *Papua* was just starting to be used. His very businesslike account of the novel transportation system is noteworthy for its attention to this sense of locatability. Bergmann seems to have been most impressed by the speed with which mission business could be conducted, given that his memories of the plane are largely prose itineraries:

> On the 26th of March we flew back to Kajabit. Since the weather was so nice, the pilot said we could once again look to fly inland. . . . The next day we left. We had loaded a lot of fuel. It was wonderful weather. Until shortly before the Elimbalim there wasn't a cloud in the sky. We flew over and landed in Mogei. We first flew over Ogelbeng

> and dropped off a letter. We soon got word from Ogelbeng that [Missionaries]
> Vicedom and Horrolt were in Ega. [Missionary] Löhe came to Mogei. We went to
> Ogelbeng. The airfield seems to be quite good, even dry. (Bergmann n.d.: 60)

His memories of the plane are of the speedy movement across dates, times, and places. Rather than strictly focusing on the phenomenological experience of speed as such (cf. Schivelbusch 1980), Bergmann memorializes his ability to get the mission's business done at a novel pace.

Bergmann delights in his capacity to locate himself and the plane in relation to the ground. This was not always guaranteed. James Sinclair (1978: 34–35) describes the first planes trying to land at the Wau airfield near the gold-mining operations; miners who had walked the tracks up to Wau many times could not orient themselves when in the air. It took the first pilot several attempts to locate the Wau airfield after it was constructed, since no aerial maps or routes existed yet. But even with heavy cloud cover, Bergmann boasts of his orientation in the plane. During one early, cloudy flight on the *Papua* he ended up guiding pilot Loose, then still quite new to New Guinea: "I told the pilot that he could fly down to the valley. He said a few times: Is that certain? I said yes. He was totally dependent on me because he did not know the area" (Bergmann n.d.: 56).

Being able to locate someone not just "in the wilds" but at a particular place and time at a destination airstrip or supply drop site also meant that one could communicate with those who were so located. That is, airplanes during the early days of Papua New Guinea civil aviation were as much elements in the transmission of talk as they were elements in the transmission of people and goods. The airplanes were extremely expensive postal services linking people across thousands of miles: "Previously it took three months for letters to arrive from home, for in some cases missionaries, their wives and children were thousands of miles apart. Now, however, an aeroplane left the ship [on which the mail was carried from Germany, the United States, or Australia] and mails arrived at their destination two and a half hours later. The missionary was able to reply immediately, as the 'plane waited for mails.'"[23]

Airplanes and radios combined to create an infrastructural space-time, in which particular persons and machines could be located at particular places and moments. Medical emergencies or a critical lack of provisions could be handled swiftly. Relatives could communicate with one another at a much quicker pace. The business of missionization was thus able to move more smoothly and quickly than it had in the past. The missionaries stationed in the highlands were no longer just "in the wilds" and out of reach, but part of a communication-transportation network linking the disparate corners of the mission as a whole. The aviation network, with its incipient radio control, started to transform the sense of circulatory primitivity into one in which people, things, and talk could in fact travel with relative ease. The distances were starting to shrink for Bergmann and the others who could now experience travel in a new way. This sense of immanence and immediacy only became stronger when missionaries tried to bring the *Papua* into the space-time of salvation.

CREATING CHRISTIAN SPACES

The Australia-based leader of the Lutheran Mission, Otto Theile, titled his speech about the quest for a mission airplane "A Miracle before Our Eyes," placing the work of the aviation program firmly within the sacred work of the mission, particularly given the opening up of the highlands to mission work. He said,

> At that time the question of further extension of our mission into the far inland among the newly discovered tribes . . . was agitating our minds incessantly. . . . We were aware that it would mean much treasure and many men to do effectually what we were setting our hands to do, we were especially quite alive to the great difficulties of transport. But there were the open doors, there were the opportunities! From the highlands of the inland we heard a call: "come over and help us" and within our hearts we heard the command of the Master "Go and preach the gospel!"[24]

Aviation for souls was not just an improvement in the communication network, and not just an increase in the speed with which those many masses of highlands souls could be encountered. The plane filled missionaries, and supposedly even Papua New Guinean Christians, with deep emotion and heartfelt offerings that Theile describes in operatic terms: "Missionaries and natives sacrificed of their possession to try and make it possible to acquire a plane. It is deeply touching to see on the list, how missionaries sacrificed a whole year's salary and it is pathetic to hear how the villagers at home and the Christian laborers on the plantations and on the goldfield brought all the cash they had in order to help along the cause." The extent to which the airplane was considered a sacred project is also evident from the fact that the archive of the Lutheran Church in Papua New Guinea has retained a file with some of the original receipts noting the individual contributions that the missionaries made to help purchase the plane. Even though the mission had other major donation drives related to raising funds for earlier modes of transportation (e.g., ships), receipts of this sort were not usually archived.[25]

There was also a sense that the aviation program was able to create a particular kind of converted person—someone who was truly able to move about, not just across the rainforest landscape of Papua New Guinea but above it, surpassing it. In other words there was a sense in which God was all the more present in an evangelistic project that was able to literally transcend the dirt and earth. Having an airplane would help create that ultimate movement to heaven, as the missionary R. R. Hanselmann puts it in an extraordinary plea for funds to the Auxiliary Society of the American Lutheran Church's Board of Foreign Missions:

> Aeroplane, workshop, machinery, pilots, mechanics, landing places, another one after the first one crashes, radio sending and receiving sets, electricians—all will mean many worries, many prayers, and much money. We don't need all this if we stay out

of the interior, but as certain as the Lord wants us to bring the Gospel message to those in an area as yet untouched by anything of civilization and Christianity, so sure it is that He has His people who will help to solve the transport problems, may they cost what they will. And especially, since the area is apparently the last primitive corner in our universe (making mission work a serious business, since the Gospel is to be brought to all ends of the world and THEN COME THE END), it seems that God wishes to give every member of our Lutheran Church an opportunity to do mission work as it has never been done before.[26]

The successful combination of these different spatiotemporal formations brought about an important event in history that was to foreshadow an ultimate end of history: "The Lutheran mission was, as far as it is known, the first mission in the world to use aviation as a tool in spreading the gospel. The *Papua* had made history."[27]

The Lutheran missions linked speed, lightness, and heavens together in a way that was immediately recognizable to missionaries and mission supporters long used to stories of muck and mud. Once the Roman Catholic and Seventh-day Adventist threat in the highlands appears, the mission raised funds for the *Papua* even though it was roughly equivalent to the entire yearly operating budget of the mission at the time. The Lutheran Mission's use of airplanes was a way to structure its missiological project. As Huber (1988) has discussed in regard to the use of boats in the early years of the neighboring Catholic missions, the space and time in which missionization took place was organized by the introduction of the *Papua*. Even though the mission often tried to downplay its large institutional and infrastructural footprint as simply a "secular concern," the mission project itself cannot be understood outside of these forms, where speed and lightness were characteristics not only of modes of travel, but of modes of Christian evangelism.

THE MENACE IN THE SKY

But the question of speed and lightness—the capacity to fly over the land in an instant—also made aviation for souls suspect. In a story that will be repeated throughout the chapters of this book, whenever Papua New Guinea seemed to be too accessible, the administration started to worry that they would lose control of the territory. That is, the sense that Papua New Guinea's interior was inaccessible was so baked into the discourses about the colony that relative accessibility often came with suspicions about illicit access. In the case of the Lutheran aviation system, those suspicions came in two distinct flavors.

The first was a general suspicion in the colonial press about the seemingly tight connection between God and technological progress that the *Papua* represented. What happens to God when he is made accessible by machine? For one thing, other objects connected with those same machines may be conflated with the mission project. This fear is made quite explicit in a 1942 cover image from the *Pacific Island Monthly* magazine during World War II captioned "Menace in the Sky" (figure 3).

FIGURE 3. Cover of *Pacific Islands Monthly* linking God and airplanes. (*Pacific Islands Monthly* vol. 12, no. 8, National Library of Australia, nla.obj-310385031)

The menace in the sky—Japanese bombs being dropped on Papua New Guinea and other Pacific territories—seems particularly menacing from the perspective of Europeans because they imagine Pacific Islanders to have connected sky, God, and airplane. The text on the cover reads: "For 150 years, the native peoples of the Pacific Islands have been taught by Europeans to look into the sky for hope and salvation. To-day, their world is crashing around them. The Europeans are fighting for their lives: while out of the sky come only terror, destruction and death. The outlook is black—but it is the darkness before the dawn."[28] Note that airplanes had been around only since the 1920s. The 150 years referred to here is the 150-year history of missionary operations in the Pacific. The cover image and text present a direct conflation of the space and time of God with the space and time of the Allied and Axis bombers.[29]

As the time grew closer and closer to the outbreak of the war in Europe, the Lutheran airplane played a crucial role in a second series of accusations against the Lutheran missionaries. Rumors swirled that German Lutherans not only were Nazi Party members, but were teaching local people to salute Hitler and, if necessary, defend the Fatherland. The infrastructure of the aviation program now seemed to constitute the ingredients of a propaganda machine much speculated on in Australian newspapers: "The Lutherans had a secret radio transmitter, a miniature factory for production of swastika flags and armbands, and always maintained excellent aerodromes."[30] As long as Papua New Guinea remained remote and inaccessible, worries about illicit access could be kept under control. But the success the Lutherans had had in developing a communicative infrastructure became part of the concern that Lutherans were too autonomous, too easily made into a larger circulatory network of wartime materiel and propaganda. The Lutherans' ability to bring in trade goods by airplane likewise became the basis of rumors: "Among the presents sent out to the natives to win their sympathy were cheap trade mirrors with a picture of Hitler on the back."[31] One Australian brigadier-general was quoted as saying that the Lutherans had five hundred airplanes ready for use in the war, not just the lonely *Papua*.[32] Papua New Guinea aviation expert Ian Grabowsky knew that the Lutherans had only one plane, but nonetheless he worried that with the right pilot and payload it might be used to bomb all the Australian planes in Papua New Guinea "in half an hour" (Sinclair 1978: 222).

As Christine Winter (2012) discusses in detail, several of the former and then-current German nationals working as Lutheran missionaries in Papua New Guinea were active and involved Nazi Party members. In that sense, the Australian fears about the missionaries spreading pro-Nazi sentiment were not outlandish, even if the specific rumors listed here were not true. And as Peter Fritzsche (1992) argues, aviation was a central part of the German nationalist imagination in the decades leading up to the war. However, my point here is that these fears were in many places talked about in terms of the circulatory potential of the Lutheran communicative networks.

In the end, the *Papua* had an even stranger role to play, taking part in neither a heavenly haul of souls nor a Nazi attack on Australia. When war in Europe was declared in 1939, the two German laymen employees who at that time piloted and took care of the *Papua* took off for the highlands in hopes of escaping over the border into Dutch New Guinea. At one point, during a refueling stop, an Australian colonial officer held them and tried to get them to swear an oath of neutrality, which they refused to do. Realizing that the men had just onboarded enough fuel to make it over the border, the Australian had them sign instead an oath saying that they would not use their fuel to escape. The men signed the oath, flew to another Lutheran station, dumped out the fuel about which the oath had been made, filled the engine's tanks with new fuel, and made a desperate flight over the border to Merauke in Dutch New Guinea.[33] From there they traveled by boat to Japan, crossed into the Soviet Union, rode the Trans-Siberian Railway into Germany, and joined the Luftwaffe (Sinclair 1978: 222). The *Papua* was never recovered, and the Lutheran aviation program had to start from scratch when, after the war, American and Australian Lutherans tried to reconstitute the vast mission program.

Although missionary modes of circulation often center on Bible translation, this did not exhaust Lutheran missionary concerns with circulation, where properties of speed, of lightness, or of movement itself were as crucial a project as Bible translation.[34] This Christian model of circulation emphasizes the movement of "the gospel message" as a project in which the qualities of movement take on moral properties. Here I have attended to the infrastructural networks across which texts like Bibles or letters appear and the ways in which the Lutherans themselves conceptualized the spatiotemporal movement of texts, people, and objects along such paths.

Colonial actors focused on Papua New Guinea as a space in which movement was almost impossible, requiring the extraordinary intervention of novel technologies to transform the space and the people residing in it. Aviation and radios worked together to open up the territory to Lutheran intervention and a potential Christian transformation. But given the extent to which colonial actors saw Papua New Guinea as a space of circulatory primitivity, the easy movements of the Lutherans soon came under suspicion. Secular observers at the time thought of the use of airplanes by missions as the height of greed—missionaries flying over the land consuming souls as if in a Christian gold rush. One of the main lessons that the postwar Lutheran organization seemed to learn was that making themselves appear too accessible also left them open to accusations of greed, treason, and immorality. As I argue below, this is most apparent in the contradictory ways that the Lutherans used the extensive postwar radio network they developed in conjunction with the CRMF.

RADIO NETWORKS AND THE CULTIVATION OF REMOTENESS

If the prewar technological innovation of the aviation program and radio network was that people could be locatable "in the wilds," the postwar problem when reestablishing the aviation program and (especially) the radio network was that people needed to maintain their remoteness. There were multiple reasons for this, and I focus on two of them in the remainder of this chapter. On the one hand, missionaries criticized themselves when they seemed to be overly connected to one another. Implicitly, and sometimes explicitly, they asked why people would come all the way to colonial Papua New Guinea if not to get out into remote territories. On the other hand, colonial administrators expressed deep skepticism of missionaries who were too connected. Even though there was no longer a wartime paranoia of Nazi influence coming into rural Papua New Guinea, there was a concern that a too-connected mission would make it too much like a state within a state. The administration subsidized the missions to run things like education systems because it was too expensive and difficult for the administration to do it on their own. If Papua New Guinea could be so connected, then at least part of the administrators' rationale for taking this laissez-faire attitude toward mission education systems was erased.

During World War II, when the civil administration was taken over by the military, surviving Lutheran missionaries were evacuated to (or incarcerated in) internment camps. Many of the Lutheran mission stations were destroyed and, as I noted above, their licenses for radios and for use of the *Papua* were rescinded.[35] Given the large number of German citizens among the Lutheran missionaries prior to the war, the ability for the mission to be reestablished afterward was very much in doubt. With postwar restrictions on German organizations and people, the structure of the various Lutheran missions had to change. First, though, they had to see if the mission would be allowed to operate at all. Arriving back in Papua New Guinea in 1945, American Lutheran Dr. John Kuder and his colleague Dr. Theodore Fricke were tasked with trying to convince the military administration that the Lutherans should be allowed back in. With the stipulation that many of the German missionaries would be barred from reentry, the administration finally relented and allowed the Lutheran missions to begin operations again. Dr. Fricke sent an ecstatic telegram to the Lutheran Mission Board in the United States: DOORS OPEN SEND MEN.[36]

Prior to the war, there were several different Lutheran missionary organizations working in Papua New Guinea: the Neuendettelsau and Rhenish missionary societies from Germany, as well as missionary arms of both the Australian and American Lutheran Churches. In the postwar era, these distinct groups were consolidated under the single name Lutheran Mission New Guinea. This new composite group was placed in the hands of John Kuder, who remained the superintendent of the mission until 1969 and who also served as the first bishop (1956–73) as the mission transitioned into being the Evangelical Lutheran *Church* of Papua New Guinea.

The rebuilding process was long and difficult. The north coast of Papua New Guinea had been occupied by Japan and by the US Army. Many of the Lutheran buildings, roads, and other forms of physical infrastructure from before the war were destroyed during the fighting. However, the army left so much equipment in its wake that jeeps, radios, tents, and other supplies were sold to missions and other returning colonials for pennies. Well into the 1950s, the Lutheran Mission's radio engineer used army surplus material from the war as a source of spare parts for radio repairs.

In December 1949, the Lutherans requested a new radio license as part of their effort to rebuild their massive organization. In 1950, they made contact with the CRMF, which wanted to create a private radio network for several Protestant mission groups in Papua New Guinea. In 1952, the CRMF applied for radio transmitter licenses to connect remote mission stations, a majority of which would be Lutheran stations at the beginning. After considerable resistance from the administration, the CRMF private radio network was licensed in 1954. It remained an independent private network until the 1970s, when the administration eventually insisted on all CRMF radios moving onto the administration network.

TWO-WAY RADIO NETWORKS:
PRIVACY AND CIRCULATION

So what was a two-way radio network? How did people connect to one another? What sorts of communication and communicative routines did the technology afford speakers? Without having transcripts of conversations, I am limited in my discussion to the ways in which the radios themselves allowed for different kinds of interactions and how users talked about their communicative routines. As it turns out, the missionary radio network was at once private—almost secretive— and intensely open, with speakers on the network unable to limit the reach of their voices. In this section, I examine the modes of privacy and channel construction that the network operators created through the regulated circulation of crystals and schedules. I will look at the ways that users dealt with the network's threatening openness, a capacity to verge on broadcasting, in the following section. Although I do not think that the Lutheran Mission's leadership was overtly thinking in these terms, the postwar problem of communications was a matter of trying not to make the space of the mission too accessible, as if the lesson learned from the *Papua* was that there was something dangerous to the mission's future if the space of Lutheran activities became too easy to navigate.

The colonial missionary radio network had a set of features that worked together to produce a fragile form of circulation, one that often appeared to be on the verge of collapse and one that users of the network were constantly fretting over. First, creating discrete linkages or nodes in the network required the restricted circulation of material objects. In particular, access to the missionary network depended on the circulation of piezoelectric radio crystals and radio schedules that set the boundaries of membership. The network was a private network to the extent that its communicative nodes could be kept limited. Second, the missionaries who used the network were constantly trying to keep the network from spilling out into the domain of broadcast communication and an ungovernable number of social relations. Once the radio network was in operation and communicative links existed among missionaries, the network operators worked endlessly to limit both the amount of talk on the network and the number of potential listeners by appealing to missionaries' own sensibilities of their roles as pioneering evangelists in a rugged and remote terrain. Valiant men of God did not sit around broadcasting their complaints or passively listen in on others'. Third, using the network required that users make a set of category distinctions that were necessary if the missionary network was going to remain autonomous from adjacent administration networks. Simply speaking into a radio transmitter wasn't enough to be a part of the network. One had to speak in the proper way and on the proper topics—avoiding, in particular, any talk "of a commercial nature"—or else the network could get dissolved by administration bureaucracy. Each of these features—restricted circulation of material, constant attention to the potential collapse into broadcast forms, and categorization of speech—points to the ways in which the colonial missionary radio network in Papua New Guinea was the ideological object of users' reflexive understanding about the kinds of communicative linkages they were creating.

As mentioned above, two-way radio networks worked more or less like walkie-talkies. A number of people all tuned in to the same frequency. Only one person could send a message at a time, while everyone tuned in to that frequency could receive the message simultaneously. For a complicated network like the CRMF missionary one, with over three hundred stations connected at its height in the late 1960s, it was necessary to have control stations that managed radio traffic, given the one-after-another turn taking that the system demanded.[37] Being part of a two-way radio network meant that one tuned in to a specific frequency used by everyone else on the network and "worked into" (i.e., one's radio traffic was controlled by) a base station specific to that network.

In order to transmit messages on the network's frequency, one had to have a specific crystal cut in such a way that it resonated at the appropriate frequency. The thickness of the crystal wafer determined the frequency at which it resonated. Once machined and calibrated, the crystal wafers were housed in boxes that were plugged directly into the radios. In the 1950s, most teleradio transmitters had space for two to six different crystals to be inserted, and one had to toggle a switch to send electricity through whichever crystal and frequency one wanted to use. Each radio network would be assigned one or two frequencies. In order to operate on a network, both sending and receiving transmissions, one had to be sent the proper crystal or crystals for that network's frequencies. In the missionary radio network files, radio engineer Carl Spehr often mentions having just "sent a crystal" to missionary stations as soon as the colonial administration had approved their license. While the administration radio engineers at Port Moresby likely had crystals for all frequencies that they licensed within Papua New Guinea, remote government stations across the territory would not necessarily have had access to transmit on the private missionary network frequencies. The missionary radio network was, to that extent, at a remove from the administration's representatives in the field. Thus, it was the controlled circulation of crystals that made the network private.[38] Without the regulation of crystals there was no regulation of the limits of the network.

Control of the network as a limited, private channel of communication also depended on the constant verbal approval of a base station, which controlled radio traffic of each outstation trying to transmit on the network. Because the missionary radio network was so large and included so many different mission stations, the network I am talking about had three different control or base stations that handled traffic for outstations within their respective areas: Madang and Lae (the Lutheran controlled stations) and Rugli (the main CRMF station in the highlands near Mt. Hagen that managed traffic for all other missions on the network). Base stations worked together to produce another material object—the radio schedule, or "sked"—which was mimeographed and sent to each mission station as the arbiter of lawful communication times (figure 4).[39]

Each mission had several different times throughout the day when only it could use one or the other frequency. The first sked time of the day for each mission was the general call-up, when traffic for the day was organized. For example, in 1966 the Lutheran Mission's general call-up happened from 0715 to 0745 hours on the 5895 frequency, one of the two frequencies used by the CRMF radios. The two Lutheran base stations at Lae and Madang would give general information and notices to their outstations, and all outstations were supposed to listen in at their radios during this time. A missionary at Lutheran headquarters in Lae or Madang would then hail each outstation one by one, asking the missionaries at each station if they had any questions or requests for later sked times ("Boana—do you have any traffic? Malolo—do you have any traffic?"). The missionaries at the hailed outstation were required to respond. They could either say "no traffic" or request to speak either with a specific person or department at mission headquarters or with a different outstation. The base station at Lae or Madang would take down all these requests, and then parcel out appointments during the remaining Lutheran sked times for each station to speak to whomever they needed to be in touch with. There were some blank spaces in the CRMF sked, particularly in the evening, when people could use the network on an ad hoc basis. The Lutherans seem to have monopolized these times to such an extent that the other missions usually did not have a chance to use them.

In addition to the base stations that controlled radio traffic, the administration in Port Moresby monitored, or at least had the capacity to monitor, all traffic. For this reason, users of the network had to speak in English. In the case of radios used by some of the Papua New Guinean crew members of the mission ships, Tok

MISS.	3196 SKED	TIME	5895 SKED	MISS.
		0600		
		0615		
SSEM	X	0630		
CMML	X	0645		
AMAF	X	0700		
BAP	X	0715	X	LMNG
NGLM	X	0730	X	LMNG
UFM	X	0745	X	METH
COC	X	0800	X	UFM
COC	X	0815	X	UFM
BAP	X	0830	X	APOS
METH	X	0845	X	EWIBM
ANG	X	0900	X	LMNG
LMNG	X	0915	X	ANG
WM	X	0930	X	ANG
NAZ	X	0945	X	UFM
		1000	X	S
		1015	X	O
AOG	X	1030	X	T
AOG	X	1045	X	A
SIL	X	1100	X	CRMF
		1115	X	CRMF
CMML	X	1130	X	LMNG
CMML	X	1145	X	NGLM
CMML	X	1200	X	UFM
CMML	X	1215	X	UFM
NGLM	X	1230	X	LMS
NGGM	X	1245	X	LMS
COC	X	1300	X	LMS
COC	X	1315	X	LMS
LMS	X	1330	X	ANG
APOS	X	1345	X	ANG
		1400	X	UFM
		1415	X	CIMC

MISS.	3196 SKED	TIME	5895 SKED	MISS.
		1430	X	EWIBM
		1445		
NAZ	X	1500	X	S
		1515	X	O
LMNG	X	1530	X	T
		1545	X	A
ANG	X	1600	X	UFM
ANG	X	1615	X	UFM
SSEM	X	1630	X	ANG
SSEM	X	1645	X	ANG
LMNG	X	1700	X	LMS
LMNG	X	1715	X	NGGM
CMML	X	1730	X	APOS
CMML	X	1745	X	APOS
BAP	X	1800	X	CRMF
METH	X	1815		
METH	X	1830		
AOG	X	1845		
NAZ	X	1900		
LMNG	X	1915		
LMNG	X	1930		
LMNG	X	1945		
LMS	X	2000		
ANG	X	2015		
		2030		
		2045		
		2100		
		2115		
		2130		
		2145		
		2200		
		2215		
		2230		
		2245		

FIGURE 4. A "sked" showing when different mission stations had scheduled times to use the radio network. The Lutheran Mission's times are marked LMNG (Lutheran Mission New Guinea, as it was officially known in the postwar years). Archives of the Evangelical Lutheran Church of Papua New Guinea. (Photo by author)

Pisin was allowed by special license. Vernacular languages were not allowed on the radio network. This means that aside from maritime licenses, all users of the network were assumed to be white Europeans.

CONNECTING THE ISOLATED, BUT ONLY SO MUCH

As newspaper reports about radio users "in the wilds" suggest, the rationale for the private radio network was the extreme isolation of mission stations and the white European missionaries living at them. Demonstrating the isolation of the mission stations was one of the most important burdens of the CRMF application for their private radio network. As part of the 1954 application for the network, the Lutherans put together a list of their European-staffed mission stations with comments about how many white women and children were present and how remote the station was. For example:

KALASA:
Missionary in Charge: Rev. F. Wagner.
Family: Wife
Comments: Isolated station between Ulap and Finsch[hafen]. Station several hours walking distance from coast. Sets [*sic*] up on top of a series of rocky terraces.

MUMENG:
Missionary in Charge: Rev. G. Horrolt
Family: Wife; 1 girl-9 years
Comments: Isolated mission station. 1 ½–2 hours walk to government station.

OMKALAI:
Missionary in Charge: Rev. Brandt (on furlough);
Family: Wife, 1 girl-8 years, 3 boys-6, 3, 2 years.
Comments: Isolated highlands station. Not accessible by plane or vehicle.[40]

Correspondence between the CRMF director and the Lutheran Mission president shows the two men debating which stories of isolation, difficult communications, and medical emergencies would be most effective as part of the 1954 application packet.[41] The application materials depict a highly functioning, albeit atomized, mission organization that only needed the capacity to talk to different stations: "The missions have the doctors and the hospitals, but lack the communications for them to serve even their own children."[42] In other words, there were concentrated spaces of colonial Christianity but each was almost autonomous, an individual space of pioneering evangelism in a rugged, difficult-to-travel terrain. Notably, almost all of these stories about medical near-misses included in the network application involve European missionaries and their families, not the Papua New Guinean population. That is, the remoteness and isolation emphasized here is white remoteness.

However much the application for the network depended on the demonstration of social and geographic remoteness, the actual experiences of using the radio network once it was running seemed to constantly create too many social connections. Most apparent from the Lutheran archive is the fact that the Lutheran missionaries quickly started hogging all of the radio time to talk to base stations or to other outstations. At regular intervals, Lutheran radio engineers had to send out the kind of pleading messages to the Lutheran Mission staff discussed at the beginning of this chapter: please stop running overtime into other sked slots and stop using up all of the unscheduled times, since by doing so they were keeping the other missions that were part of the network from being able to communicate.[43] In his 1968 report to the assembled members of the Lutheran Mission at their yearly conference, radio engineer George Groat gave the network users a good dressing-down for talking out of turn, using the network for improper kinds of communication, and not using the appropriate radio jargon: "over and out" is nonsense, given that "over" assumes that you are awaiting a response but "out" means that you are *not* awaiting a response. You should say "off and clear" instead. He tried to enforce the use of a particular register for radio interactions: "Ask control for clearance before going ahead with your traffic. Think your communication out clearly before sked time. Don't ramble on. Abbreviate wherever you can for easier copying by the recipient of your traffic."[44] He was frustrated that he had made these same pleading announcements for years to no avail. The Lutheran missionaries had gone from being isolated Christian evangelists to chatty Cathys who couldn't stop talking with one another in anarchic disorder.

In some radio networks at the time, a certain amount of free-form chatter was routinized and grudgingly tolerated by the colonial administration. Sinclair (1984: 193) briefly discusses the network used in the Papuan islands region by planters, missionaries, and government officials in which everyone agreed that 4:30 to 6:30 p.m. would be an "unofficial small-talk radio schedule" known as the "Rum Sessions." The Department of Posts and Telegraphs in Moresby monitored the sessions as part of its regular monitoring of all networks. "So long as the proprieties were observed, however, the Department was loath to intervene. The rules of the game were well understood by all: no profane or indecent language could be used, and no purely commercial messages exchanged, for this would deprive [the Department of Posts and Telegraphs] of lawful revenue. Then someone broke the rules," and in 1959 the administration ordered that the Rum Sessions had to end. The Papuan islands network that hosted the Rum Sessions had only twenty-five radio sets; the CRMF network had over three hundred in 1968. This kind of free-form Rum Sessions chit-chat was impossible, yet the Lutherans at least kept trying to do it.

And while access to transmitting on the network was tightly controlled by the circulation of crystals, one could hear any sked one wanted. If hydroelectric power or long-lasting batteries were available, missionaries could listen in on a potentially endless supply of news or gossip or information about the medical maladies or airplane travel of various missionaries. Users of the network were not supposed to listen in except during their general call-ups in the morning and when they had a sked, but they were of course aware of the fact that within their private network there was very little privacy. In a letter to the Lutheran Mission superintendent, the head of CRMF, Claude D'Evelynes, writes: "If you wish to discuss any of these matters with me over the air we could make a sked for 5 a.m. on 3196 and be fairly sure of privacy."[45] In other words, you could try to schedule an appointment to talk in the middle of the night, but that would at best cut down on people listening in, not avoid it altogether.[46]

Although the network was based on a sense of white colonial isolation that needed to be overcome, it quickly started to generate too many moments of contact. The isolated nodes of the network were still supposed to be isolated. That is, you cannot be a missionary if you are just idly chatting, gossiping, or eavesdropping on the radio all day. Missionary self-conceptions as romantic and pioneering evangelists did not include that much chit-chat. The culture of colonialism more broadly is one of isolation, and talking about one's experiences of remoteness is part of the colonial project (Ardener 1987). Technological limitations, romanticized self-conceptions, and religious conversion all contributed to the ideological and practical work done to make the missionary radio network capable of managing but not eradicating those feelings of isolation. More generally, the network could keep its shape as a private missionary network only if it could keep from becoming a broadcast station.

MERGING INTO OTHER NETWORKS

A major limiting condition on the licenses that the administration granted to the mission network had the effect of blurring the boundaries between the private and the administration networks. It was common at this time to separate commercial from noncommercial messages on wireless networks. The missionary network licenses were granted with the restriction that any discussions of commercial or business interests would result in fees payable to the Department of Posts and Telegraphs in Port Moresby, one shilling per three-minute conversation (in 2024, this is approximately equivalent to a charge of five US dollars every three minutes). That is, even if the mission network was private, it was to be run as if it were part of the Posts and Telegraphs department of the colonial administration whenever "business" was discussed.

The administration assumed that most traffic would be chargeable (i.e., commercial) except for those limited sets of "conversations relating to the safety of life and property and the spiritual welfare of persons." For the administration, noncommercial traffic should only include things like "medical consultations, urgent medical supplies, whereabouts of personnel in cases where questions of safety are involved, aircraft movements and vital weather information in emergency."

Yet the CRMF director assumed that all traffic should be free except for the limited sets of conversations about trade stores or the sale of mission plantation copra (coconut). Food for missions could be "health and safety," while supplies for mission schools could be "spiritual welfare." Even Carl Spehr thought the CRMF director's position was extreme, summing up his thoughts in a handwritten postscript to his boss: "I am sure that the Post-Master General and Rugli [i.e., CRMF] do not agree on the interpretation of 'Spiritual Welfare.' Rugli claims it means 'all mission matter'; the Post-Master General claims it means what it says."[47]

The member missions of the CRMF wanted to negotiate a five-pound flat rate to pay to the administration each year, in essence sidestepping the whole question of how to disentangle business from spirit in day-to-day affairs. But the CRMF director was adamant that any fees were a ridiculous intrusion on the autonomy of the network and an unfair burden on the Christian missions. Thus began a never-to-be-resolved debate about what exactly constituted commercial traffic on the missionary network. In his history of telecommunications in Papua New Guinea, Sinclair (1984: 194) says of the CRMF mission network that "there is no doubt that a lot of traffic was passed that should, by any reasonable criteria, have gone to P and T [Posts and Telegraphs], so contributing much-needed revenue to the national telecommunications system." For the almost state-like Lutheran Mission, which ran plantations, trade stores, hospitals, schools, and supply houses, "commercial matters" as opposed to spiritual or safety matters were difficult to distinguish. Missionaries kept logbooks that tried to bureaucratically police the domain of the commercial, but nobody really knew how to log most calls.

In effect, this ambivalence about the boundary between spiritual and commercial radio traffic on the network meant that it was impossible to fully separate the mission and administration networks. The demand to log any calls of a commercial nature meant that the private mission network became, at moments, a subsidiary of the administration network. The isolation from the administration that was the initial rationale for the mission network was subverted by actually using it, which was perhaps the goal of the administration.[48] But it was a goal that the missionaries resisted. They wanted to be independent of the administration even as they depended on it for support and subsidies.

The autonomy of the network therefore depended on the categorization of talk: what was a commercial exchange and what wasn't? The network could stay independent only so long as it kept track of the distinction. In addition to the regulation of speech through crystals and skeds, and the limitations on the amount of speech in the desire to manage but not eradicate isolation, the network was able to be a network only to the extent that users paid constant attention to the impossible line between the commercial and spiritual in their everyday talk of planes and weather and trade stores and conversions.

THE LIMITS OF A NETWORK

These different kinds of limitations—or forms of channeling—not only produce a network with defined, if always collapsing, boundaries and linking nodes. They also produce a certain kind of social space: a geographic and racial imaginary that distinguished the speech on the network from the world outside it.

Pockets of mission activity were linked to one another through a network that depended legally on their continued extreme isolation from other white, English speakers. Yet the Lutheran speakers on the network were continually chided about their abuse of the radio skeds and their endless talk and social connectivity. Likewise, the need to log all traffic of a commercial nature meant that speakers were constantly monitoring their relation to an adjacent network of administration personnel and practices, but doing so in ways that guarded their separation from the administration. The network of isolated, white, colonial speakers produced a porousness and superfluity of social connections that had to be constrained. The network needed to manage and control colonial isolation, not banish it.

The circulatory primitivity of the Territory of New Guinea was exacerbated rather than overcome by the Lutheran Mission's extensive communicative and transportation networks. Given the administrators' concerns that they were too large and powerful in their domain of influence, the Lutherans had to minimize their own footprint. In the run-up to World War II, rumors of Nazi factories and fighter squadrons hidden in the jungles kept the administration suspicious of German national missionaries (and the aviation program came to an abrupt halt when the Lutheran lay aviation engineers ran off with their only plane). The assumption of communicative freedom that seemed to open up with aviation into and out of the highlands during the "gold rush for souls" came to a halt, and that freedom was more circumscribed in the postwar years. In order not to repeat the same prewar dynamics, the administration had to try to keep tight control over the radio network and the Lutherans had to try to insist they still needed it because of their remote outstations. The communicative technologies of Papua New Guinea were opening up, yet the structural tensions between the administration and the mission meant that communications needed to be kept curtailed.

Even as telecommunications have dramatically improved in recent years with the introduction of mobile phone access in rural Papua New Guinea (see Foster and Horst 2018, Foster 2024), the sense that communication systems have to be used sparingly and respectfully remains part of the memories of missionary life. The Bible translation organization known as SIL International developed its own radio network and worked with the Mission Aviation Fellowship to create a network of planes and helicopters to transport their translators. Unlike many of the garrulous Lutherans who were constantly chastised in annual meetings for talking too much, the SIL translators seem to have largely been able to keep their radio use to a minimum. However, the translator who worked in the Waria Valley, where I did research in the first decade of this century, was an exception. Ernie Richert was known as a larger-than-life character. The story that both Waria Valley people and other SIL translators consistently told about him was that he treated the aviation network not as a sacred resource capable of occasionally mitigating remoteness, but instead like a taxi. He would call up on the radio network in the morning and demand to have a plane come pick him up that same day. This was unheard of, yet he apparently did it on more than one occasion. And it was still one of the first things people told me about him almost fifty years later. He did not use the aviation system in a way that maintained a feeling of remoteness at all, and as the Lutherans discovered before him, that made one an object of scorn and some suspicion.

Because Papua New Guinea had both many mountains and many languages, it created a space in which it was almost impossible to build economies of scale: even if the mountains could be conquered, the languages were still there, requiring more and more missionaries on the scene who valorized local-language Bible translation to engage with the local communities—more and more missionaries who then had to be connected by radio. But if circulation actually had become simple, then all of a sudden the administrators might have wanted to take over the secular aspects of their work. That is, the non-integration of the many denominational mission organizations was acceptable only to the extent that the Territory of New Guinea continued to suffer under circulatory primitivity. Lutherans needed to organize communicative networks to eradicate distance among their colonial outposts, but were at risk of losing their colonial autonomy the moment distances actually seemed surmountable.

When it came to languages, too, remoteness was an artifact of Lutheran work rather than a natural outcome of conditions on the ground. In the following chapter, I look at how the circulation of men and languages through Lutheran plantations seemed, for a long time, to create not connections, but religious and subjective boundaries.

2

Tok Pisin and the Linguistic Infrastructure of the Lutheran Missions

People have been trying to kill Tok Pisin for as long as the language has been around. In regard to other languages spoken by colonized communities, scholars and activists speak of language death. For Tok Pisin, it is better to speak of attempted language murder. While this book has taken many unexpected twists and turns since I first started working on it, one of the fundamental issues I have kept returning to is how so many love to hate Tok Pisin.

The desire to destroy Tok Pisin took many forms. People have, for example, talked about trying to "slay the dragon of Pidgin," using an allusion to biblical verses like Isaiah 27:1 about the Leviathan: "In that day the Lord with his hard and great and strong sword will punish Leviathan the fleeing serpent, Leviathan the twisting serpent, and he will slay the dragon that is in the sea." To "slay the dragon" in Isaiah is to redeem Israel, to defeat evil, and to bring about the end of earthly troubles. "Slay[ing] the dragon of Pidgin," as the Australian minister for external territories Paul Hasluck put it, would redeem Papua New Guinea, allowing for some other radically new and better English-based future.[1] Less poetically but just as violently, the UN demanded in 1953 that the language simply be "eradicated" (as I discuss in chapter 5). Others have talked about trying, if not to kill Pidgin, then to engage in a little assisted suicide, helping to slowly transform the language into something more or less identical with standard Australian English through a process of gradual incorporation of more and more English content and grammar.

And it is not just colonial agents who have these deadly desires. Papua New Guineans have often insisted (and continue to insist) on the removal of Tok Pisin from Parliament, from the school system, or from the country more generally (see Slotta and Handman 2024). Sir Michael Somare, the first prime minister, who is

59

now widely revered as the father of the nation, once argued, during a 1976 parliamentary session, against proposals to make Tok Pisin a national language with official status. In itself this was a common enough argument at the time. The only thing that makes it remarkable is that he made the comment—in Parliament—while speaking in Tok Pisin.[2] Finally, people sometimes speak as though Tok Pisin is so fragile it will come undone with just the slightest prodding. An interlocutor from the Waria Valley once said, in response to my request that he translate an ancestral ritual couplet into Tok Pisin from the Guhu-Samane language, that to do so would rupture the language (*em bai brukim Tok Pisin*). Whether it is figured as the Leviathan to be defeated or as a suicide to be assisted, or as a fragility on the verge of disintegration, Tok Pisin is often depicted as being at death's door. The debate has often just been whether it needs a "great and strong sword" or only a slight push to send it to the other side.

Not everyone hated Tok Pisin. A few, like American linguist Robert A. Hall Jr. and some of his allies, took great pains to standardize and spread it. They argued that Tok Pisin was the only possible way of dealing with what was called "the language problem": the problem of how to facilitate communication where there seemed to only be "insuperable barriers" of linguistic difference, as a director of Papua New Guinea's Department of Education, W. C. Groves, put it. "One of the greatest problems in this Territory is the multiplicity of vernaculars," he wrote. "Not only in schools, but in every contact between Administration and Native, and between Native and Native, the problem of linguistic complexity arises."[3] With so many dead set against Tok Pisin, though, Groves had to remind his readers that "in New Guinea, the problem of finding a lingua franca has already been solved."[4] Tok Pisin was the solution to the language problem that everyone refused to see.

In addition to Hall and Groves, some Christian missionaries ended up using Tok Pisin, although sometimes, like the Lutherans whom I discuss in this chapter, they did so belatedly and through gritted teeth. The administration and missions eventually published Tok Pisin newsletters—and a weekly newspaper, *Wantok*—starting in 1970 (for Tok Pisin journalism, see Schram 2023). Australian linguists, especially those working with Stephan Wurm at the Australian National University, were also prominent supporters. The most notable examples of this support came in two forms: first, a collection of essays on the future of Tok Pisin featuring many of the ANU linguists arguing in support of Tok Pisin's necessary role in Papua New Guinea's development (McElhanon 1975); and second, the speech that linguist Thomas Dutton gave at the University of Papua New Guinea advocating Tok Pisin as the language of the nation and the school system, which sparked a vigorous and sometimes angry debate that took place via letters to the editors of the national newspapers and other media outlets (collected in McDonald 1976).

Yet even these cheerleaders worked under the assumption of Tok Pisin's inevitable and desirable demise. The Catholic Fr. Francis Mihalic, arguably the most important person in the history of Tok Pisin's life as a language of the nation-state, published his dictionary of the language with the assumption that it would help promote English and eventually make Tok Pisin obsolete. Arthur Capell, professor of linguistics at the University of Sydney, concluded his review of Mihalic's dictionary with a left-handed compliment: "It is a pleasure to recommend the work as long as Pidgin is current. The only danger is that a work of this nature might by its very excellence tend to prolong the life of a thoroughly objectionable form of speech" (Capell 1959: 235). The Australian linguist Don Laycock, a very vocal advocate for the language, wrote in 1982 that the growing spread of English-language education programs would finish off Tok Pisin: "This does not mean that Tok Pisin will die a rapid, or even an easy, death. . . . But it does mean that, in perhaps fifty years' time, Tok Pisin will most likely be being studied by scholars among a small community of old men" (Laycock 1982: 267).

Forty years after this prediction, Laycock has so far been proven very wrong. Tok Pisin is today the most widely spoken language in Papua New Guinea by far, an extraordinary accomplishment in a place with over eight hundred languages spread unevenly among more than nine million people. I will discuss some of the more positive reactions to the language and the various supporters of it in this and subsequent chapters. But I do not want to tell this history of attempted language murder as one in which Tok Pisin valiantly triumphed in the face of adversity—even though it did that. In this book, I use the enduring criticisms and sometimes murderous thoughts about Tok Pisin as a lens on broader questions of communication in colonial and decolonial contexts. That is, trying to answer the question of why Tok Pisin was a favorite linguistic punching bag for so many both inside and outside of Papua New Guinea has, in the end, required that I move well outside of discussions of language as such. For this language that emerged from the widespread kidnapping and indenture of Melanesian peoples for forced labor on plantations across the Western Pacific, the central theme of many discussions related to Tok Pisin was the morality and modernity of circulation. All these threats to the life of Tok Pisin are refractions of the question of whether and how Papua New Guineans would be made connected, mobile, free, and well governed.

If one were to write a history of colonial Tok Pisin that focused only on the language and people's responses to it, it would necessarily just repeat the arguments that took place during the colonial period. When linguists like Hall and Dutton tried to defend Tok Pisin to colonizers and decolonizers in Australia, in Papua New Guinea, or at the UN, they often focused on defining the language as separate from Australian or British English. For these defenders, the goal was to prove that Tok Pisin had a real grammar with rules of use and was not just a mishmash of poorly pronounced words and half-learned syntactic structures. These arguments largely fell on deaf ears. To this day, many Australian English speakers (Australian and sometimes Papua New Guinean) still see Tok Pisin as just a shoddy version of what they speak. I don't want to argue that a different tactic could have been more effective; as I said, the community of Tok Pisin speakers has grown regardless of what people tried to do to it. But I also think that focusing just on the grammatical structuredness of the language does not really get at the enduring concerns that various colonial and decolonial actors had with Tok Pisin. Rather, I argue that Tok Pisin was the object of so much scrutiny and concern because of the ways that it reflected the possibilities and promises of circulation as modes of colonialism and decolonization. The widespread dislike of Tok Pisin despite its obvious usefulness perfectly demonstrates that even though a central tenet of the modernist imaginary of circulation is that more circulation is better, when moderns made their way to the colonies they discovered that their various projects demanded that circulation be controlled, curtailed, or transformed in various ways. The Lutheran Mission again offers an important example of this dynamic.

In this chapter, I examine how the Lutherans dealt with "the language problem." The complexity of the linguistic situation in Papua New Guinea pushed the Lutherans toward a model of language as infrastructure—as a pathway through a forest of languages, very much akin to the pathways that their road-building projects and aviation networks created. In chapter 1, I argued that the overall emphasis on the modernity of circulation was constantly upended by the contradictory forms of circulation that different colonial projects demanded. Here, I argue that a parallel ambiguity is evident in the internal Lutheran arguments about those infrastructural languages. But not all infrastructures were created equally, and the Lutherans frequently argued and changed their minds about the possibilities of movement and connection enabled by different linguistic systems. These ambivalences are especially clear when it comes to Tok Pisin, a language that was itself born of a process of circulation. They used languages as infrastructures to try to clear pathways into Papua New Guinea but, as in chapter 1, the emphasis on circulatory primitivity meant that easily accessible spaces and peoples were suspect. In that sense, Lutherans worked to define Tok Pisin as a language without life, depth, or soul as part of a broader erasure of the circulation of Papua New Guineans in labor contexts. To do so, they valorized a set of church lingua francas as well as what they thought of as Christian forms of circulation.

IN THE FOREST OF LANGUAGES

As I discussed in chapter 1, the Lutheran missionaries often lamented the loneliness of life at their disconnected mission stations. They worried about their health and how their families might fare in case of emergencies. They lamented how long it took for news and letters to travel to their stations. The unmanageable chattiness that the radio operators tried to tamp down was just one way that this loneliness bubbled up. The missionary R. R. Hanselmann momentarily imagines what a different kind of mission life might be like in his report on transportation costs to the Lutheran Auxiliary Society in 1934:

It is entirely out of the question that the entire mission staff could live as a colony near Madang, in order to eliminate many transport expenses. Indeed living together would expel all present isolation for members on distant stations, would bring medical aid to the door within a moment's notice, mail would be received on steamer dates and not weeks later, and it would mean much socially and spiritually to every member of the staff—but how detrimental it would be for the work.[5]

It would be a wonderful change if the whole mission could be together (or, when the radio network started, if the whole mission could just chat), but then why go to Papua New Guinea at all? Hanselmann rules out the idea that there is much, if anything, of evangelistic value to do in towns. The true objects of missionization were out in the remote corners of the territory, not in the easily accessed town centers.

But in fact there were many young men in towns and Lutheran centers to whom missionaries could have ministered if they were interested in doing so. The problem was that these young men were laborers, working in ethnolinguistically mixed groups in which communication happened through the use of Tok Pisin rather than vernacular languages. For many decades, Tok Pisin–speaking laborers were not considered targets of evangelism, even if the very same people would become so as soon as they returned home and started speaking their first language again.

If circulation was the primary problem of colonial New Guinea, the reason for missionaries being in such far-flung and remote stations to begin with, how was this population of circulating laborers and the language they spoke so invisible to the Lutheran missionaries? Why not create the conditions of idyllic, socially satisfying, missionization that Hanselmann described with a dedicated subgroup of missionaries working with the concentrated populations of men in towns and on plantations? But the existence of Papua New Guineans in town and of Tok Pisin as a language used by them was not seen as strong proof against the circulatory primitivity that governed the colonial imagination. By denying that Tok Pisin was a proper language, the colonials could maintain the idea that Papua New Guinea is characterized by a lack of circulation: the communicative system that facilitated the migration of laborers was bracketed as a non-language.

If Tok Pisin was not going to be used, would the Lutherans then use the vernacular languages of the communities they evangelized? Even at the end of the nineteenth century, before the estimated number of languages in Papua New Guinea had reached into the several hundreds, it was clear that there was a level of linguistic diversity that the missionaries had not anticipated. This was clear just by looking at the Huon Peninsula, where the mission was initially based. The first mission stations, at Simbang and later Sattelberg, were located in the area of Kâte speakers. The mission as a whole was based in nearby Finschhafen, in an area of Jabem speakers (see map 1). Although Sattelberg and Finschhafen are quite close to each other geographically, their inhabitants are separated by a language-family boundary: Kâte is in the Papuan, or non-Austronesian, language family; Jabem is in the Austronesian language family.[6]

Not only were Kâte and Jabem two of the first languages that the Lutheran missionaries used, but they became the lingua francas of the mission as its workers spread across the Huon Peninsula and points south. This meant that Lutheran missionaries and their "native evangelist" helpers not only had to teach local people about Christianity, but also had to teach them one of two languages in which Christian evangelistic materials were prepared. In the early twentieth century, most official mission literature was printed in either Kâte or Jabem, and many children in the burgeoning Lutheran school system learned one or the other language as part of their education. Likewise, when Lutheran missionaries from the Rhenish Mission started work around Madang, they used a language known as Gedaged (or Graged, or Ragetta) as their mission lingua franca.

Which of the two church lingua francas—Kâte or Jabem—was used in any given part of the Neuendettelsau Mission was based on the language family of the vernacular language spoken there. If a non-Austronesian language was spoken in the area, Kâte was used; if an Austronesian language was spoken, Jabem was used. This policy obviously required knowledge of local languages and language families, and some of the missionaries devoted considerable time to language study and linguistic description. Otto Dempwolff, a German linguist and doctor, was first to posit, on the basis of Lutheran Mission reports, that the Austronesian language family spread across coastal New Guinea and throughout the island Pacific. These classifications became the basis of the administrative organization of church communities. All the congregations that used Kâte as their mission lingua franca belonged to the Kâte Circuit, and all the congregations that used Jabem as their mission lingua franca belonged to the Jabem Circuit.

But why would Lutherans, of all people, decide to promulgate languages that people did not natively speak? Martin Luther was the champion of vernacular-language Bible translation. Luther thought the Catholic Church's use of Latin kept the laity from having knowledge of, and interactions with, God. Luther advocated for "a priesthood of all believers" that could partly do away with Roman Catholic hierarchies that mediated between God and the faithful. Luther's translation of the Bible into German set off the modern era of translation, in which the Protestant norm is that one is supposed to read the Bible in one's own first native language. Johannes Flierl wrote that "only by acquiring a knowledge of the native's own language was it possible to completely understand and instruct him. Our Lutheran Mission holds to the principle of instructing the native in his own vernacular" (1936: 26).

Yet the definition of "his own vernacular" was somewhat elastic. Given the problem of circulation, the church lingua francas were both helpful and local enough: Kâte could stand in for all non-Austronesian languages; Jabem could stand in for all Austronesian languages; Gedaged could cover the entirety of the north coast around Madang. For the Lutherans, there was a nonspecificity to Papua

New Guinean languages below the level of language family that made them interchangeable. As one Lutheran missionary later put it, "All New Guinea languages have practically identical thought categories, ideas, and concepts."[7] Sometimes the hyperdiversity of Papua New Guinean languages engendered a sense of primitivist sameness that seemed to offer a way through the circulatory primitivity: these church lingua francas that embodied local categories well enough could be the infrastructural routes through a fragmented social field.

Questions of spiritual access and connection were discussed in more practical terms when the Lutherans dealt with infrastructural issues of transportation. Landscape, language, and infrastructure are all connected in a complex whole, as in the example of the Rhenish Mission's promotional material from roughly 1935, aimed at members of the Iowa Synod of the Lutheran Church in the United States.[8] American Lutherans supported overseas missions in the Madang region of Papua New Guinea and in the area around Chennai [then Madras], India. The two regions are presented in abbreviated form through a series of contrastive statistics that are meant to give the American reader a flavor of life "on the mission field."

Described in terms of infrastructural problems and possibilities, the Indian mission field is depicted as a wide-open space of mobility compared with Papua New Guinea's impenetrability: "Roads—Fairly good highways and railroads. Considerable auto travel." Note that for a target population totaling "about one million souls," only fifteen missionaries are allocated to India at this point. In Papua New Guinea, travel is arduous and slow: "No railroads, driveways or bridges, except foot and bridle paths and an occasional hanging bridge suspended by vines, or a log laid across the deep ravine. Boats and canoes are used along the sea shore but very little on rivers, these usually being turbulent mountain streams." Within this impenetrable zone live a relatively small number of people. Indeed, until 1933 the population of the Lutheran section of the Territory of New Guinea was counted at roughly forty-six thousand. It was only a few years prior to this notice that several hundred thousand people were "discovered" in the highlands. The Papua New Guinea field was difficult to access and had an extremely tiny population in comparison with the area around Madras, yet at this point twenty-seven missionaries had been sent out there, almost twice as many as were in India, with many more needed.

The discrepancy arises from the interconnection of the landscape and languages: just like the dense foliage that kept the missionaries from evangelizing by "auto," the density of languages kept them rooted to ever-smaller corners of the Papua New Guinea field. In India, all is simple: "Language of the people—Telegu (which our missionaries learn in about two years)." In Papua New Guinea, all is complicated: "Language of the people—Many different languages and dialects divide the people into countless tribes and clans. The language selected to become the universal one of our Mission is Ragetta [i.e. Gedaged], a Melanesian vernacular. In the far inland the Papuan or mountain language, Kâte, may have to be added. Every missionary is compelled to learn at least two native languages besides Pidgin English which is gaining ground right along."

Beyond just the distinction in the number of languages—one Indian versus hundreds of New Guinean ones—is the fact that Telegu has a long literary history. By contrast, in Papua New Guinea the missionaries had to develop orthographies for all of these languages. Processes of recording and transcription are likened to pathways through dense jungle in a later internal history of the mission:

> Already in 1886, the flying foxes of Finschhafen were well-equipped with ultra-sonic squeakers and echo-sensitive ears and wingtips to find a pathway through thick jungle in the dark, tropical night. By comparison, Senior [Johannes] Flierl was ill-equipped to penetrate the jungle of languages that confronted him. No tape recorders, no word processors, and no computers were available to him and his fellow missionaries. In their wisdom, they decided to make only a narrow pathway through this jungle by using one or two local languages, which they hoped everyone would learn. (Hage 1986: 409)

Kâte, Jabem, and Gedaged were these narrow paths, linguistic roads that were used, as one missionary said in defense of them, "in those days when travel and transportation were so very difficult."[9] However, the Lutherans were deeply ambivalent about whether languages as communicative roads could all equally allow for communication between souls and God. At points, they talked as if all languages could act as infrastructures of connection to the divine, while at other points they claimed that each potential convert had to be addressed in terms of her or his native language, as when Flierl and many others argued for using only the local vernacular. The use of church lingua francas expressed both positions at once: they were roads through the dense and imposing jungle, itself an image of the opacity of the population's linguistic forest, but they were also keyed to particular language families, Austronesian and non-Austronesian. As I argue below, the depth of the lingua francas—the sense in which they connected to local souls—was secured only through comparisons with what the Lutherans saw as Tok Pisin's surface-level capacity to connect laborers but not souls.

Missionaries were so invested in the sense that Kâte, Jabem, or Gedaged was the language of the people (even when it was promulgated by the mission itself) that they refused to give up on the different languages. In the 1930s, Neuendettelsau Mission leaders fiercely debated which of the lingua francas to use, but neither the Kâte proponents nor the Jabem proponents were able to win out (the Rhenish and later American missions around Madang kept using Gedaged).[10] In the post–World War II era, with American and Australian financial support very low and all former German support ruled out as a possibility, it would have made sense economically to bring the nearly bankrupt mission together under a single lingua franca. Theologically it made sense to unite the future church under a single linguistic umbrella, so that only one Evangelical Lutheran Church of New Guinea might eventually exist. Thus,

> the introduction of three unifying languages [the lingua francas] did not produce a solution either of the problem of language, or of the problem of the unity of the Church. What happened was that three Churches had come into being. They were all Lutheran but they had nothing more to hold them together than the fact that they had all grown out of the work of a mission, and that they all reflected the character of the Papuan people. (Vicedom 1961: 52)

According to Vicedom, the "controversy about languages was never settled" (ibid.: 53) and by the postwar era it seemed that the lingua francas were too well entrenched. John Kuder, the superintendent of Lutheran Mission New Guinea, lamented in 1953 that they might have been able to unite the missions under one language prior to the war, but at that point it was a lost cause. It was a few years after this unhappy admission from Kuder that the members of the Lutheran Mission resolved at their 1956 annual meeting to "accept" Tok Pisin in those emerging situations where a church lingua franca was inadvisable (Hage 1986: 413). But this move toward Tok Pisin was made with all the enthusiasm of a prisoner headed to the gallows. In his retrospective account of Lutheran education, under the subheading "Reluctant acceptance of Pidgin," Hartley Hage writes: "If missionaries had been able to agree on the use of only one church vernacular, the practical need for using Pidgin would hardly have arisen within the church" (ibid.). Hage refers to mission fathers like Flierl when he writes: "Little could these men know that the centenary of their arrival would be celebrated in a language for which they had the lowest possible esteem" (ibid.: 409).

How does a mission—especially a Protestant mission oriented toward the text—use a language it despises? More importantly, what traces of that dislike might be left on the language? In the next section, I argue that with the use of Tok Pisin as a secular channel—a desubjectivized language for the circulation of laborers—whatever emphasis there was on interior subjectivity could reside contrastively in the Lutheran lingua francas. It was thereby possible to bracket off the colonial movement of laborers as a temporary disturbance of the more fundamental, permanent circulatory primitivity of Papua New Guinea.

TOK PISIN, THE "HORROR OF HORRORS"

The most important early colonial proponent of Tok Pisin was the Roman Catholic Mission. In the 1930s, the Catholic Society of the Divine Word decided to make Tok Pisin a liturgical language and started to produce the necessary literature. Fr. Joseph Schebesta compiled a dictionary and was preparing it for publication when he was killed in World War II. The manuscript dictionary was published by Fr. Leo Meiser in a very limited run in 1945, although it became the basis of

Fr. Francis Mihalic's influential and widely used dictionary published two decades later (Mihalic 1968).

Even Catholics who were working to promote the language were vocal about what appeared to them as Tok Pisin's flaws. Chief among these flaws was what they considered its tendency toward constant and radical change. In Meiser's preface he states that "this dictionary cannot be considered as an exhaustive and final compilation, but only as a collection of words in current use among those who speak the language" (Meiser 1945: 2). It is unclear how this differs from a dictionary for any other language, yet the rate of change is something for which Meiser and many other later supporters of the language had to apologize. But this capacity for change marked Tok Pisin not as a living but rather as a dying language. Arthur Capell argued that later Australian policies were "definitely aimed at causing Tok Pisin to commit suicide, albeit as painlessly as possible, by taking more and more English over into it" (Capell 1955: 72). As he notes a couple of pages later, "It is only a question of time" (ibid.: 74). Capell argues here for something like a linguistic version of the Australian policy toward Aboriginal Australians, whereby the latter would slowly "die out" as a separate ethnic group the more they were forced to marry and have children with white Australians.[11]

The perceived instability of the language—and the possibility that it was in the midst of self-harm—provoked a strong contrast with the other Papua New Guinean languages that missionaries dealt with. According to the missionaries, those vernaculars were deeply rooted in the land, so much so that they produced an impenetrable jungle that had to be cleared with focal languages that could stand in for all the New Guinea thought categories. Tok Pisin, by contrast, looked like no language at all from the colonial perspective.

As Hage noted in the quotation above, the early missionaries "had the lowest possible esteem" for the language. Flierl was particularly adamant that Tok Pisin could not be used in missionary work. In commenting on other missions in Papua New Guinea, he wrote that the Seventh-day Adventists "show their predilection for Pidgin English, this 'horror of horrors.'[12] The Catholics also favour Pidgin English very much. Bishop Vesters told the conference at Rabaul that it was a simple and easy vehicle of conversation with the native. The Lutheran and Methodist representatives opposed this statement of the Bishop. It was a superficial language" (1936: 26). The Lutheran position on Tok Pisin remained negative well into the mid-twentieth century. Otto Theile, an Australia-based leader who worked with the Lutheran Mission in Papua New Guinea, argued that pidgins spoken in both Papua New Guinea and Aboriginal Queensland were useless in missions work. In a speech titled "Missionary Methods," Theile condemns anything but "the vernacular": "Among themselves they [i.e., Aboriginal Australians and Papua New Guineans] use the vernacular, and I am convinced that if we would understand their innermost thoughts we must be able to converse with them in the vernacular.

We can therefore, not support the proposals that for primitive natives Pidgin or English be adopted as a means of bringing to them the Gospel of Jesus Christ. They must hear the message in their own tongue."[13] Theile's speech is definitive: Tok Pisin was seen as a language that could not reach the soul. It was not a language that constituted a perspective from which to speak; Theile reserved the latter category for those innermost thoughts that had to be turned inside-out in order for the conversion process to take place (Keane 2007). Instead of the linguist Capell's image of a language that was committing suicide, we get here the Lutheran missionary image of a language that was simply never alive. In this view Tok Pisin lacks dimension, staying at the surface of evangelism rather than plumbing the soul's depths. As another missionary said in a different context, Tok Pisin "is a language without a father," a genealogical bastard that could not anchor any sense of self or past.[14]

What Theile leaves out, however, is that the church lingua francas like Kâte and Jabem that the mission was using in the Territory of New Guinea were vernacular languages but *not* the vernacular languages for most of the converts in their domain. Kâte and Jabem had only about a thousand speakers each at the time of Flierl's arrival in 1886. But in 1959 the Lutherans estimated that over two hundred thousand people spoke or could understand some amount of Kâte.[15] The Jabem circuit was smaller, but it too involved a vast increase in the number of speakers of the language in comparison with the situation when Flierl first arrived. Theile plays with the meaning of *vernacular* here, assuming that anything vernacular and local in Papua New Guinea was intimate and interior for any Papua New Guinean. The possibility that Kâte or Jabem as a lingua franca could reach the souls of converts only emerges contrastively when put in relation to Tok Pisin's travel along the surfaces of the self.

Lutheran complaints about Tok Pisin sometimes focused on its linguistic limitations. In a tradition that extends to contemporary white settlers and missionaries in Papua New Guinea, the Lutherans delighted in what seemed to be the absurdities of Tok Pisin. Because pidgin languages often have relatively small vocabularies, they also have highly productive ways of making compound words or circumlocutions. Some of the more inventive of these—such as *trousis bilong leta* ("envelope," from Eng. "trousers of the letter")—were used as evidence of the limitations of Tok Pisin rather than as testaments to the communicative creativity of people in coerced-labor contexts. Some circulated only as jokes, having never been attested in any verifiable source. No opinion piece railing against Tok Pisin was complete without mention of such howlers of circumlocution as the supposed term for "helicopter," *miksmasta bilong Jisas Krais* (from Eng. "Mixmaster of Jesus Christ"), in which the spinning beaters of the Sunbeam brand of standing mixer were seen as evocative of the spinning rotor blades of a helicopter up in the heavens.[16] Whether this phrase was ever used even once by a cook or other household servant, it has lived on as part of the lore of Tok Pisin's insufficiencies and absurdities. In 1950, Tok Pisin was closely tied to colonial labor contexts, since that was where men learned to speak it and where they primarily used it with one another and, to a limited extent, with their colonial overseers. Among the Lutherans it was considered useful only as a language for barking orders on their plantations or circulating simple bits of secular information.

The threat that the lingua francas might only be conduits for secular information is explicitly addressed in Stephen Lehner's paper presented to the annual Lutheran Mission conference in 1930. Lehner disparages Tok Pisin as an insufficient channel for evangelism over several pages. He gives the usual examples of what he thinks are the most ridiculous circumlocutions and an extensive quote from the Tok Pisin version of the Proclamation of Annexation read to local people when Britain, as represented by Australian soldiers, took possession of German New Guinea at the start of World War I: "British new feller master, he like him black feller man too much he like him alsame you picanin alonga him."[17] Tok Pisin is the language of last resort, for example "when as a result of mixed marriages Pidjin [*sic*] will be the language of the newcoming generation." The only real option is using a vernacular if one wants to actually reach the innermost self where Christian conversion happens, a space of subjectivity inaccessible to Tok Pisin. "If he [the missionary] has an opportunity to use a New Guinea language, which is so rich in detailed expressions, there should be no doubt as to which is to be used. May traders use Pidjin and may Governments even give Proclamations in it, and may an Anthropologist use it to find out facts:—a missionary cannot use this language if he wants to arouse the hearts of the people."[18] Against the gibberish of Tok Pisin, or at least the gibberish version of Tok Pisin spoken by colonizers, Lehner holds up the native language as the only route to real conversion. But he has to catch himself at the end of the paper—the Lutherans do not, in fact, use the mother-tongue languages of their potential converts:

> I hope that these pages do not give some people the idea regarding the introduction of one or two centralized languages, for which many of the tribes should give up their mother tongue. I admit that doing this is only a compromise forced by the fact that there are too many different languages, but not the ideal solution to the problem. Unfortunately it is impossible to cultivate 20 to 30 languages and produce school material and literature in all of them. But the introduction of another New Guinean language, even if it is not of the same structure, is still quite different than introducing a European language in order to get away from the difficulties that the many tribal languages present.[19]

Lehner has to apologize for a Lutheran policy that seems to go against all of the principles he laid out in his opposition to Tok Pisin. He implies that the use of the lingua francas is a logistical issue only—if they could use all the native languages, they would. But even the nonlocal lingua francas are superior, since they are less different from a local language than Tok Pisin or English would be.

Lehner was not the only one to equate the use of Tok Pisin with colonial administration, and church languages with salvation. Georg Pilhofer reported on a conversation he had with an administrator in the highlands in which the latter urged him and the rest of the Lutherans to use Tok Pisin rather than Kâte or Jabem.[20] Pilhofer replied, "No Protestant Mission will teach the Gospel in Pidgin. Only the Catholic Mission can do that. For they are, first and foremost, concerned with acquainting their followers with ritual forms and formulas. We are not against Pidgin as a means of communication between white and black. However, for the actual mission work we decline to use it" (ibid.: 3). Catholic forms and formulas, administrative proclamations, anthropological inquiries: these are all acceptable uses for Tok Pisin since, according to the Lutherans, they do not have to create a channel to the depths of the person.

KEEPING TOK PISIN IN FLUX

All Lutheran missionaries learned and used Tok Pisin, but for a long time their approaches to Tok Pisin were disorderly and slapdash. In contrast to the Catholics, who began early on, in the 1930s, to create a Tok Pisin orthography, the Lutherans seemed to actively work to keep Tok Pisin in a state of disorder. Two documents that have been filed next to one another in the Lutheran archives demonstrate the extent to which Lutherans wrote the language idiosyncratically.

The first is a Tok Pisin translation of the famous hymn "Nearer My God to Thee," which appears to have been produced by Jerome Ilaoa, a Lutheran missionary from Samoa, in 1933. His first text is in the top row of each numbered line, with spelling or grammar that differs from standard Tok Pisin in italics. The second row is Ilaoa's text written in the contemporary Tok Pisin orthography. The last row is my back translation:

NEARER MY GOD TO ME [*SIC*]. BY JEROME ILAOA. 1933

1 Klos tu, o God, long yu
   Klostu, o God, long yu
   Near, oh God, to you

2 Klos tu long yu
   Klostu long yu
   Near to you

3 *Kuros e kin* bring im mi
   Kros i ken bringim mi
   The cross can bring me

4 Klos tu *a*long yu
   Klostu long yu
   Near to you

5 Trabel *en* pen i kam
   Trabel na pen i kam
   There is trouble and pain

6 Mi no k*i*n lusim yu
   Mi no ken lusim yu
   I cannot leave you

7 Mi laik i go along yu
   Mi laik go long yu
   I want to go to you

8 Klos tu *a*long yu
   Klostu long yu
   Near to you

9 Insai*d* long *santu hart*
   Insait long bel holi
   Inside your sacred heart

10 Mi laik i hai*d*
    Mi laik hait
    I want to hide

11 J*e*sus yu dai *for* mi
    Jisas yu indai pinis long mi [alt.: Jisas yu indai pinis long
       kisim bek laip bilong mi]
    Jesus you died for me

12 Mi no k*i*n *fraid*
    Mi no ken poret
    I cannot be afraid

13 Taim *soul* i karim p*a*in,
    Taim sol [alt: tewel] i karim pen
    When [my] soul is pained

14 Mi ken i kom *a*long yu
    Mi ken kam long yu
    I can come to you

15 Klos tu long yu o God
    Klostu long yu o God
    Near to you oh God

16 Klos tu long yu
    Klostu long yu
    Near to you

Aside from several small changes, this translation from the 1930s looks roughly similar to contemporary Tok Pisin (so much for the argument that it is changing at an extraordinary rate). The changes needed to make it conform to contemporary usage are largely minor. Word-final voiced obstruents are usually devoiced in Tok Pisin (e.g., word-final /d/ is pronounced /t/), and contemporary spelling reflects that (*haid/hait* in line 10; *fraid/poret* in line 12). The phrase *sacred heart* in line 9 is rendered as *santu hart*, both ignoring the Tok Pisin word for heart (*bel*) that is used in a later stanza in this translation and displaying the Catholic tendency to render theological terms in Latinate form (*santu*).[21] Within this largely phonemic spelling, there is a lack of standardization: the preposition *long* is sometimes *along* (lines 4, 7, 8, and 14); the transitive marker *-im* is not connected to the verb in line 3. The predicate marker *i* is used with first-person verbs, although this is not done in standard Tok Pisin. The worst problems are in line 11, where (1) the English preposition *for* is used in the benefactive construction "died for me" rather than using something like *bilong kisim bek laip bilong mi*, "to save you [lit., to get your life back]"; and (2) the completive marker *pinis* is left out, which in some forms of Tok Pisin at the time would have meant "Jesus passed out" rather than "Jesus died."

If the Lutherans had regularly used an orthography and grammar that matched the hymn translation above, one could talk about a regular Lutheran Tok Pisin norm emerging. However, right next to this document in the archival record is a version of the "Our Father" prayer in Tok Pisin, translated by a bilingual German- and English-speaking missionary:[22]

DAS VATER-UNSER IN PIDGIN [THE OUR FATHER]

1 Pappa belong me fellow he stop on top,
   Papa bilong mipela i stap antap
   Our [EXCL] father is above

2 Name belong you he tamboo,
   Nem bilong yu i tambu
   Your name is taboo

3 fashion belong you he come,

pasin bilong yu i kam
your ways came

4 something he stop along bell belong you all he make him
      on top all the same you me make him down below,
   samting i stap long bel bilong yu ol i mekim antap olsem
      yumi mekim daunbelo
   *something that is in your heart they do above like we
      [INCL] do below*

5 Kaikai belong me fellow, all time you give him me fellow,
   kaikai bilong mipela oltaim yu givim mipela
   you always give us [EXCL] our food

6 loose him trouble belong me fellow past time all right,
   lusim trabel bilong mipela pastaim, orait
   first remove our [EXCL] troubles, then

7 you me loose him trouble belong brother belong you me;
   yumi lusim trabel bilong brata bilong mi
   we [INCL] remove my brother's troubles

8 you look out, Satan he no try him me fellow too much,
   yu lukaut Seten i no traim mipela tumas
   watch that Satan does not test us [EXCL] a lot

9 alltogether something havy he stop belong skin belong me
      fellow you loose him;
   olgeta samting hevi i stap long skin belong mipela yu lusim
   remove the burdens from our [EXCL] bodies [lit., skins]

10 alltogether bush, alltogether strong, alltogether light too
      much belong yu all time.
   olgeta bus, olgeta strong, olgeta lait tumas bilong yu oltaim
   all the forests, all the powers, all the light really always yours

11 Him he true.
   Em i tru.
   It is true (amen)

Not only is the orthography completely wedded to standard English, but several lines are notably ungrammatical or semantically questionable. Line 10 lacks a verb. The translator does not seem to understand the distinction between inclusive *we*, which refers to speaker and addressee (marked INCL above), and exclusive *we*, which refers to speaker and others but *not* the addressee (marked EXCL above).

For example, God is included in the "we" who create God's will on Earth (line 4) and who forgive those who trespass against us (line 7).[23] Orthographically, the language is presented as nothing more than bad English, and if one is reading from an English vantage point it reads as close to gibberish. It follows none of the more phonemic spellings used in Ilaoa's hymn. And yet, when rendered in an orthography that obscures the etymological links to English that are so transparently presented in the original document (see the second row of each numbered line), even this jumbled version of the language starts to look much more familiar, as can be seen in the transliterations I have provided between the translated and English lines.

Unlike the Catholic dictionary, which adopted early on an orthography much closer to what appears in Ilaoa's hymn, Lutheran missionaries' attempts at employing Tok Pisin kept the language unstable, verging on the edge of linguistic disorder. Pastor Ilaoa seems to have made an attempt at developing Tok Pisin into a liturgical language, writing it in an almost phonemic spelling system that would have been easier for newly literate Papua New Guineans to use. But one of the only other attempts at creating a liturgical text backs away from this project, using a version of Tok Pisin that underlines, in grammar and spelling, the ways in which the language can seem a garbled version of English. Ilaoa's hymn looks like an attempt to create an accessible text, whereas the "Our Father" translation looks more like something that would be used as evidence for why Tok Pisin should not be used in evangelism at all.

FROM LABOR NETWORKS TO CHRISTIAN NETWORKS

Lutherans were happy to let Tok Pisin languish in this disordered form because Lutheran missionary efforts were focused on rural, remote, vernacular language speakers. This was true to such an extent that they completely missed the chance to evangelize to the people they were transporting to the coast to engage in Tok Pisin–mediated labor. Like their Catholic counterparts (Huber 1988), the Lutheran missionaries initially funded a portion of their work in Papua New Guinea through coastal copra (coconut) plantations, cattle ranches, and dairy farms (Wagner and Reiner 1986). Papua New Guinean men worked on these plantations, usually for three-year labor contracts during which they earned extremely low wages, living in multilingual workers' housing. Towns were also filled with other "labor lines" (labor housing) for local white-owned businesses or for the colonial administration. Here was an available group of men who were within easy reach, men who often already had some sort of connection to Lutheran missions, and men who were known to the missionaries in charge of the plantations.

Yet it was not until the Christian literacy expert Frank Laubach visited Papua New Guinea in 1949 that the idea of evangelizing to the men in the labor lines was given concerted attention and thought within Lutheran missionary circles. Laubach was an American Congregationalist missionary who originally worked in the

Philippines in the early twentieth century. He developed a phonics-based method for rapidly teaching literacy to adults, a method that people at the time described as "miraculous" in its speed and effectiveness. An article in the *Pacific Islands Monthly* magazine about his visit to Papua New Guinea suggested that Laubach's method had been used to teach illiterates in Indonesia to read in an hour, or even just fifteen minutes.[24] Laubach's method usually involved a quick trip to an area to create minimalist literacy primers and run a few classes that both taught the content and demonstrated the teaching method. Under the label "Each One Teach One," this method required that each student then teach another friend. Through this snowballing increase in students, Laubach claimed that he was responsible for teaching literacy to millions (Roberts 1961). In 1949, Laubach was on a UNESCO-sponsored tour of Asia, squeezing a five-week visit to Papua New Guinea into an itinerary that also included Thailand, Pakistan, and India.

Laubach came to the Lutheran headquarters just outside the city of Lae for the first stop on his New Guinea tour. He wanted to give a demonstration of his method to administrators and missionaries. A small number of men then working in Lae as laborers, who were also speakers of various languages that were known to different missionaries, were brought in as students in these initial demonstration sessions in which Laubach was explaining his method. Initially, there was no thought of developing literacy materials for the language of the labor compounds, Tok Pisin, since the missionaries were all squarely oriented around the idea of missionizing to people in what they thought of as the more monolingual, mono-cultural context of remote Papua New Guinea.

It was Laubach himself who seemed to see how useful Tok Pisin could be to a broader evangelistic project. And while it may not have been part of the initial plan, literacy materials were developed for Tok Pisin during the Lae demonstration sessions. During the demonstration, Laubach managed to have the superintendent of the Lutheran Mission, John Kuder, work with a number of people as Tok Pisin speakers—that is, as speakers of a language developed and used in a multilingual context of colonial labor (see figure 5). In doing so, Laubach also helped the Lutheran missionaries see Tok Pisin–speaking laborers as objects of evangelism, since Laubach's mass literacy methods were part of a larger Christian evangelical project to create Bible readers. Writing about Laubach's visit afterward, Kuder wrote in a letter that Laubach

> saw how convenient the use of Pidgin was through an actual demonstration, which was all the more effective because it was unplanned. People of different languages came together for a service here in Lae and in order for everyone to be understood Pidgin was extensively used. People from the interior, people from the mountains and from the coast all used and understood each other through Pidgin. Dr. Laubach was much impressed.[25]

The Lutheran missionaries seem to have been impressed too. Long held up by the Lutherans as a non-language incapable of cultivating a Christian subjectivity,

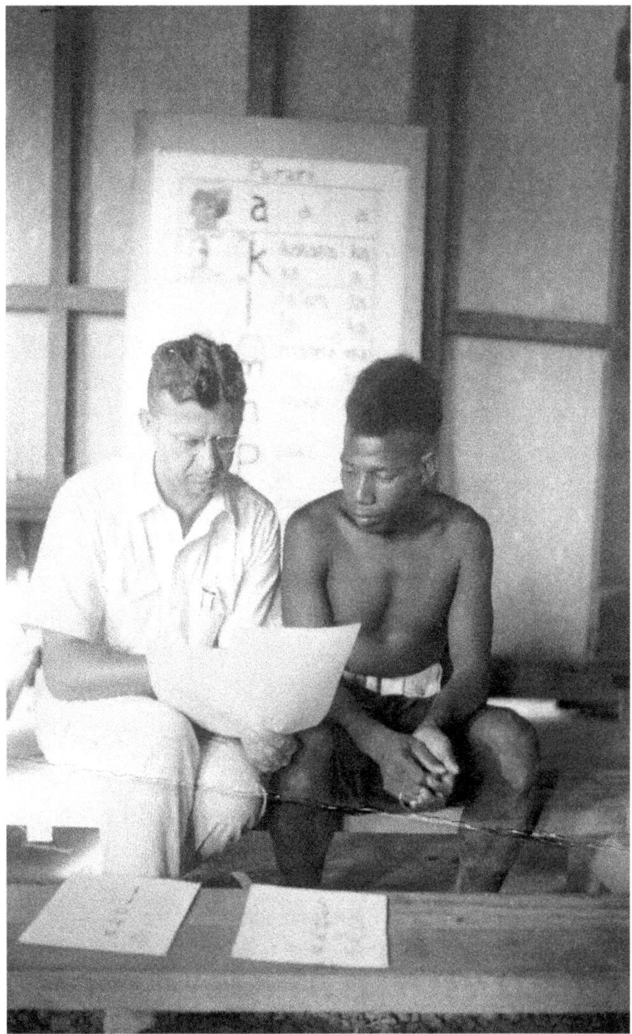

FIGURE 5. Reverend John Kuder, superintendent of the Lutheran
Mission, teaches a man (identified only as a "police boy") to read Tok
Pisin during the Lae literacy conference in 1949. "Police boys" were
laborers who worked for the colonial police force. Some of Frank
Laubach's literacy materials for the Purari language can be seen on
the board behind Kuder and his student. (Archives of the Evangelical
Lutheran Church in America, TALC 16.8.1. b5 f19)

Tok Pisin took a great leap forward with Laubach's visit. Not long after Laubach
left, Kuder began to inquire with the British and Foreign Bible Society in London
about the possibility of publishing a New Testament in Tok Pisin. This eventually kicked off a nineteen-year ecumenical project involving several of the major
missions of Papua New Guinea, culminating in the 1969 publication of *Nupela*

Testamen na Ol Sam, the Tok Pisin New Testament with Psalms, which remains the number-one best-selling book in the country to this day. More generally, it marked a shift in Lutheran missionaries' thinking about Tok Pisin, from a language they refused to countenance as anything other than a laughable joke or conduit of secular information to a serious medium for the circulation of Christianity. Yet it is worth pointing out that even Laubach initially pitched the idea of translating Bible materials into Tok Pisin as only a temporary bridge to English, with texts gradually adding in more and more English until Tok Pisin itself was extinguished.[26] Laubach raised the profile of Tok Pisin a great deal, but even he thought of it as a language without a future.

The sudden upswing in Tok Pisin's fortunes after Laubach's visit was mirrored by the sudden attention the Lutherans started paying to urban laborers in labor compounds, since Tok Pisin was considered a language of laborers. In the years following Laubach's visit, the mission started having missionaries and Papua New Guinean evangelists work with laborers. In their annual reports, missionaries wrote about how they tried, in what was known as "compound work," to minister to the needs of the "boys" (a term that was applied to all male laborers regardless of age) in between all of their other work that was focused on the in situ autochthonous communities adjacent to colonial towns like Lae or Bulolo. In a report summarizing work ministering to the Lae Wampar group during 1951, the compound work is described as having "only just started."[27] Comments throughout the early 1950s show a few missionaries begging for the money and personnel necessary to actually have a dedicated outreach to these groups.[28]

These reports indicate that at least part of the mission felt obligated to expand their ministry to the men who were bearing most directly the brunt of colonial exploitation, yet much of the rest of the mission required convincing that this was a worthy use of limited resources. At the annual mission conferences, selected missionaries were asked to give papers on issues that were causes of controversy or disagreement. At the 1953 conference, the missionary Theodore G. Braun gave a paper on "The Native Labor Program of the Mission."[29] The paper as a whole covers the incipient program that a few missionaries were starting to work on, but its final part is a plea to the mission more broadly to think of laborers as evangelistic subjects in need of care.

At this point in the early 1950s, amendments to the labor laws governing local people meant that indenture contracts were finally being phased out of the labor system. Braun asked that the missionaries likewise change their attitudes regarding people who were starting to work at least nominally by choice rather than through coerced recruitment. Men being trained for skilled labor, those in the army or the police constabulary, trade unionists: all required ministering. Braun invoked the common motivators—the specter of Roman Catholics and atheists gaining influence—to try to push his fellow missionaries toward seeing this work as important, and urged anyone who was thinking of doing this work to learn Tok Pisin.[30]

Braun pointed in particular to the mobile, fluid, multicultural nature of labor compound communities—some of the features of these spaces that contrasted most sharply with Lutheran imaginations of rural villages as homogeneous and immobile populations—and tried to reframe these as positive features of Christian opportunity rather than disappointing contrast: "Wherever possible, compound congregations should be started, even if the population is in great part a floating one. More emphasis could be placed on the fact that Christians are brothers. We ourselves are a body of four nationalities. Our program should be so adaptable that it meets changing trends and conditions and does not become fossilized."[31] In other words, Papua New Guinea is a site of missionization only when an image of circulatory primitivity can be maintained. Braun had to convince his Lutheran coworkers to recognize spaces of labor mobility and circulation as spaces for Lutheran missionary work.

His paper ends with a strong plea to the missionaries to think beyond the confines of their rural districts (or "circuits" in Lutheran missionary terms) and accept that substantial change was already happening in the postwar Territory of New Guinea:

> In summary, we are interested in native labor because it represents an important phase of native life. It is a time when a native is in contact with the white man and it has played, and will continue to play, a large economic and social role in the life of this country. If we remember what our calling is, namely to preach the Gospel by word and example, we will not go far wrong, especially if we avoid a picayune outlook which tries to tell us our work only extends as far as our circuit or job.[32]

Note the ironies, then, of a mission group always in desperate need of funds to support its work in rural and remote parts of Papua New Guinea, always in desperate need of being able to join together in more populated areas, having to be pushed to see the people closest to hand as worthy of attention. The mission ran plantations in coastal, semi-urban areas to help fund the work in remote locales. The mission brought workers from those remote locales to the coast to work on the plantations in order to fund the missionaries' work in the rural hinterlands. But at no point prior to Laubach's visit did anyone think that the men who had been brought out from those same hinterlands could be objects of evangelistic attention themselves while they were speaking Tok Pisin at those plantations.

A GOOD ENOUGH CHANNEL

By 1954, with Laubach's visit and the beginnings of the New Testament translation project, it is clear that the president of the mission, John Kuder, was contemplating a partial shift to Tok Pisin, even while maintaining his negative attitude toward it: "Because Pidgin gives us access to so many people the question arises whether we should not cultivate it rather than use it merely as a necessary evil?"[33] Lutherans discussed two main reasons for this official recognition. First, they were battling with other denominations for dominance in the highlands. Teaching the Lutheran lingua francas to potential converts during yearlong confirmation classes was taking too long. Other missions were picking off the students by offering immediate baptism. Reluctantly, in 1956, the Lutherans allowed the use of Tok Pisin in these hotly contested new highlands areas in an effort to keep as much of their "flock" as they could. Second, the missionaries were starting to make more concerted efforts to turn the mission into a church, and to have local people take over for the American, Australian, German, and Samoan missionaries. Yet, because these expatriate missionaries were never able to decide on a single church language, the Papua New Guinean Lutherans had no single language with which to communicate with one another. Tok Pisin was partly accepted because it was the only language in which meetings among members of the Kâte, Jabem, and Madang synods could take place.

In the early 1950s, one of the Lutheran missionaries began to work in limited ways with the Catholic Fr. Francis Mihalic on standardizing Tok Pisin and translating the New Testament into it (see Cass 1999). The translated New Testament was published in 1969, an official orthography in 1970, and a grammar and dictionary in 1971. Yet even when codifying the language, the missionaries' orienting horizon was always an English-language future with Tok Pisin on a modernizing suicide mission. Mihalic, the missionary most responsible for standardizing Tok Pisin, writes in the preface to the first edition of the dictionary that the codification of Tok Pisin is just meant "to span the gap to that farther shore" of English-language fluency (Mihalic 1968: ix). In other words, missionaries did not suddenly disagree with the anti–Tok Pisin rationales that were articulated in earlier decades. They continued to disparage Tok Pisin in familiar ways even as they started to use it.

The extent to which Lutherans worked to maintain Tok Pisin outside of its use as a religious channel, even as they started using it for that purpose, is most clearly on display in 1971 correspondence between Kuder and John Sievert, who had worked, before his retirement, with Mihalic on the Tok Pisin New Testament translation. Kuder complained about Sievert's replacement on the Tok Pisin work, Paul Freyberg, who was taking too long with his translation of the Lutheran statement of faith. Before getting to Kuder's comments, it is important to note that Kuder had been working on the statement of faith for at least five years. Hammering out the theological differences among the different Lutheran missionary societies was a seemingly never-ending task. Kuder also worked hard to make the statement of faith specific to and appropriate for the Papua New Guinean context. It was almost like his parting gift, as the mission was formally in the process of being nationalized, going from a Euro-American-run mission to a church that would be run by Papua New Guineans. This final stamp of theological authenticity and truth in the statement of faith was meant to set the new church on the right path. Kuder had been worrying over it for years, and yet he notes in his comments to Sievert that Freyberg is taking too much care with the Tok Pisin translation:

> I can't see that this is going to be done in the immediate future. What seems to me would be a much better solution would be that a few of us who are not quite so good in Pidgin as Paul is [come together] and that we should get it out the best we can. Then it can be worked over and revised where necessary to bring it into line with our changing use of the Pidgin itself[—]to have somebody prepare what we think is a perfect copy is like Sisip pushing the stone up the mountain. He never reached it.[34]

Even though Kuder was deeply concerned about this document, he was ready to insist upon what he thought would be a middling translation into Tok Pisin. One would always have to "bring it into line with our changing use of the Pidgin" because the Tok Pisin itself is always changing to an extent that does not seem to be true of other languages. That is, trying to get a Tok Pisin translation into proper order is Sisyphean because of the instability of Tok Pisin itself.

As is clear from Kuder's comments, a few Lutherans like Freyberg thought that Tok Pisin could be a channel to the soul, or they at least worked under that assumption. Certainly, after Kuder left and the leadership of the church moved into Papua New Guinean hands, Tok Pisin came to be an important part of Lutheran practice. In most Lutheran communities, Tok Pisin eventually took over from Kâte, Jabem, and Gedaged. But ambivalence about Tok Pisin was ongoing during the mission era. It was recognized as useful for uniting the mission, given the missionaries' incapacity to find a single church lingua franca, yet it was kept separate from those lingua francas and the vernacular languages of the people. Kuder's refusal to let Freyberg continue his work on the translation—his refusal to even admit that a proper Tok Pisin translation was possible—points to the ways in which Tok Pisin was maintained as a language that could only travel on the surfaces of the labor migrations that the Lutherans in general tended to ignore. Even with Kâte and Jabem sidelined and Tok Pisin on its way to becoming the main Lutheran language by the time of Papua New Guinea's independence, many Lutheran missionaries maintained a sense that Tok Pisin was still a secular channel connecting laborers, rather than one connecting souls and God. As the language enabled the movement of laborers, Tok Pisin was marginalized, erasing this history of colonial labor circulation to promote instead the Lutheran lingua francas as channels of Christian circulation to the supposedly remote and immobile populations further inland.

CONCLUSION

Richard Bauman and Charles Briggs (2000) contrast the theories of John Locke and Johann Gottfried Herder as the two main apostles of modernist language ideologies, the one advocating a rational and transparent language of logic and the other describing the particularistic languages of ethnonational groups. In the terms I have been using here, Locke imagined language as a conduit for information transfer, in which the success of circulation of truth depended on the perfectibility of the language. The more it was an accurate reflection of reality and no more, the better the circulation of information. Herder was instead invested in imagining language as a code, a system that imprinted itself on the speaking subject, affecting the way that speakers engaged with the world.

This opposition has become one of the main organizing principles of linguistic anthropology. Locke has become the totem of the Enlightenment, universal truth and objectivity, the analytic philosophy of language, and an emphasis on reference and the circulation of information. Herder has become the totem of the Counter-Enlightenment, relativism and subjective perspectivism, a culturally informed approach to understanding language, and an emphasis on pragmatics and context. However, information channels and cultural codes are more deeply interconnected than this story of opposed language ideologies implies. Some linguistic forms can be channels because of the way that speakers or observers reflect on them as kinds of code. Some linguistic forms can be codes only if they are seen as making particular kinds of connections. But with the division of the study of language separated between Locke and Herder, between information conduits and cultural codes, linguistic anthropologists have not paid enough attention to the cultural formation of channels.

Tok Pisin's history, especially its history within the Lutheran Mission of enforced disorder, shows how hard it is to keep these stories separate. This is especially apparent in the ways that the standard story opposes a focus on truth and universalism against a focus on particularity and subjectivity. The view from nowhere is made possible in the Lockean imagination because language can be perfected. What is especially interesting in the Lutheran case is that Tok Pisin was delinked from a subjective self not because it was perfect—a laboratory instrument for understanding the world—but because it was so deeply flawed. It changed too quickly, it did not have its own center, it was committing suicide by slowly being eaten up by English. For about seventy years, the Lutherans both used the language and tried to keep it in that imperfect state. Positing that it lacked the subjective depth that could link soul and God, which they assumed came from the structuredness of a stable linguistic code, the Lutherans thought of Tok Pisin as a language of secular labor infrastructure and no more.

One version of the modernist imaginary of circulation holds that greater circulation produces greater modernity. Yet the Lutherans' project of Christian evangelism, in which intrepid missionaries circulate the Gospel to immobile Papua New Guineans and thus compel them toward more circulation, was at odds with the actually existing forms of labor migration that many Papua New Guinean men were engaged in with the help of Tok Pisin. Papua New Guinea was mountainous and multilingual, but it became specifically a space of circulatory primitivity when colonial actors saw it through their contradictory lenses of modernist imaginaries of circulation.

One of the legacies of the colonial trope of circulatory primitivity in multilingual Papua New Guinea has been a constant emphasis on questions of access and channels. For the Lutheran missionaries, it was only the stable and seemingly immobile codes of indigenous languages of remote Papua New Guinea that could be the communicative channels to God. To downplay circulation, to maintain an image of immobility, Tok Pisin's communicative channels were minimized as the shallow and suspicious networks of temporary labor experiences. Likewise, as I will show in chapters 3 and 5, Tok Pisin's capacity to allow for different kinds of illegitimate or unwanted circulation was the concern that continued to unite a disparate community of colonial and anticolonial actors.

3

Telepathy Tales

Tok Pisin, Communist Radio, and Other Channels of Illegitimate Circulation

FROM IMPASSABLE TO POROUS

For all the talk about the ways that circulation seemed next to impossible in Papua New Guinea for various kinds of colonizers, there was another form of commentary that emphasized instead the incredible ease and speed with which Papua New Guineans could communicate, move, and connect with one another. A good example, reproduced in its entirety below, is a brief item in the Australian tabloid newspaper *Smith's Weekly* from 1946, when a large number of Australian troops were still stationed in Papua New Guinea in the immediate aftermath of World War II:

TELEPATHY?

Discharged from hospital and awaiting reporting to his NGIB [New Guinea Infantry Battalion], Putari acted as interpreter in an ANGAU HQ [Australia New Guinea Administrative Unit headquarters].

A cheerful cuss, even his wound had failed to upset him. But one morning he was very down in the lip.

Asked what was wrong, he replied "Sumting no good'e come up alone brother bi'ong me." (Sioni, his brother, was with the battalion three hundred miles away.)

Nothing we could say or do would cheer him up. Some of us were inclined to laugh but the Major, an old New Guinea hand, said:

"I've heard of this sort of thing before. Make a note in the diary and get in touch with his battalion for information regarding his brother." It was five days before we got a reply to our sig [signal], and it read "Sioni accidentally killed by aircraft propeller."

Date was that noted in the diary.[1]

The item—published on the paper's "Unofficial History" page that collected stories sent in from Australian soldiers—was presented as a kind of oddity, something for the Australian audience to shake their heads at. But stories about Papua New Guinean or Pacific Islander telepathy appeared with surprising frequency in newspapers and magazines that circulated among the colonial classes in Papua New Guinea, so much so that their regular presence in the media suggests a more serious set of concerns than just the exoticizing entertainment of a Sydney tabloid reader. In fact, the story of Putari's telepathic communication encapsulates a recurrent fear within the modernist circulatory imaginary: for Australian colonizers and foreign missionaries, Papua New Guinea might be horribly difficult to traverse and the people might be almost impossible to communicate with, but what if that is only true for them? What if others can communicate across the territory with ease? If so, how can colonizers access this form of communication? Or are they destined to always be on the outside of it?

All of the main features of what I will call a telepathy tale are present in the brief article about Putari's telepathic update regarding his brother. Two different kinds of people, with disparate modes of communication, are put in contrast with one another: the telepathic "natives" capable of receiving news without any obvious means of doing so, and the critical "moderns"—who, as narrators in these stories, act as stand-ins for the reader—capable of forensically analyzing the accuracy and timing of the telepathic message through a technologically enabled communication system (it's unstated how the "sig" was sent to Putari's brother's battalion three hundred miles away, but it was likely by teleradio). "An old New Guinea hand"— that is, an Australian who had been in the colony for a long time—is in this case set between the two, and can affirm that this story of telepathy is not singular, but just the most recent in a long line of similar tales.

In addition to the communities and their corresponding modes of communication are the two languages. On the one hand is Tok Pisin, presented here in particularly disheveled orthographic form. It can only gesture vaguely at what exactly happened with Sioni, through the nonspecific claim that "sumting no good" occurred. On the other hand is English, perhaps the maximally efficient version of it used for clipped military signals over radio. In English, we get the gruesome particulars of Sioni's accident. But if Tok Pisin and telepathy seem to suffer in the comparison with English and radiotelegraphy by not capturing all the details of the deadly event, their trump card is the message's timing: telepathy and Tok Pisin allow for instantaneous notification across three hundred miles, in contrast to the five long days of waiting for the battalion's reply in English.[2] Telepathy moves faster than the electric charge of the telegraph or the waves of the radio, and it does so without any of the cumbersome wires, machines, stations, or operators that had been needed for Australian families to learn of the deaths of their own loved ones in the recently concluded war.

As with other modernist morality tales of technology leading to a disconnection from nature and from one another, the moral of this civilizational story is that "natives" have a capacity for connectedness that cannot be captured through telecommunications and that has become inaccessible to the moderns. For American Lutheran missionary Frederick Henkelmann, this was a consequence of constant warfare and social fragmentation. That is, for the modern looking down at what he perceived as the circulatory primitive, what he saw as a warfare-based lack of movement may have produced this other kind of connection: "Because the heathen regards every stranger as an enemy, he has developed his psychic powers to a superlative degree." Henkelmann then quotes from another text, shifting his explanation into a more overtly racial frame: "'Gifted spiritually to a profound degree, to the negro the spirit of another is transparent' (Rutlidge) [*sic*]."[3] Circulatory primitives may neither be able nor want to move about freely, but they have supernatural capacities for connection on those occasions when separation has been forced on them.

In this chapter, I look at the ways in which the circulatory imaginary of Papua New Guinea could sometimes get turned on its head. Instead of worrying over the impassibility of Papua New Guinea, colonizers could start to feel like it was an all-too porous space, with communicative capacities that were far too promiscuous—to borrow John Durham Peters's (1999) phrase—for colonial regulation and monitoring. As Tracey Banivanua Mar (2016) discusses, colonizers in the Pacific both emphasized the remoteness and inaccessibility of Pacific communities and yet also did a lot of work to regulate and limit the movement of people in them. By looking at the colonization of Papua New Guinea in terms of the discourses on circulatory primitivity, three seemingly distinct issues can be analyzed as inverting the prevailing imaginary from circulatory primitivity to circulatory porousness: stories of Papua New Guinean telepathy, fears of communist radio propaganda, and concerns about Tok Pisin being used for anticolonial projects. While stories of Papua New Guinean telepathy were a steady part of more lighthearted colonial reportage, the later fears of communist radio and Tok Pisin–enabled insurrection suggest that telepathy-like communicative systems that cross ethnic and cultural boundaries also cross over into categorization as threats to colonial order and colonial borders.

Telepathy tales not only cover the specific stories of telepathic communications, but more broadly point to colonial stories of magical, unregulatable modes of communication within what should be a context of secular modernity (see Mazzarella 2017). They are colonial stories because they are framed by the sense that the Pacific (and Papua New Guinea in particular) is a place in which circulation is impossible for colonizers. If local people are able to circulate, then those circulations must be supernatural, illegitimate, or simply non-modern. So while folkloric accounts of dead family members announcing their own deaths are relatively common cross-culturally, there is a particular colonial version of these tales that starts from the perspective that legitimate communications in the Pacific are close to impossible without the technological expertise of colonizers. Telepathy tales provide narrative form for colonial concerns about illegitimate circulation (see Bayly 1996, White 2000, Luckhurst 2002, Gage 2020).

In the middle of the twentieth century, such colonial stories of illegitimate circulation took on a particular Cold War flavor. As Scott Selisker (2016: 49) argues in the American context, anti-Soviet partisans often focused on the illegitimate means by which communism was spread, via what seemed to be propaganda, brainwashing, or viral infection. Soviet influence was proof of how minds could become too porous (cf. Taylor 2007, Luhrmann 2020) if care was not taken to reinforce the boundaries of individualist selves. Concerns about control at a distance, about being able to affect others' minds, were bound up with concerns about Soviet aggression. As I will discuss more at the end of this chapter, Tok Pisin itself was seen by some as a potential medium for communist infiltration.

Telepathy tales, stories of surreptitious communist radio propaganda, and fears of Tok Pisin–based anticolonialism all feature moments in which the labor of Papua New Guinean colonial subjects is disrupted through secret communications transmitted to porous listening subjects. The sense of porosity present in these examples is particularly important because the porousness of the listener is what helps blur the boundary between code and channel: being open to telepathy means that there is no obvious material form mediating distance in time and space (see Guillory 2010).

One of the broader arguments of this book is that when you take problems of circulation as your perspective, language and other infrastructures can be viewed together under the single frame of being elements of communicative networks. But from a more standard linguistic anthropological account, language and media usually are separated. Using Roman Jakobson's (1960) definitions, language is important primarily as a code, whereas things like two-way radios or telephones are the technological bases of channels. Codes in this sense are defined as grammatical and semantic systems, the basic norms and knowledges that constitute a language as a system of communication. Channels, however, are the spaces or linkages created and maintained to enable the code to pass from a speaker to a hearer. But in contexts in which the nature of communication seems mysterious, secret, and immediate—as is the case with the colonial telepathy tale—there is no clear distinction between a system of communication and the medium through which elements of the system pass.

In the context of colonial frontiers organized by experiences of colonizer remoteness and uncertainty about the possibility of communication, where code and channel sometimes seemed to both be in doubt, telepathy tales were the basis on which other kinds of suspect communications came to be interpreted. The features that I identify here—secrecy, labor disruption, and porosity—together created a communicative framework in which the code/channel opposition came to be blurred in this colonial space. For the circulatory moderns, Papua New Guinean telepathy offered instantaneous information transfer, but it did so at the cost of a sense of mental autonomy and self-control. Telepathic circulations made colonial subjects temporarily—and maybe even permanently—unwilling to work or unable to be governed by the administration through their forms of modern circulations.

TELEPATHY AND THE MYSTERIES OF KINSHIP CONNECTIONS

Stories about telepathic messages being sent among Pacific Islanders popped up throughout the first half of the twentieth century. They appeared in articles and letters to the editor in the *Pacific Islands Monthly*, a news magazine that catered to expatriates across the Pacific, as well as in Australian newspapers discussing Pacific Islander peoples. Australian private diaries and letters also make offhand mention of indigenous telepathy (e.g., Nelson 2007: 74, Taylor 2016: 333).[4] In many cases, a particular story of telepathy would make reference to a much wider collection of stories on this topic that circulated among expat Europeans about Pacific Islanders. In fact, a July 1933 item in *Pacific Islands Monthly* from Henry Dexter of Milne Bay was a call to readers to send in their stories of islander telepathy in order to create a written record of the many stories that were then in circulation orally.[5] It is fair to assume that the small but substantial collection of these stories in print represents only a fraction of the stories that were told in colonizer circles. But even if there were only a few such tales, the belief that there was surely a large corpus out there was an important component of the telepathy-tale genre itself. Any one story could be presented as representative of countless others just like it, as when the "old New Guinea hand" in the opening example says, "I've heard of this sort of thing before."

Telepathy tales have two somewhat distinct flavors: kin-based death notices and intercommunity news (I'll discuss the latter in the next section). The stories that involve unexplainable knowledge of the death of a close family member get told in elaborate detail, partly because they are treated as relatively unthreatening curiosities, fodder for reflection on "modern man" and his modes of circulation, more than as phenomena of administrative concern. For example, in a 1954 item published in *Pacific Islands Monthly*, a telepathy tale is told as a personal reminiscence of an unexpected interruption of a conversation the narrator was having with his friend over drinks one night in the Cook Islands. The two white men had been talking about the planned atom bomb tests in French Polynesia and their shared sense that this was proof that modern man was not in tune with nature anymore. "So the conversation drifted along, and we expounded some kind of theory that people who live simple lives close to nature have certain instincts or intuitions which we, as superior civilized beings, have irretrievably lost." At just that moment, a normally happy domestic servant named Mina cried out when a lamp-glass shattered, devastated by the immediate and certain knowledge that this indicated that her father, eight hundred miles away on a remote island, had just died. Like Putari in the earlier example, Mina was inconsolable. Weeks later, the telepathy was confirmed. Once again, it was a white man, this time with access to a boat rather than a teleradio, who verified the story. The narrator relayed this information to his friend with whom he had been discussing the atom bomb tests:

> "By the way," I said, "do you remember the scene at my place when the lamp-glass broke? Well, Mina's father *is* dead. I've checked with Skipper Andy, off the schooner, and he well recalls the night on Manihiki, for he was ashore at the time and remembers asking what the crying and wailing in the village was about. Believe it or not, the old man died, as far as we can check up, at exactly the same time as that glass broke."
>
> Burton gazed at me for a long time. I can still see the look of amazement on his face. "But Mina," he said finally. "How the deuce did *she* know?"
>
> EDITORIAL NOTE: In 20 years, the PIM has heard of a number of such cases of what may be telepathic communication between natives of the Pacific Islands.[6]

Although published in an outlet that featured news reporting on colonial administrative and business concerns, this item appeared in the magazine section. It was placed alongside a number of other pieces that were presented as first-person realist reportage, but all veered closer to the genre of short story. The author, who used the nom de plume "Periti," was a regular contributor to *Pacific Islands Monthly*, usually writing about Polynesia. Periti's contributions ranged from poetry to realist fiction items like this one to straight news. In this story, the narrator's description of his philosophizing friend Burton echoes the double-voiced descriptions of the bourgeoisie in Dickens novels that Mikhail Bakhtin (1981) was so fond of analyzing: "Burton was about sixty-five, looked about fifty, had a keen mind, a droll sense of humour and a private income. A very fine fellow, too." Yet it is a short story that strains to be taken as fact, emphasizing the mundane details and by-the-way conversational notes. And if the writing seems too on-the-nose, too perfect to be anywhere close to a truthful accounting of an evening in the Cook Islands among two expats, the editorial note is there at the bottom of the page to affirm that this story represents many others just like it, too many to be considered purely fictional. In telepathy tales, there is always some authorial or editorial voice insisting that any one story is echoed by dozens of others. The rational, calculating perspective of the modern—the one who cross-references battalion diaries or the date and time of ritual wailing—likewise counts up these instances of telepathy, creating an archive of them, as Henry Dexter of Milne Bay was hoping to do.

Telepathy tales often concerned domestic servants, as is true of the two examples with Putari and Mina. Domestic servants would have been the only local people allowed in white colonizers' homes for the most part, and thus the only people whom colonizers might see in such unguarded moments of emotional shock. Importantly, telepathy interrupts their labor: it stops Mina from continuing her work and makes Putari too sad to be discharged back to his duties. One gets the sense that the colonial observers may register these moments only because their laborers stop laboring. Telepathy tales not only mark illegitimate circulation, but also lead to the loss of colonial power over local labor.[7]

The way that telepathy tales interrupted colonial labor through "natural" rather than "technological" modes of communication is a prominent part of an article titled "'Black Magic': How Do Islanders Communicate?"[8] The author, who wrote under the name L. Poole and who contributed several articles in the 1950s to *Pacific Islands Monthly*, was responding to a letter to the editor in an earlier issue. A ship captain had written in regarding one Malaitan (Solomon Islands) community's telepathic knowledge of the death of a relative who had been working on the ship. The confused captain said at the end of his letter to the editor that "probably some PIM reader can tell me" how the community knew that there would be a dead body to collect on his ship.[9] Poole took up this charge, explaining that many communities, "too numerous to mention," in the Coral Seas, Torres Strait, and other nearby areas, "were all adepts at sending messages of this sort— certain groups having a system of communication as correct as our wireless." But this telepathic communication system was due to the "natural-born gift of people directly attuned to earth vibrations" rather than to technological advancement. Poole claimed that drums, well known to be a system of communication in parts of the Sepik River area for example, were not necessarily used to send messages themselves, but rather "were extensively used to stir up the warlike feelings of the people when they were expecting the receipt of such tribal messages." As mysterious and possibly foreboding as colonizers might find the drumming communications of the Sepik, Poole says that these were just the audible announcement that later and completely inaudible telepathic messages were incoming.

As with the Lutheran missionary Henkelmann's comments that telepathy was caused by warfare and isolation, in Poole's account islander telepathy was not a mode of modernist circulation in the sense that it produced greater health, commerce, or information transfer. It was rather circulation that was produced by and encouraging of further isolation, most clearly visible to the colonizer in the ways that telepathy could be used to circumvent demands for islander labor: "In urgent cases [telepathy] was the only means of communication, and it was used to warn many a tribe of the approach of blackbirders [labor recruiters], giving the kanakas time to hide in the bush where, in those days, sailors dared not penetrate." Telepathy was not just non-modern and a means of resistance against a system of coerced labor, but highlighted the extent to which much of the Pacific remained impassable to the modernist colonizers.

In many communities, there are traditions of supernatural knowledge of distant family members' deaths. Dreams sent by spirits or the "wailing of the banshee" could foretell the imminent death of a loved one or announce their passing. But if such spiritual messengers were part of the ontologies of the Pacific Islanders who feature in these tales, the colonial men and women who told the stories did not seem to know anything about them. The focus instead was on the temporally and materially immediate experience of knowledge. Part of a broader colonial and racist discourse that insisted that non-Western peoples did not have the same autonomy of self or mind, telepathy tales highlight the ways in which technologies of communication seemed to rationalize (in Max Weber's sense) spiritual connection. Confined to kin-based news only, these sorts of telepathy tales were ways of defining a divide between the modern world organized by technology and no longer governed by kinship on the one hand, and the "primitive" world connected to nature and defined by family on the other. Pacific Islanders were so connected to both nature and family that their thoughts could be linked together. There was no objectified linguistic code that traveled on a technological channel of connection, but only minds united by kinship and earth vibrations.

TELEPATHIC NETWORKS AND COLONIAL CONTROL

This porosity of mind, code, and channel allowed circulatory moderns to imagine their communicative others in relatively unthreatening contexts where kinship interrupted colonial labor. But telepathy took on different valences when it crossed into contexts beyond immediate kin-linked notifications of death. In the second major kind of telepathy tale, the channel of communication was unknown but the messages spread rapidly across different communities. Many of these tales were attributed to some variation of what was called the "bush telegraph." In reporting focused on Islanders, Aboriginal Australians, or white Australians, the term *bush telegraph* most often referred to the rapid spread of news (if it was considered true) or gossip (if it was not). Similar terms like *coconut wireless, coconut radio,* or the French *radio cocotier* seem to have been more common in Polynesia than in Melanesia. They tended to refer to the mundane, if still rapid, spread of rumors across wide social networks and territories, rather than to immediate, telepathic knowledge of the mortality of distant family members. These terms riff on the telecommunication systems that were widely transformational at the end of the nineteenth century and the beginning of the twentieth, uncannily bringing together technological advancement with the natural resources of "non-modern" environments. Indeed, short notes about the coconut radio or bush telegraph occasionally appeared in newspapers and magazines just one column over from notices of actual radio and telegraph connections being installed in various outposts across the Pacific.[10]

Stories of the coconut radio or bush telegraph as rumor mills or grapevines were sometimes treated as relatively harmless facts of life in the Pacific. The capacity for the colonized to know information faster than the colonizers was something to be remarked upon but not necessarily moralized about. Hank Nelson (2007: 74) notes that during World War II, "even without obvious human carriers, news seemed to travel quickly. On 19 January 1942 on Witu Island, Gladys Baker at Langu Plantation was told by the 'natives' that Rabaul had been bombed, and soon after her radio went silent they told her, again accurately and within hours of it happening, that Rabaul had fallen."[11]

Yet there were times when journalists and other colonial authors considered stories of the rapid interisland or intercultural transfer of knowledge a source of deep threat to colonial stability. And when that was the case, commenters often fell back on tropes of telepathy to shore up what seemed to them to be the unexplainable speed of message circulation. In these instances of the rapid sharing of news among much wider beyond-kin networks of people, telepathy took on a potentially more sinister aspect, seeming more like broadcasts than point-to-point telepathic communication.

Colonial accounts of such intertribal or intercommunal messages made a correlation between the importance of a message to be conveyed telepathically and the success or accuracy of the message transfer, as if the currency of broadcast mental telepathy was emotional resonance. In a "School Section" of *The Age* in 1952, Melbourne area children were instructed that "scientists incline to the theory that only real 'thought transference' can explain the rapidity with which certain kinds of emotionally charged 'news' can travel among primitive people. It was undoubtedly true, for instance, that the negroes of the southern parts of the United States knew of the death of Abraham Lincoln long before their white masters, who had the telegraph and railroad to assist them."[12]

Since the emotional importance of a message could be assumed in the case of a family member's death, this feature of telepathy tales is remarked on explicitly only in stories about messages that spread to larger networks and involved other topics. A report in the *Sydney Morning Herald*, written in March 1942 as Papua New Guinea was just starting to get pulled into World War II, made the connection explicit:

> You can't try to explain this 'bush telegraph.' District officers and magistrates who have spent 15 years among the New Guinea natives will not hazard a guess. The news just travels mysteriously through the jungles almost with the speed of an electric telegraph. . . . In recent weeks the natives have given erroneous reports of parachute landings by Japanese troops, of mysterious ships off the coast. *But when dealing with matters of deep concern to the natives themselves* the accuracy of these strange reports is unquestioned.[13] (emphasis added)

Two features of wider broadcast telepathy—islander proclivities for gossipy embellishment and broadcast strength being based on emotional resonance—could sometimes lead to dangerous effects. If telepathic messages were about things that local people cared about (or were embellished to seem that way), uncontrollable mobs could form. Coconut radio messages were blamed for an unruly crowd in Papeete that had spread the news that an incoming ship was loaded with pots of gold (it was only copra). More consequentially, the March 1942 article just cited talks about how the telepathic features of the bush telegraph caused so much chaos and "mob hysteria" that "control was lost" after the announcement of the change-over from a civilian to a military government in Papua New Guinea.[14]

Telepathy tales of family death notifications wouldn't be newsworthy if they were incorrect—if, for example, Mina was mistaken about her father's demise. At best, they would be proof of indigenous irrationality. But even incorrect telepathic transmissions across ethnic lines could be newsworthy, because colonizers worried that they could instigate mobs or violence. At such times, telepathy tales stopped being curiosities and started being threats to colonial order.

These interethnic telepathy tales are in some ways akin to the hysteria over chapatis that circulated in colonial India in 1856 and 1857. For unknown reasons, chapatis (small, round flatbreads) were sent from one village to another across northern India in a pattern of circulation that many have compared to chain letters (Guha 1983, Bayly 1996, Downs 2000). The British were alarmed not only by the fact that they could not figure out the meaning of the chapati circulation, but also because one of the only things they could determine was that the chapatis were being circulated at a rate equal to or faster than the colonial postal system (Downs 2000: 81). In retrospect, the British in India thought that the chapatis had in some way signaled the start of the First War of Independence (or Indian Mutiny), which began a few months after the chapatis were first noticed. Later on, nationalist historians tended to agree with this account. Today, scholars suggest that the chapatis may have circulated so widely precisely because nobody, Indian or British, knew exactly what they signaled and they could add whatever meaning seemed most fitting. While they may have been part of a religious ritual aimed at warding off a cholera epidemic then circulating in the region, they were in other ways empty signifiers, able to materialize a growing and multifaceted sense of insurgency or discontent.

If the chapati circulation remained a mystery, it at least offered a material medium for inspection by the British administration: village watchmen who were taking the chapatis from one village to another could be questioned, and the chapatis themselves could be examined or tasted. In contrast, the bush telegraph and indigenous telepathy, while being pegged to more specific propositional content, offered no such material trace. There was no visible channel of communication to control. Both systems were able, in their different ways, to cultivate paranoid reflections on colonial circulation through the unanswered questions of either content or medium.

The formula for the interethnic telepathy tale was so well established that a parodic inversion of its form even made the papers. According to the July 1947 issue of the *Pacific Islands Monthly*, a young man in Mangaia (the Cook Islands again) got drunk and broke into the colonial administration's radio room and started sending messages in Morse code asking when the next ship might be coming. Someone at the Rarotonga station actually replied to his poorly tapped-out message, but the young man couldn't understand the Morse code answer that was sent too quickly for him to parse. Meanwhile, a colonial administrator had a telepathic sense to go check on the radio room, found the young man, and took him into government custody for trespassing.[15]

Here the roles are reversed, with a "native" operating the wireless and the inquisitive administrator having a telepathic sense that some trouble was afoot. Getting his hands on a telecommunication technology that was usually kept away from him, under lock and key, the intoxicated Pacific Islander bungles the message. Even when he has the proper technology in his hands, the article suggests, he is unable to take advantage of its ability to quickly send and receive detailed albeit mundane information about transportation. Instead of ending with the forensic certification of "native" telepathy (as when the narrator and captain compare notes to ascertain that the lamp-glass shattered at the exact time of Mina's father's death), the story ends with the Pacific Islander in jail awaiting trial.

In contrast to the stories of instantaneous family death notifications or the non-supernatural reports of gossip on the coconut radio or bush telegraph, interethnic telepathy tales that might incite chaos or violence were rarer. Yet they were established enough to be useful as a model for colonial concerns about uncontrollable communications among Pacific Islanders. Clearly, colonial actors were concerned that these "non-moderns" might take up radio, telegraphy, or telephony in unknowable or untrackable ways (although the story of the drunken attempt at communicating on the radio in Mangaia was perhaps useful in allaying fears that any attempts like that would work).

Any form of communication outside of colonial control became a version of a telepathy tale, a story of a non-modern subject too easily influenced from outside and susceptible to external messages. As I discuss in the next section, echoes of these concerns appear in the ways that administrators and other colonial actors worried over communist communications and Tok Pisin–based interactions. Concerns over communists and Tok Pisin speakers were versions of telepathy tales told somewhat differently.

"THIS PROGRAM COMES TO YOU
FROM RADIO MOSCOW"

Telepathy tales did not just happen in the context of colonial "great divide" narratives attempting to separate the world into circulatory moderns and primitives. Messages coming unbidden into one's mind without obvious ways of turning them off or managing them are, in fact, a consistent feature of communication-based technophobias. Contemporary concerns are focused on social media saturation, yet each new medium has produced its own version of the fear that humans may be too porous, too open to messages from the outside (Peters 1999). If there are telepathy-as-telegraphy tales that emphasize primitivist access to distant kin and emotionally resonant truths, or ones that emphasize female-based spiritual connection to the dead (Tomlinson 2019, Manning 2021), there are also telegraphy-as-telepathy tales that point to an ongoing fear that modernist communications make their users too susceptible to outside influence (for a discussion of the ways that young women were considered too susceptible to the dangerous influences of others through unregulated telegraphic communications, see Standage 1998). In other words, there is a constant fear that modernist communication systems turn moderns into "primitives" by making them subservient to the minds of others, incapable of using their autonomous rational, critical faculties. Tales of radio-as-telepathy or social-media-as-telepathy are stories of propagandistic or mesmeric claims on other minds.

A wide range of fictional stories in English have delighted in playing up these connections, with some entries celebrating telegraphy and other modern communication technologies as the salvation from primitive modes of control-at-a-distance, and others seeing telepathy as the way to free one from the domination of social control. The novel *Dracula* by Bram Stoker (2018 [1897]) is a story of a primitive non-modern who takes mesmeric control over women in the heart of the British Empire. When Count Dracula travels to London to prey on and then telepathically command its citizens, a strange quintet consisting of a doctor, a scientist, a lawyer, an aristocrat, and a cowboy from the United States band together through their copious use of telegrams, letters, and journals to defeat the monster (Richards 1993). Scientific telegraphy defeats primitive telepathy, but just barely. In a reversal of values, the science fiction classic *The Chrysalids* by John Wyndham (2020 [1955]) tells the story of a postapocalyptic and highly repressive frontier society whose purist dogma is transmitted by the relatively old media of scripture and signage. Freedom is available only for a small band of young children who are able to communicate telepathically. At the end of the book, when they are about to be captured and killed by their own kin, the children are rescued by members of a highly evolved society living in New Zealand (so remote as to have largely avoided the apocalypse that destroyed North America) in which neo-primitivist Rousseauian characteristics of telepathy, freedom, cooperation, and peace are shared among all. As Peters (1999), Taylor (2007), and others have noted, the boundaries of the mind seem only to get more fragile as modernist concepts of autonomous self-mastery get stronger and more important.

The expat colonials of the mid-twentieth-century Pacific brought a well-established archive of telepathy tales with them, then, whether they were stories that celebrated the immediacy of connection that "natives" unalienated from nature enjoyed or stories that feared the control-at-a-distance that an emotionally resonant (but possibly untrue) rumor could evince. Within this context, the Cold War's dualistic structure of competing "worldviews" that could infect one side from the other was tailor-made for telepathy tales that would stoke fears of new media. Indeed, the main players in the Cold War both tried to use telepathy in their global conflicts. Soviet researchers attempted to harness telepathy to help create the New Soviet Man (Velminski 2017), even as the CIA attempted to weaponize telepathy for defense purposes (see Lemon 2013, 2018: 104–5).[16] The apparent "brainwashing" of captured American GIs during the Korean War typified fears that communist influence could be anywhere, as the 1962 movie *The Manchurian Candidate* dramatically showed (Selisker 2016). Less mystically, both sides engaged in extended propaganda wars through the medium of radio (Nelson 1997). Radio waves were the more mundane version of telepathic influence at a distance (on radio as a prosthetic extension able to touch listeners, compare Blanton 2012).

In Papua New Guinea, broadcast radio was strictly a state project, run by the Australian Broadcasting Corporation (ABC). According to a government report on mass communications, the administration considered radio the most successful medium for connecting with local people.[17] Early broadcasts during the war were celebrated for their ability to explain the basic outlines of the conflict and encourage Papuans to aid allied soldiers (Baskett 1991: 92–96). In the postwar years, radio remained in ABC hands, although non-state groups—missionaries in particular—were invited to produce short programs. The Christian Radio Missionary Fellowship (CRMF), whose two-way radio network I discussed in chapter 1, tried unsuccessfully for over a decade to get a license for its own broadcast network. We can look at the CRMF's negotiations with the administration to get a sense of how the latter thought about the threat of unregulated media, and how the specter of the telepathy tale was never far from its considerations. While the administration felt that radio connection among colonizers who worried over remoteness and isolation was a legitimate issue, the concern with broadcast radio was that the boundaries of the colony and of the minds of its inhabitants would become too porous.

The CRMF originally applied for a missionary radio broadcast franchise at the time of its 1954 application for the private radio network. The application for the broadcast franchise was denied, as it was in 1959, 1963, and 1965. Across all that time, the geographic and social space described in the broadcast license application was fundamentally opposed to that described in the two-way-radio network license applications. The CRMF applied for the private network to overcome missionary isolation in a far-flung, mountainous terrain, yet the simultaneous plan to create a broadcast radio system was based on the claim that the broadcast system would be able to "deter the natives from congregating around missions and government posts with the attendant danger of the breaking down of tribal law and authority."[18] Suddenly we have moved from an opaque and difficult-to-navigate Papua New Guinean terrain to one in which there is already far too much movement of colonial subjects. Instead of solving a problem of isolation, the broadcast system would solve a problem of social porousness, organizing and regimenting these "native" subjects so that they would remain evenly spread across the territory as a whole.

In both missionary and administration writing about broadcast radio for Papua New Guinea, the problem to be solved is consistently the problem of making Papua New Guinean listeners less accessible to outside influences. In the 1950s–60s Cold War context, there was a growing concern that Papua New Guineans, especially rural men who were employed temporarily as urban laborers, would be influenced by communism. Australian fears about communist influence in the Pacific need to be understood in terms of Australia's own colonial ambitions for the region, which in the years leading up to 1960 involved plans for Australian control over Melanesia as a whole.[19]

The fact that the Communist Party in neighboring Indonesia was gaining strength in the late 1950s and early 1960s added to Australia's concerns about Papua New Guinea's potential to go red. In pressing the case for the missionary broadcast radio system, one missionary argued that "the people in the Rabaul area were being adversely affected by the lying Communist propaganda from Peking Radio, and . . . there was an urgent need for the Missions to have radio facilities to tell the people the truth and guide them through the troubled waters that inevitably lie ahead as they are given more and more independence."[20]

While there are many instances of people discussing Radio Peking or Radio Moscow, few examples of broadcasts on these stations are available now. One of the few I have seen is from 1952, when an administration officer reported hearing English-language broadcasts from both Radio Peking and Radio Moscow that were jamming the shortwave signal that Radio Australia beamed into Papua New Guinea. In other words, Radio Peking and Radio Moscow were broadcasting on frequencies adjacent to those used by Radio Australia's 9PA channel. Because they were broadcasting from different countries, there was little that could be done about the long-distance transmission of shortwave programming into the territory. An extremely alarmed colonial officer stationed in Rabaul took quick notes on a broadcast he heard in 1952 that denounced US aggression on the Korean Peninsula, denounced the UN as a stooge organization legitimizing Western colonialism, and hoped for Stalin's long life and health (a hope that would be dashed the following year). The program ended with a sign-off that ensured that listeners knew the origin of the message: "This program comes to you from Radio Moscow." The only suggestion that the Australian officer could give to counter the broadcasts was that ABC needed to both switch the frequency for the 9PA broadcasts it was sending to Papua New Guinea and do some of its own work of jamming the communist radio broadcasts to try to close up the borders of the territorial space once again.[21]

In meetings between missionaries and administrators that took place biannually in the postwar years, communist radio influence was a recurring topic of conversation. Missions and administration were jointly convinced of the damage communist radio was doing, and convinced that at least some in Papua New Guinea were being moved by these broadcasts to have communist sympathies. John Kuder, head of the Lutheran Mission in the postwar years, mentions briefly in a 1961 report how close Radio Peking's broadcast frequency was to Radio Australia's Port Moresby signal and how easy it was to hear "what kind of fare our New Guineans are lapping up."[22] Rev. Wesley Lutton of the Methodist mission was likewise concerned that communist radio was not just available for local people to listen to but was proving to be extremely popular as well. According to the official record of the 1961 Mission-Administration conference, Rev. Lutton

> was, he said, quite sure that the communistic world had its aim directed at Papua and New Guinea because they probably thought the people were ripe for Communism. Everyone was familiar with the tendency in this country to look for something for nothing and consequently there were cargo cults, and Rev. Lutton believed that the Christian leaders in this Territory should try to counteract that tendency. Radio Peking was very much on the air and so was Radio Moscow and many people in the Territory listened to them.[23]

Beyond just a radio presence, the colonial Legislative Council of Papua New Guinea discussed their worries that "our friends in Moscow" could just enter the colony at any time.[24] And in fact the Australian security service, ASIO, kept tabs on the few people in Papua New Guinea who were actually suspected of being communists. In 1961, one young man, who was in Papua New Guinea as an agricultural cooperatives officer, was arrested and expelled for seeming to promote the idea that Papua New Guineans should stop laboring, rise up, and overthrow their colonial masters.[25] Similarly, the anthropologists Peter Worsley and Max Gluckman were denied entry to Papua New Guinea because of their links to the Communist Party (in 1952 and 1960, respectively). Both cases were discussed in the Australian Parliament and were the subject of sustained media attention across Australia.

Communists seemed then to be everywhere, making themselves accessible to Papua New Guineans at every turn. Even worse from the administration and missionary perspective, they were doing so in ways that seemed to possibly be entertaining the Papua New Guinean population. Thus, Radio Peking had to be jammed, new radio stations put up, communist agitators expelled, and communist organizations disbanded.

In what ways would the communist message be attractive to Papua New Guineans? There were two explanations that kept reappearing. The first was that communism spread because of resentment. In discussions about communism at the Missions-Administration conferences, the primary question was how to improve what was referred to as "race relations" so that resentment and bitterness, and eventually communism, was not cultivated (note that there was not a sense that resentment and bitterness was a current concern).[26] A few missionaries, Geoffrey Baskett most vociferously, used this threat of communist takeover to push the administration to abolish at least some of the segregationist laws in towns.

The colonizers' other explanation for why Papua New Guineans would turn to communism was their purported naiveté and gullibility: these listeners were not autonomous enough to know how to critically encounter the radio messages. Colonial administrators worried that the Papua New Guineans might believe anything they heard. This attitude lasted well into the 1970s (and continues today in terms of how people discuss Papua New Guinean uptake of viral social media content). For example, in Edmund Carpenter's (1972) remarkable monograph on radio in Papua New Guinea, he suggested both that New Guineans took radio extremely seriously (p. 1) and that they understood almost nothing, particularly if the broadcasts were the English-language programs from Voice of America or Radio Peking (177; see also 170–71, 173).

Here the problem was not managing the impermeability of Papua New Guinea and the consequent isolation of colonial zones of whiteness through a point-to-point network (as was the case with the CRMF radio system, as discussed in chapter 1), but creating a bounded territory that could deflect a spreading Red Menace that was creeping into the as-yet-innocent minds of Papua New Guineans. Reports of communist radio transmissions jamming official state-sanctioned broadcasts appeared with the sort of regularity that was true of telepathy tales earlier. These reports and rumors updated the telepathy tales for Papua New Guinea's radio age. Ungovernable communications beyond the level of individual family members were dangerous threats to colonial order. Even if there was no scientific mystery about how the communist radio made its way into the territory, as was the case with the original telepathy tales, there was still a sense of subterfuge and porousness: other people were able to focus the minds of Papua New Guinean subjects in ways that administrators, missionaries, and other colonial actors found almost impossible.

TOK PISIN, LABOR, AND COMMUNICATIVE SECRECY

One of the contexts that helped encourage the circulation of telepathy tales was the colonial concern about the apparent difference in circulatory capacities of the colonizers and the colonized. Whereas colonizers experienced loneliness, remoteness, rough patrols through difficult territory, and confusion in the face of a dizzying array of languages, colonized Papua New Guinean subjects seemed to the colonizers to be able to communicate with mysterious ease. The new media and communication technologies might help a little, although they could not crack the nut of linguistic hyperdiversity. But that only underscored the impression that local people had access to some other hidden, supernatural capacity for communication that worked in ways that were beyond regulation and monitoring—even if the answer, in at least some cases, was just Papua New Guineans' tendency to be multilingual (Sankoff 1977). And even the new media that might aid in the colonial project seemed susceptible to subversion: communist radios jamming Australian state broadcasts offered a less mysterious but, for paranoid colonizers, no less effective version of an interethnic (indeed, international) telepathy tale.

Tok Pisin always seemed to hold out the hope of solving at least one of the communicative issues in the Territory of New Guinea by providing a common language for a wide and, during the postwar years, rapidly growing range of people. Yet the stories of Tok Pisin's growth in the postwar years recapitulated this basic circulatory story of colonizer difficulties paired against the surreptitious ease of communications among the colonized: Tok Pisin was seen as an impoverished means for basic communication from the colonizer to the colonized and yet at times as a medium of mysterious and sophisticated interethnic circulation.

Tok Pisin was, in the eyes of many colonizers, a brute-force solution to the problem of linguistic hyperdiversity, in the sense that for them it was less a language than a supplementary set of verbal cues that aided in physically moving laborers around (see chapter 2). As a government anthropologist, F. E. Williams, put it in 1936 regarding interactions between colonizers and local people in Papua, "at present the means of communication are pidgin Motu, pidgin English, telepathy, and swearing" (Williams 1936). But the supposed simplicity of the language was a feature, not a bug: colonizers thought that as long as Tok Pisin was nothing but a simple language, it did not have the grammatical or representational capacity to be used to foment trouble. For example, in Rabaul, colonizers were astounded to wake up one morning in 1929 to a general strike among laborers, since they believed that the linguistic and cultural differences among the laborers and the simplicity of Tok Pisin made such organization impossible (Gammage 1975). Part of the problem was that few colonizers bothered to learn Tok Pisin (see Wedgwood 1953: 107), and instead only spoke English with some Tok Pisin terms (*long, bilong, -im*) thrown in, what actual Tok Pisin speakers used to call "Tok Masta" (from Eng. *talk master*), the boss's language. In a 1956 "Territories Talk-Talk" gossip column in *Pacific Islands Monthly*, the pseudonymous author "Tolala" noted that the linguist Robert A. Hall Jr.'s work to standardize Tok Pisin's spelling and change its name to "Neo-Melanesian" was an attempt to remove the "master-slave" taint of the language. In a parenthetical comment that points to how happy at least some expat residents of Papua New Guinea were with the status quo, Tolala writes, "Why all this shuddering about 'master-slave' business where Tok Pisin is concerned, I cannot understand."[27] That is, Tok Pisin was fine as it was, in all its orthographic and linguistic messiness, since it was only needed for relatively basic speech acts of ordering workers around.

Given the extremely low expectations that many had for Tok Pisin, then, the discovery that it might be capable of something more than just communicating basic commands was both a disturbing surprise and a fact with potentially supernatural valances. In part *because* planters thought that it was just a bastardized form of English without the capacity for complex communication, Tok Pisin speakers on plantations were able to invent forms of disguised talk that allowed them to discuss, for example, the plantation owner or manager without being detected. This eventually came to be a distinct register, called *tok bokis* (from Eng. *boxed talk*) or *tok hait* (from Eng. *hidden talk*), used both to keep European colonizers out of the communicative loop and to talk with other Papua New Guineans about taboo matters. Below is one example of the sort of hidden talk that was used in mid-twentieth-century Tok Pisin on plantations in which the boss was referred to as "ABC radio" (Brash 1971: 17):

A:	Yu harim ABC nius long morning?	Did you hear the ABC news this morning?
B:	Nogat, em i tok wanem?	No, what did it say?
A:	I nogat gutpela tok—tok win bilong kranki man tasol.	Nothing important—a load of rubbish.
B:	Tru ah, atink yumi no ken harim tok long dispela nius—yumi inap sekim tok bilong en.	Is that so? Well I don't think we have to worry too much about what it says—we can ignore it.

The possibility that colonial laborers could be concealing something from their overseers by using Tok Pisin was first raised in a set of 1949 articles by a Catholic missionary/school teacher/plantation manager, Albert Aufinger, who begins his article by asking, "Do secret languages exist in New Guinea? This is usually denied, even by Europeans who have spent considerable time in the country" (Aufinger 1949: 90). The tone of this two-part article is one of shocked surprise. He discusses the secret Tok Pisin register that uses regular words to refer to hidden meanings, as with the "ABC radio" example, as well as a form of "backwards" Tok Pisin used in both oral and written forms that reversed the order of the phonemes of a word. He suggests that this kind of language game was a postcontact invention as local people took up literacy practices. One example of this phenomenon that he provides is "Alapui kow, atsam i mak!," which is the backwards version of the phrase "Iupala wok, masta i kam!" ("You all [get to] work, the boss is coming"). Aufinger concludes (114): "After what I have said, one will hardly go wrong in assuming, whenever one suddenly surprises a group of natives and they go on talking about apparently inconsequential and trivial matters, that they are unobtrusively continuing in secret language the same discussion which, until the white man came on the scene, they had been conducting in straight language."

Aufinger was just starting to recognize that many communities in Papua New Guinea have well-established speech registers that use different forms of lexical substitution and metaphor for talking to spirits, for talking about taboo topics and people, or for talking about politically fraught issues. What linguists call avoidance registers (see Fleming 2015), these are known by different names across the country: "veiled speech" in Melpa (Strathern 1975), "turned over speech" in Kaluli (Feld 1982), "pandanus language" in Kewa (Franklin 1972), "mountain language" in Awiakay (Hoenigman 2012), to name just a few. Schieffelin (2008) examines the relation between these avoidance speech registers and the development of Tok Pisin versions in Christian contexts. The plantation workers that Aufinger cited were using well-established communicative practices for indirection and avoidance, in this case using Tok Pisin to secretly discuss the colonial powers rather than using their indigenous language to obliquely discuss taboo topics.

A later and likely more influential piece than Aufinger's article was Peter Lawrence's book *Road Belong Cargo*, a widely read ethnography of the 1960s phenomenon of Yali's so-called "cargo cult," a new religious movement that was primarily conducted in a secret register of Tok Pisin (Lawrence 1964: 84, Brash 1971: 326). For both Aufinger and Lawrence, it was the capacity of Tok Pisin—as the language of school, administration, and plantation—to be used deceptively that was concerning or alarming. Even when treated in a more lighthearted way, as in Bob Browne's "Grass Roots" comics that appeared in the English-language *Post Courier* newspaper (collected in Browne 2006), there was a sense that Papua New Guineans were using Tok Pisin in ways that were opaque to colonial actors, especially those who really only knew Tok Masta.

From the later 1940s through the 1960s—in these situations in which people coerced into labor regimes had invented and spoke a language the colonizers considered useful but insipid—there was a growing recognition that Tok Pisin might not be as simple as it seemed. Anti-administration feeling and anticolonial ideologies were setting in, it was feared, through a hidden form of communication in the very medium that the colonizers had long discounted as incapable of abstract or complex representation.

Like the interethnic telepathy tales or the communist radio broadcasts jamming Radio Australia, Tok Pisin's secret forms were a matter of colonial paranoia about speech that was uncontrollable. Propagandistic radio and interethnic telepathy were forms of communication that could come to Papua New Guineans whether the Australians or even the Papua New Guineans themselves wanted it. In Peters's (1999) terms, they were forms of communication that emphasized the ways in which people were too porous, too open to the influence and even remote command of others. Tok Pisin offered a slightly different take on these communicative fears. As the language of labor—the language of, as the "Territories Talk-Talk" column had it, master-slave dynamics—the paranoid concern here was that the act of colonial rule was in fact spreading the capacity for anticolonial communications. The strange fear about Tok Pisin was that when colonizers used it and imagined themselves to be spreading it, they were in fact only enhancing the ability of laborers to upend the colonial order. If the paradigmatic case of propaganda saturation is a radio that cannot be turned off constantly broadcasting state news, Tok Pisin became a secretive subversion of this problem: a language of labor whose anticolonial capacities could not be turned off. Tok Pisin's trick, in Aufinger's telling, was that this language of labor was also acting like both the communist radio and a telepathic message on the bush telegraph: sending signals that colonizers could in this case hear, but ones that they could never trust that they understood.[28]

In Aufinger's analysis, Tok Pisin goes from being a tool of colonial labor to becoming the communicative medium that threatens its future, all without the awareness of the plantation overseers. Necessarily a language of interethnic communication, Tok Pisin's version of the telepathy tale comes from its mysterious ability to communicate secrets out in the open. If the original telepathy tales offer mysterious media of unstoppable communication, and if communist radio jamming offers technologically knowable but still unstoppable communication, Tok Pisin manages both tricks at once: it is a secret and a "straight" version of a language unstoppably spreading throughout the territory.

The link between Tok Pisin and communism was most explicitly and publicly made in 1955, when the American linguist Robert A. Hall Jr. published a short book called *Hands Off Pidgin English!* It was written for the Australian public in response to a 1953 UN demand that Tok Pisin be "eradicated" from the Territory of New Guinea as quickly as possible (I discuss this in detail in chapter 5). In defending Tok Pisin, Hall for the most part used a line of argument about the adequacy of the language that linguists would repeat throughout the second half of the twentieth century: Tok Pisin was a stable, growing language with rules of its own separate from those of standard English; it was meeting the communicative needs of local people; and it should be encouraged in this growth in order to rapidly expand education to as many Papua New Guineans as possible.

Hall was a strange ambassador for Tok Pisin. A professor of Italian at Cornell University, he had a long-standing side interest in pidgins and creoles.[29] He had also worked in the US Army Language Training Institute during World War II, developing materials to rapidly teach GIs languages in combat areas, including Tok Pisin as well as Romance-language manuals (Moulton 1961). Perhaps stemming from his time with the army, Hall was a rabid cold warrior of the sort that flourished in the United States and Australia in the 1950s, and his defense of Tok Pisin made this particularly clear. What were the stakes of "eradicating" Tok Pisin for Hall? Nothing short of the advancing domination of a Soviet empire. If Australia gave up on—indeed, tried to suppress—the language of "the people," then not only would Australia lose whatever goodwill existed between it and its colonial subjects, but the "Russians" would quickly move in to take Australia's place. Making comparisons to the 1940s civil war in Greece in which anticommunists self-defeatingly tried to eradicate the popular (demotic) register of the Greek language associated with communist forces, Hall was sure that any Australian attempt to eradicate Tok Pisin would be the first step on the path to Papua New Guinea's loss to Soviet aggression. In Hall's view, Tok Pisin would be an excellent medium for Soviets to surreptitiously spread communist propaganda if Australia tried to get rid of it. A report to the government in response to the UN's recommendation to eradicate Tok Pisin that was clearly influenced by Hall's main points also comments on the idea that if Papua New Guineans were forced to use English, they would start to feel inferior and this would "leav[e] the way open for subversive groups—influenced by those who, for their own purposes, loudly profess to treat the natives as equals."[30]

In that sense, Tok Pisin was always threatening to become an uncontrollable means of communication. Australia needed to nurture and guide it, rather than shun or eradicate it. Hall seemed to suggest that the Soviet antipathy to Tok Pisin that was expressed in the Trusteeship Council debate was nothing more than a ruse—an attempt to trick Australians into giving up on their best means of real communication with their subjects. Even as he promoted Tok Pisin as a language in its own right, he tied it to the problem of communist propaganda, suggesting that Australia had best be the one to use it, or else others would do so in their place. Hall's advocate in the Department of Education, W. C. Groves, likewise argued that the use of Tok Pisin could keep the kind of resentment and bitterness that bred communist sympathies at bay, because Papua New Guineans using Tok Pisin would not be embarrassed by their lack of knowledge of English.

Rumors of communist radio and secret Tok Pisin languages came together in the September 1953 issue of *Pacific Islands Monthly*. A brief item reported that neighboring Indonesia was now broadcasting in Tok Pisin and Motu on Radio Australia frequencies. Even worse, the radio receivers recently distributed to Papua New Guineans in rural villages had an unadjustable, fixed frequency, so it was impossible to tune to a different station if Radio Indonesia cut in. What was supposed to be a medium of Australian propaganda became instead a medium of Asian communism. The reporter writes:

> I was informed in Moresby that, to assist in the work of establishing a common language—the Territories' biggest single problem—the Education Department has distributed no less than 5,000 Sparrow receiving sets (supplied by the Crammond firm in Brisbane) to native villages. They are on a fixed wave-length, and the plan is that from 4.30 to 6p.m. each day the villagers can listen to a half-hour of Pidgin, and an hour of Motuan, or any other selected language, broadcast from the Moresby station.
>
> Some people are wondering if it is more than coincidence that a powerful Indonesian station should be broadcasting regularly on what is approximately the Sparrows' fixed wave-length, *and in Pidgin*. So far, the monitors have heard no recognizable Red propaganda—only apparently harmless social stuff.
>
> Port Moresby officialdom is aware of the danger. Indonesia is drifting steadily under Communist influence.[31]

The fixed-frequency Sparrow sets were distributed in order to help solve "the Territories' biggest single problem" of a common language, yet this immediately became co-opted into a telepathy tale of its own, in which potentially communist propaganda would be impossible for local people to avoid if they used the very radios that the administration had provided for them and asked them to listen to. Regardless of whether Australia made Tok Pisin its primary language of instruction, the threat of uncontrollable communications remained as the inverse paranoia of a colonial world focused on the mountains and languages hindering its own circulatory projects.

CONCLUSION

Telepathy tales shift from curiosities to threats when they move away from just stories about communication among close kin. When the servant girl Mina realizes that her father has died, the colonial conversation about it can focus on the contrast between modernity and tradition, between technological media of communication and telepathic ones. But when people in one village alert those in another to some issue of concern, maybe some news about the colonial government itself, telepathy tales instead lead to questions of colonial opacity, of whether colonizers will quite figure out or have access to colonized peoples.

Stories of supernatural or secretive influence and communication extend beyond the colonization of the Pacific. Count Dracula is a figure from the mysterious East who stands in contrast to British colonial order and science. His supernatural control-at-a-distance over others is contrasted with the expository telegrams, letters, notes, written journals, and phonograph journals that make up the content of *Dracula*'s epistolary format. In the Pacific, the primary telepathy tales were told as straight journalism or with more literary flair, but they were always told in the plural: every story hinted at hundreds more just like them. The stories constituted a robust genre of colonial imagination, one that easily could be extended into further thinking about uncontrollable communications that had the potential to disrupt colonial labor by making connections to the too-porous minds of Papua New Guineans.

The overall conceptualization of colonial Papua New Guinea as a space of circulatory primitivity, in which colonizers could not seem to move people, goods, or information with any ease, also produced an interest in its opposite—"native" telepathy that was able to circulate information in mysterious, supernatural ways that were not open to the colonial moderns. One version of the modernist imaginary of circulation says that more circulation is better. But these tales show that there was always a countervailing claim that circulation had to be managed and curtailed, qualitatively channeled in ways that could produce the right kind of remoteness or the right kind of subject.

The robustness of the genre of telepathy tales—and of the opposition of telepathy tales to circulatory primitivity more broadly—affected the way that other new modes of communication also came to be part of colonial Australia's work in Papua New Guinea. Communist radio and Tok Pisin, not normally two things that would seem to be closely connected, become species of the same paranoia about the capacity for intervillage or even international communications outside of Australian control. A circulatory perspective gives us a way to conceptualize not only the colonization of Papua New Guinea but, as I show in the next chapters, its decolonization as well.

PART TWO

Bureaucracies of Decolonial Connection

4

———

Demanding Independence
on Behalf of Others

*The Trusteeship Council and the Trust Territory
of New Guinea*

In moving from discussions of the Lutheran Mission and colonial administration in the Territory of New Guinea in part 1 of this book to discussions of the UN Trusteeship Council and the bureaucratic attempts to decolonize the Territory of New Guinea, I am making a claim for a communicative perspective as an organizing frame for analysis. Local people sometimes confused the Trusteeship Council's visiting missions (biannual territory inspection trips) with Christian missions, to the chagrin of the UN delegates, but in most respects there was little overlap. The connecting link is the way in which the modernist imaginary of circulatory primitivity continued to be the overarching context through which the Territory of New Guinea was seen and dealt with. In this first chapter of part 2, I lay out the particular institutional and historical context of the Trusteeship Council and the communicative networks that it was trying to create between New York, Australia, and the Territory of New Guinea.

MAKING DEMANDS FOR DECOLONIZATION

Nationalist independence projects were difficult enough when centered on the complex ties between colonizer and colonized, but the postwar decolonization era saw a number of even more complicated demands for independence, mediated by the various groups of anticolonial nations that formed in the 1950s. In these contexts, third parties—whether parts of the UN, the Non-Aligned Movement, or other anticolonial formations—in essence made demands for independence on behalf of other colonized peoples. Using versions of the historicism that had been broadly foundational to the colonial project (Chakrabarty 2000, 2010), the nations that had decolonized early assumed that their brothers and sisters across

109

the colonized world would be repeating their experiences soon enough and tried to help that historical progression along. They found it necessary to triangulate multiple entities in a complex voicing structure in which more vanguardist groups could enunciate demands for independence that may or may not have been on the lips of colonized peoples in a given territory.

If colonialism is defined partly by the colonizer's sedimentation of ethnic or linguistic differences into communities to govern ("you are a people"), then narratives of nationalism assume that there is a performative event of self-enunciation in the demand for sovereignty ("we [are] the people") (Lee 1995). From within that framework, to demand sovereignty for others ("they are a people"), who themselves may not be making that request, seems to sit uncomfortably between those two more recognizable forms. In this part of the book, I examine the bureaucratic moments when an organ of the UN that was then being driven by a coalition of anticolonial nations made demands on Australia to decolonize the Trust Territory of New Guinea. This was a complex speech event in which a part of the UN claimed to be speaking for Papua New Guinean peoples: not *we the people demand independence*, but *we the UN demand independence on behalf of these people*.

Although Papua New Guineans were, in fact, demanding that Australia change its colonial policies at the time, in many cases their demands would have looked like requests for more, not less, colonial involvement: more educational facilities, more health services, more opportunities to participate in the cash economy. Alternatively, they were making demands for equality and autonomy that were illegible as political demands to the delegations at the UN, who instead glossed these movements as quasi-religious "cargo cults" (see Worsley 1957, Burridge 1995 [1960], Jebens 2004, Schwartz and French Smith 2021). But the fact that the UN delegations recognized relatively little evidence of local Papua New Guinean demands was not a deterrent to their efforts. If anything, it spurred further denunciation of Australia's colonial rule, since the anticolonial bloc assumed that every group wanted to be self-sovereign and that a lack of such demands could only be caused by repression or bad administration. In this ritual moment in which factions of the UN Trusteeship Council attempted to voice a demand for independence on behalf of the Trust Territory of New Guinea, we see contests over the framing of the demand itself and the ability of the various participants to be seen as part of the same political here-and-now. The anticolonial delegations of the UN had to claim that Papua New Guinean peoples were already full participants capable of sovereignty while also claiming that the UN had the legitimate capacity to author Papua New Guinea's demands in the absence of anything that UN delegates could themselves see as a demand.

Just as the canonical narratives of nationalism have emphasized these performative demands as moments of national self-making, canonical narratives of nationalism have also focused heavily on the mass media as network formations that promote nationalist identities and circulate demands for sovereignty. Anderson's

(1991) influential discussion of the role of realist reportage in newspapers and novels has been widely debated and discussed for several decades. Others have since argued that radio, television, film, and the internet likewise cultivate their own national imaginaries (Hayes 2000, Williams 2002, Whitaker 2004, Kunreuther 2014). Yet the call to national sovereignty documented in this and the following chapters happened through a set of narrowcast rather than broadcast channels, in the form of bureaucratic information flows from New York to Canberra to Port Moresby and back again. Indeed, the demand for independence itself was largely phrased as a bureaucratic demand for information: what target date was Australia planning on for the independence of Papua New Guinea?

In making this argument, I add to a growing literature that is rethinking the centrality of the nation-state form in the decolonization era. At the broadest level, some scholars argue that indigenous communities have engaged in decolonial projects outside of the nation-state across the history of the colonial experience (for a discussion of the Pacific context, see Banivanua Mar 2016). In terms of the twentieth-century history of decolonization itself, Kelly and Kaplan (2001) argued, contra Anderson, that the nation-state became the assumed form only after World War II. And as other authors have recently discussed, even the early years of the postwar decolonization movement did not necessarily assume national territorial sovereignty in the nation-state form as the ultimate aim.

In some cases, demands for an end to colonization were demands not for independence, but rather for greater integration with the metropole, as when leaders in francophone Africa and the Caribbean demanded to be incorporated into a greater France (Cooper 2012). In other cases, more relevant to the discussion here, some hoped to create self-determination through a coalition of the decolonized in which territorial sovereignty was important largely as a precursor to creating this broader formation, rather than as an end in itself. Adom Getachew (2019), for example, outlines some of the attempts made by a transatlantic coalition to create a countervailing group that could stand against the European empires. Some of this was supposed to happen through UN organs, the Non-Aligned Movement, or groups similar to them. Even though these and similar plans had largely been undone by the 1970s, Getachew and others (e.g., Wilder 2009) are hoping to recover some of these forgotten futures of the early decolonization movement as a way to think outside the sometimes failed promises and confines of the nation-state form. My goal here is to further expand on the sense of the communicative networks through which decolonization demands were made, focusing especially on networks that existed outside of, or in addition to, those linking only colonizer and colonized.

The first part of this book covered a more canonical topic in the anthropology of the Pacific and the anthropology of colonialism. We have well-established ways of thinking about the role of Christian missions in projects of both evangelism and colonial subject formation. But, with a few important exceptions (Downs

1980, Riles 2000, Denoon 2012), the UN and in particular the Trusteeship Council have not been front and center in the anthropology of the Pacific. This is partly due to the limited role of the Trusteeship Council. Probably one of the council's most consequential decisions was when it urged the World Bank to produce a report on Papua New Guinea in 1965 that then shaped postcolonial economic priorities (though in many cases by outlining goals and programs that Australia decided to work in opposition to). Outside of the World Bank report, the council's strongest effects may have been due to Australia's concern about its global standing, which it measured through the ways in which it related to the council and its other members, especially the United Kingdom and the United States. Was Australia being treated as an equal partner to these larger global powers? Was the Trusteeship Council trying to embarrass Australia?

White Australian residents of colonial Papua New Guinea associated the Trusteeship Council with a sense of scolding paternalism. For example, when a movie theater was discovered to be offering race-segregated screenings, its owner was mockingly warned that "you better watch out or we'll tell on you to the UN" (Craig Volker, personal communication). As I discuss elsewhere (Handman 2024), the Australian national press followed the recommendations and pronouncements of the UN about Australia's rule in Papua New Guinea with great interest, often taking umbrage at what the media class saw as illegitimate interference in sovereign Australian issues. Conservative 1950s anticommunist sentiment in Australia made many suspicious of the UN as a puppet of the Soviet Union. Minimally, it was a left-leaning institution demanding an unrealistic political idealism.

As the extensive amount of material in the National Archives of Australia attests, politicians and civil servants in the Department of Territories and the Department of External Affairs spent an incredible amount of time and energy managing the relationship with the Trusteeship Council. Although it may not have produced many changes in the day-to-day administration of more rural locales, where anthropologists have tended to do most of their research on Papua New Guinea, the Trusteeship Council was responsible for hurrying Australia toward a number of consequential decisions regarding the educational system, local government, and ultimately the timing of independence itself.

MANDATES, TERRITORIES, AND TRUSTS

The Trusteeship Council was one of the original main bodies of the UN (figure 6). Its purpose, composition, and responsibilities are laid out in Chapter XIII of the UN Charter. In contrast to the General Assembly, the Security Council, the Economic and Social Council, the International Court of Justice, and the UN Secretariat (all of which were also brought into being by the charter), it is the only main organ of the UN whose work has wrapped up. As of 1994, the Trusteeship Council is no longer in regular operation.[1]

FIGURE 6. The UN Trusteeship Council chambers on June 18, 1954, as delegates are about to begin the annual review of the Territory of New Guinea. Beside the window is an exhibit of maps and photographs from the territory. (UN Photo/MB, UN7662270)

The council had oversight of territories that had been placed under the international trusteeship system, also established by the UN Charter (Chapter XII). According to the charter, trust territories in the international trusteeship system were supposed to come from three sources: (1) territories that had formerly been League of Nations mandated territories; (2) territories detached from enemy states as part of World War II; (3) and territories voluntarily placed under the trusteeship system by states responsible for their administration. Most of the eleven trust territories were former mandated territories; only Italian Somaliland became a trust territory through the second route. No trust territories emerged through the third route—colonial powers were unwilling to voluntarily place any of their possessions under trusteeship.

The Trusteeship Council was composed of several categories of member states of the UN. Each state that acted as an administering authority for a trust territory had a seat on the council. Throughout the 1950s, there were seven administering authorities: the United Kingdom (administering Tanganyika, the British Cameroons, and British Togoland), France (administering the French Cameroons and French Togoland), Belgium (administering Ruanda-Urundi), the United States (administering the Pacific Trust Territory), Australia (administering New Guinea and Nauru), New Zealand (administering Western Samoa), and Italy (administering Italian Somaliland). In addition to the seven administering authorities, any permanent members of the UN Security Council that were not administering authorities (i.e., the Soviet Union and [nationalist] China) were given permanent seats on the Trusteeship Council. Finally, as many other member states would be elected to three-year terms on the council as were necessary to have an equal number of administering and non-administering states on the council. During the period discussed here, there were always seven administering powers and seven non-administering powers.

The trusteeship system had several important differences with the League of Nations mandate system that it replaced. The first difference had to do with the horizon of possibility for each mandated territory. Mandated territories had been divided into three classes: A, B, and C. The A mandates, former territories of the Ottoman Empire, all gained independence between 1919 and 1948, eventually becoming Palestine/Israel, Jordan, Iraq, Syria, and Lebanon. The B mandates consisted of most of Germany's African territories, which were assumed to be on a slow but progressive track toward eventual independence: Ruanda-Urundi, Togoland, Tanganyika, and the Cameroons. The C mandates were former German and Japanese territories in the Pacific as well as one in Africa: New Guinea, Western Samoa, Nauru, the South Pacific Mandate, and Southwest Africa. These C mandates were considered so backwards that it was not possible to think in practical terms of independence happening in the foreseeable future. Within a few years of the UN's founding, all class A mandates were independent. The trust territories were the class B and C mandates, with the exception of Southwest Africa (now Namibia), a class C mandate that South Africa refused to place in the trusteeship system.

In contrast to the mandate system's three tiers based on the territory's level of "advancement," the trusteeship system gave all trust territories the goal of self-government or independence. As such, the trusteeship system seemed to be oriented toward decolonization from the beginning. In fact, ten of the eleven trust territories were independent by 1975, only thirty years after the founding of the trusteeship system (Louis 1978: 116). It was an unexpectedly rapid process, with the result that one of the main UN bodies was considered entirely obsolete not long after it was first established.

Although the UN is now most associated with its "Universal Declaration of Human Rights" and with the advancement of decolonization in the second half of the twentieth century, scholars have argued that this outcome was in many ways a surprise to the architects of the UN system (Louis 1978, Mazower 2009):

> Indeed, many left the founding conference at San Francisco in 1945 believing that the world body they were being asked to sign up to was shot through with hypocrisy. They saw its universalizing rhetoric of freedom and rights as all too partial—a veil masking the consolidation of a great power directorate that was not as different from Axis powers, in its imperious attitude to how the world's weak and poor should be governed, as it should have been. (Mazower 2009: 7)

However, the Bandung Conference in Indonesia in 1955 resulted in the Non-Aligned Movement a few years later and helped develop a visible anticolonial voting bloc led by India, Indonesia, and Egypt. These new anticolonial nations became a significant force in UN deliberations.

So while decolonization was written into the trusteeship system as the universal end-point for all territories, the speed of decolonization was unexpected. The administering authorities of trust territories were caught off guard by the way that the Trusteeship Council became an organ of decolonization, beginning in the mid-1950s and continuing through the rest of its active existence. Most of the architects of the trusteeship system assumed that it would be in operation for seventy-five to one hundred years or much longer (Louis 1978). As I will discuss further here and in the following chapters, the US played an important part in speeding up this timeline within the Trusteeship Council when it started to occasionally vote with the non-administering delegations in 1956. This allowed the non-administering authorities to pass resolutions with more forceful demands that the administering authorities quicken the pace toward self-determination in the trust territories. This was a radical shift from the League of Nations Permanent Mandates Commission, which had been staffed by former colonial administrators who saw things from the perspective of the colonial powers.

Not only was the Trusteeship Council organized in a way to give equal voice to administering and non-administering delegations, but it was also given additional powers in the form of bureaucratic oversight of the administering authorities. The new, postwar international order was going to be maintained with paperwork. In addition to asking for annual reports as the mandates commission had, the Trusteeship Council oversaw the trust territories through their management of three other forms of upward and downward information flows. First, a subset of delegates would be chosen to go on biannual or triannual visiting missions to each of the trust territories. During these fact-finding visits, the administering authority would try, through a guided tour of the territory, to stage-manage a presentation of its efforts toward political, economic, social, and educational development, invoking the primary categories of trust territory oversight. Second, subjects living in the trust territories could petition the council to demand actions or to seek redress of grievances. This could happen during the visiting missions, usually in large, often outdoor meetings in which local communities gathered to speak to and hear speeches from the members of the visiting missions. But subject peoples could also mail petitions to the council or even, on occasion, formally address it in person in New York. Third, the council could vote on resolutions that made recommendations to the administering authorities about future governance plans based on the annual reports, visiting mission reports, and petitions. Those recommendations were required to be addressed in subsequent annual reports prepared by the administering authorities, and checked on during the next visiting missions. Each of these three forms of information collection and distribution spawned other kinds of documents and flows. Files in the Australian archives, for example, show that the Department of Territories created a standardized form for responding to Trusteeship Council recommendations.[2]

One of the most important features of all of this bureaucracy was that the council could make demands on administering authorities' future actions in addition to commenting on past actions. This orientation toward the future—with self-government the imagined telos, even if that was originally considered a century into the future, rather than just a few decades away—was the primary difference from the mandate system. It was the engine for the bureaucratic system of information flow embodied in the annual reports, the visiting mission reports, the petitions, and the recommendations themselves.

One of the most significant pieces of information that the Trusteeship Council tried to elicit from each of the administering authorities was the target date for the attainment of independence. The non-administering authorities had frequently tried to demand target dates for the attainment of independence throughout the history of the council, and those demands increased throughout the 1950s. The 1955 Bandung Conference, led by India and Indonesia, was an important event for organizing a broader anticolonial coalition of recently decolonized nations. It was a precursor to the establishment of the Non-Aligned Movement in the early 1960s, in which India, Indonesia, and Egypt took leading roles in trying to end colonial rule around the world while also offering a nonaligned way out of the bipolar Cold War political order defined by the opposition between the United States and the Soviet Union. As Dipesh Chakrabarty (2010: 53ff.) has discussed, the Bandung conversations included what he calls a "pedagogical" project. The Bandung leaders wanted to end the oppression and inequality of colonialism while at times also holding on to a sense of themselves as "more advanced" countries within the anticolonial project (see also Pham and Shilliam 2016, Lee 2010). They would lead the "less advanced" colonized peoples into the anticolonial future. Representatives of these delegations saw themselves as providing the political model that other colonized territories needed to emulate, in some ways putting those other colonies into a developmentalist "waiting room of history" while working toward decolonization.

Demanding target dates for independence was part of this project. When the non-administering delegations tried to include target-date recommendations in these reports, these were either final target dates (when sovereignty would be transferred to the local people in a territory) or intermediate target dates (when particular benchmarks would be reached in the areas of political, economic, social, or educational development). The most contentious of the intermediate target dates were those for political development, since these were inevitably dates for establishing whatever would be the precursor to an independent or at least self-governing territory. That is, intermediate target dates for political development were seen as being only a small step away from final target dates for independence (this, at least, was how Australian civil servants viewed the matter from Canberra).

In 1956, the US started to vote with the non-administering authorities on the issue of intermediate target dates (I discuss this policy shift in more detail in a later section). After debating the 1956 visiting mission's report on its visit to the Territory of New Guinea, the council voted to include in its recommendations a greater emphasis on target dates. Set apart from the rest of the report in its own section— "VI. establishment of intermediate target dates and the final time-limits for the attainment of self-government or independence"—and then set apart again with paragraphs printed in italics was the specific performative ritual demand: to ask on behalf of the people of Papua New Guinea for information about when, exactly, Australia planned to hand over control. After noting that Australia ("the Administering Authority") has "on occasions planned regional and territorial development with tentative target dates," the council

> commends to the Administering Authority for its consideration the opinion that a more precise statement of the steps and manner in which self-government or independence is to be achieved, and the drawing up of successive targets for political, economic, social, and educational plans and programmes, would give the Trust Territory a stronger sense of purpose and direction in achieving its final goal and would tend to induce in the inhabitants a greater understanding of their future which would enable the Territory to move ahead as rapidly as possible.
>
> The Council accordingly recommends to the Administering Authority that it indicate such successive intermediate targets and dates in the political, economic, social, and educational fields as will create the pre-conditions for the attainment of self-government or independence.[3]

The next paragraph "invites" Australia, in its next annual report, "to inform the Council of the results of its consideration of these recommendations." With these explicit primary performative verbs of speaking—*commending, recommending, inviting*—the council establishes a framework in which it has the authority and capacity to do such things, implicitly in the name of the rights of man, and particularly in the name of the people of the Trust Territory of New Guinea, who may need help forming "a greater understanding of their future."

The 1956 visiting mission, which had happened earlier in the year, had tried to hear the voices of the people of the Trust Territory of New Guinea. The delegates held many meetings during which they hoped that local people would voice demands for autonomy, greater control of local-level government, or even something like a plebiscite. But what the visiting mission delegates heard instead were demands for more hospitals, schools, and roads—that is, more intervention by Australia rather than less. Papua New Guineans attempted to elicit a moral relationship with Australia through soliciting greater interaction with the administration (see Stasch 2015). During the visiting mission of 1953, the delegates had received a petition about participation in local government, but it was a petition from one community to have the right to *refuse* to participate in local self-governance (as I discuss in chapter 5). In some places away from the more heavily colonized islands and coasts, communities that had only recently come into regular contact with the Australian administration did not take speaking roles in these meetings that the visiting mission had set up to allow indigenous voices to be heard. They participated instead by putting on elaborate welcoming dances of reception, highly political events by which they hoped to initiate connections and exchanges for the local people, but ones that were somewhat indecipherable for the UN delegates.[4]

And yet, what seemed to be the relative silence of Papua New Guinean subjects did not get in the way of the Trusteeship Council inviting Australia to name target dates for independence. In the absence of the kinds of "we the people" ritual demands that the visiting missions were expecting to find, the council's representatives in New York put together their own bureaucratic demands on behalf of the people of the Trust Territory of New Guinea. Indeed, one of the major topics of debate in council meetings throughout the 1950s was trying to decide what they would call the people of the territory, whom they were trying to baptize, so to speak, into a national consciousness.

At times, the lack of a demand for independence from the people of the Territory of New Guinea was considered a benefit by some of the more engaged members of the anticolonial bloc. The delegate from India, Rikhi Jaipal, spoke at length in the discussions of the 1956 visiting mission report on this topic. While criticizing Australia's administration, he also argued that the lack of Australian colonial "progress" was an opportunity for unprecedented transformation. The people of the Trust Territory of New Guinea "will have no history of colonial domination or exploitation; they will have no legacy of colonial strife or bitterness; there will not be the apathy born of political frustration. Their freedom is assured and held in reserve by the international community."[5]

Jaipal was perhaps implicitly contrasting his own country's experiences with those of the Territory of New Guinea in making these very optimistic statements about the opportunity provided by what seemed to him a colonial blank slate. He reiterated the visiting mission's report that the current enthusiasm for state services and greater engagement "runs the risk of drying up if development is not sufficiently rapid" and that "if the present high hopes of the people are seriously disappointed conditions may change radically."[6] In other words, people might not be making demands now, but if Australia does not obey the recommendations for target dates, there will be demands soon enough. In the gap between 1956 and whatever time it might take for the people of the territory to experience that frustration, the Trusteeship Council—or at least the non-administering delegations of the council—would voice the demands for independence that would be coming soon enough anyway. The historicism that places the Global South in the "waiting room of history" is here used by a strongly anticolonial delegate from one of the first nations to decolonize in order to usher on that history of growing sovereignty for a different colony.

In the late 1940s and early 1950s, the UN approved a suite of statements and declarations that enshrined in global bureaucratic consciousness a particular image of humanity. The "Universal Declaration of Human Rights" (1948), the "Statement on Race" (1950), and the "Statement on Vernacular Education" (1955) each argued for a vision of the human that has a natural inclination for self-determination, a mental plasticity, and a perfectly adequate vernacular language in which to govern and learn. Even as the UN became the central institution pushing for rapid decolonization of the world, the UN documents did not seem to acknowledge the massive transformation in local communities that this would involve (see Steffek 2021: 137ff). This was especially true for the Trusteeship Council, which vacillated between recognizing the wholesale transformation of the political world that decolonization would engender and denying that very much needed to be done to transform colonized peoples into self-governing peoples.

Because the "Universal Declaration of Human Rights" assumed that all peoples wanted self-determination, any reticence about it could only come from one of two sources. First, reticence about self-determination could be due to selected cultural practices that needed to be pruned in order to let the desire for freedom shine brighter. Trusteeship Council debates about specific forms of oppression—for example, of women—worked off the assumption that if a certain practice could be eradicated, then the realization of the need for self-determination would spread further. Second, reticence about self-determination could come from ignorance (especially the kind of ignorance fostered by colonialism). If people could be introduced to the principles of self-determination, of course they would want to enact them.

When it came to the Trust Territory of New Guinea, the council's debates centered mostly on the second issue: how could the people of the territory learn about the principles of self-determination and freedom that had been kept from them? The council often assumed that it was not Australia, in particular, that had kept this good news from the people, but rather the conditions of the Territory of New Guinea itself. With so many people closed in, shielded from contacts with others by the geographic and linguistic conditions, freedom in the territory would be achieved by overcoming these communicative issues. In that sense, the focus of much Trusteeship Council work on the territory emphasized the flow of information into it. The faster and easier information could flow, the faster and easier decolonization could be enacted.

The emphasis on the speed of decolonization was formalized in 1960 with the UN General Assembly's Resolution 1514 (XV), "Declaration on the Granting of Independence to Colonial Countries and Peoples." The resolution, which begins with the assertion that all dependent peoples yearn for freedom, invalidates any rationale for continued colonial dependence: "Inadequacy of political, economic, social or educational preparedness should never serve as a pretext for delaying independence." This perspective had clearly been present in the Trusteeship Council's debates in the 1950s, although it did not then have the official backing of the entire General Assembly. Indeed, Australian diplomats had spent much of the decade coming to terms with the fact that, as one Department of External Affairs memo put it, "criteria other than that of speed of development are no longer worthy of serious consideration" for the non-administering authorities, and perhaps even for the Trusteeship Council Secretariat.[7]

LONG-RANGE PLANS AND OTHER DEMANDS FOR INFORMATION

The UN's power was always limited. With few mechanisms for punitive action, much of its power came from the idea that member states would want to avoid censure from the newly created "family of nations." The UN tried to put pressure on delegations in the Trusteeship Council, and Australia in turn tried to deflect that pressure, mainly through management of information. The council tried to elicit certain forms of information from Australia, just as Australia tried to provide only the information that it thought would help maintain the sense of its moral standing as administrator of Papua New Guinea. Across many of the remaining sections of this book, I am looking at how these relationships were negotiated through information flows: how those pushing for rapid decolonization and those pushing for continued colonization fought this battle through the circulation of forms, reports, and petitions.

The most significant piece of information the Trusteeship Council tried to elicit from each of the administering authorities was the target date for the attainment of independence. As mentioned above, the eighteenth session of the council, which met during July and August 1956, was an important one because it was at this point that Australia really had to contend with the fact that control of the council had shifted into the hands of the non-administering authorities due to the US policy shift. A general sense of Australian frustration with the idea that the UN would have the capacity to make demands on the administering authorities is especially clear in a marginal comment on a cable from the Australian delegation to the UN. The cable notes that the French government proposed to carry out a "prescribed popular consultation [i.e., a referendum] in French Togoland under UN supervision" in October 1956 and asked that the UN appoint observers to supervise the vote. A reader of the cable at the Department of External Affairs has underlined the word *prescribed* and written next to this paragraph in rather nondiplomatic terms, "This stinks!"[8] Clearly, the Trusteeship Council's emerging power to prescribe, supervise, and otherwise demand information and action was upsetting the members of the Department of External Affairs, as well as many other civil servants and politicians involved in the administration of the Trust Territory of New Guinea. From the perspective of these men, much of this situation was due to one person in the US delegation.

For most of the 1950s, the US representative to the Trusteeship Council was a man named Mason Sears, who had his first major effect on the council when he chaired the 1954 visiting mission to the trust territories of Africa. In memos and reports written after that visiting mission, Sears devoted himself to advocating an advanced schedule to move the African territories much more quickly toward independence. While this was starting to become the US policy position with respect to much of the colonized world, he pushed for it with a religious zeal. In a memoir of his time on the council—a self-congratulatory account with the grandiose title *Years of High Purpose*—Sears (1980) depicts himself as the leader of a crusade for a dramatic and novel approach to independence timetables that shook up the fusty world of Trusteeship Council diplomacy.

It's clear from diplomatic cables sent between New York and Canberra that Sears had a bull-in-a-china-shop attitude toward UN diplomacy and especially toward the other administering authorities on the council. For a while, Australian diplomats assumed that Sears was a loose cannon, and that all they needed to do to get rid of the target-date issue was have conversations with his bosses at the US State Department. For several weeks in July and August 1956, Australia and the UK sent diplomatic messages to the State Department, shared them secretly with one another, and presented their arguments against target dates as best they could. But they slowly realized that it was not just Sears who was taking a positive position on intermediate target dates, and that the US would no longer vote in line with the UK and Australia on this issue.

In these communications with the UK and Australia, the US diplomats described their position as a relatively moderate one. They were not in support of *final* target dates for complete independence (in contrast to the Soviet Union and some of the other more militant non-administering authorities on the Trusteeship Council), but only *intermediate* target dates for reaching particular benchmarks in political, economic, social, or educational advancement in the various trust territories. In reality, this US policy was largely oriented toward the African rather than the Pacific trust territories, as one part of the Cold War battle for influence on the African continent. Sears even confided to the Australian representative to the UN that target dates were important mostly in places like Tanganyika and Ruanda-Urundi, and that they were just "hocus pocus" for the other territories.[9] But it was hocus pocus that the US practiced and that Sears defended with passion when it came time to vote. A memo that circulated within External Affairs summed up the Australian sense of defeat in the face of the new US position:

> [We consider] the US position as essentially a national policy and not simply as a personal thesis of Mr. Mason Sears and we are in agreement therefore with the Australian Embassy in Washington's views on this point as expressed in their memorandum No. 1298 of 2nd October, 1956. However, while the State Department regards the intermediate target date formula has some practical administrative merit and political advantage, Mr. Sears is inclined to view it as of revolutionary significance. It was for this reason that he encouraged in the Council during the Eighteenth Session the belief that, in adopting the new principle, the United States had departed so far from its basic policy of "assisted evolution" hitherto applied in the Pacific Islands

Trust Territory that that policy should be henceforth regarded as superseded rather than merely modified. In this attitude Mr. Sears would appear to have come dangerously close to adopting the non-administering view, to which we refer in the attached memorandum, that criteria other than that of speed of development are no longer worthy of serious consideration. It might be advantageous if the State Department could be persuaded to concede that at least this aspect of Mr. Sears' thinking is incorrect, for it is from this point that that intermediate target date formula derives much of its emotional support.[10]

The war within the Trusteeship Council was practiced, then, as a set of battles about a quite specific piece of information: would administering authorities give the council dates by which independence, or benchmarks toward independence, would happen? If speed was the only issue, then the most important order of business was setting those benchmarks. Australia felt that this was making a mockery of trusteeship by reducing its object to a particular date. But the non-administering authorities on the council saw the target date as a final element of a larger set of explicit, supervisable plans. The focus on target dates meant that there was a horizon toward which each trust territory was directed.

After debating the 1956 visiting mission's report on its visit to the Trust Territory of New Guinea, and with the US now voting with the non-administering authorities on this issue, the Trusteeship Council specifically included in its recommendations a greater emphasis on target dates. The council strongly recommended that Australia set these target dates and invited the Australian delegation, in its next annual report, "to inform the Council of the results of its consideration of these recommendations."[11] In other words, give the council target dates or explain why you are directly flouting its recommendations. This last recommendation was met with indignation in the Department of Territories and outrage in the Australian press (see Handman 2024).

The Australian UN delegation was more clear-eyed than their fellow civil servants in Canberra in seeing the direction in which the UN was moving (that is, toward the 1960 resolution mentioned above, the "Declaration on the Granting of Independence to Colonial Countries and Peoples"). By the beginning of 1957, they were gently trying to suggest ways that people in the Department of Territories could adjust reports to include more specific plans and benchmarks, at least for the less controversial areas of economic, social, and educational advancement. A memo prepared by the Dependent Territories section of External Affairs (whose first page—with the date and identification of author and recipient—is unfortunately missing) recommends that in addition to continuing to oppose target dates, the Department of Territories could also provide more information in their annual reports on the Territory of New Guinea as a way to placate the demands of the UN. That is, they would manage criticism and suspicion on the world stage by managing the upward flow of information, replacing target dates with more information about plans and policies. Under the heading "Suggested Action," the memo says that "we should, therefore, whilst maintaining our opposition, endeavor (a) to remove the suspicion of our motives held by non-administering powers as a result of our outright opposition to target dates, and (b) to provide maximum information to the Council consistent with the maintenance of our long-term interests." "Maximum information" would consist of "revising the manner of presentation of our annual record of administration" and "enlarging the amount of information in the Annual Report, with more facts, statements of principle and policy, and advice of planning, wherever this is possible, and with explanations where it is not. This would greatly facilitate defence against criticism."[12]

As much as Australia resented the capacity of the Trusteeship Council to precipitate actions within specific trust territories (as the reader in External Affairs noted, "This stinks!"), at least some within their ranks argued that more information sent upward to the council could result in fewer actions taken by the council in the Territory of New Guinea. For most of the people and institutions involved, control of the territory was contested in terms of control over this information. If the council could successfully elicit a target date, they could hurry along the administering authority toward the goal of self-government. If the administering authority could instead mollify the council with elaborate descriptions of plans, then they might be able to fend off a plebiscite or a premature transfer of power.

Specific people in External Affairs or in the Australian delegation to the UN seem to have resigned themselves to a future in which target dates would take a larger and larger share of the debate about the trust territories. But for those in the Department of Territories and the Territory of New Guinea administration itself (that is, the people responsible for producing reports and enacting policy in the territory), it was a much longer road toward the acceptance of target dates or Trusteeship Council intervention more generally. In the next section, I outline some of the main figures and processes featured in the files that I examined regarding Australia's interactions with the council.

FILES AND INFORMATION FLOWS

In the Australian archives, certain civil servants and politicians appear over and over again in the 1950s Trusteeship Council files. These include two men who spent most of their time in New York and appeared frequently before the council. As a member of the Department of External Affairs, William Forsyth was Australia's permanent representative to the UN and had been the Australian delegate on the Trusteeship Council in earlier years. Stationed in New York, Forsyth often sent cables to the Department of External Affairs in Canberra as well as to the Australian Embassy in Washington, DC. Australia's special representative to the Trusteeship Council at this time was J. H. Jones (figure 7), who had worked in the Territory of New Guinea for many years and brought the kind of practical,

FIGURE 7. At left is J. H. Jones during the twelfth session of the UN Trusteeship Council in 1953. Jones was Australia's special representative to the Trusteeship Council throughout the 1950s. Pictured with him at right is A. H. Loomes, a member of Australia's Permanent Delegation to the UN. The other man in the photograph is not identified. (National Archives of Australia, A6513, 9)

grounded knowledge and experience of Papua New Guinea that many in Canberra thought was otherwise totally lacking on the council.

In Canberra, members of the Department of External Affairs coordinated with the Department of Territories, which during the 1950s was led by Paul Hasluck. A Liberal Party member for Curtin in Western Australia, Hasluck was an important architect of Australia's position within the Pacific. He hoped to create a wider sphere of influence for Australia in order to counter the perceived threats from communist nations to the north and west (see Waters 2016).

In Papua New Guinea, the Department of Territories often sent cables back and forth to the Office of the Administrator. For much of the period discussed here, the administrator was Brigadier Donald Cleland, CBE, Australia's top representative for both Papua and New Guinea. Given the different status that Papua had in comparison with the Trust Territory of New Guinea, Cleland had to deal with the UN via two different agencies: the Trusteeship Council for New Guinea, and the Fourth Committee on Non-Self-Governing Territories for Papua. Working from Port Moresby, which was officially part of Papua rather than New Guinea, he often had to contend with protests, especially from Soviet delegations, that the "administrative union" of Papua and New Guinea was harming the Territory of New Guinea. In addition to managing relationships with Hasluck and others in the Department of Territories and with the UN representatives of the two agencies that dealt with New Guinea and Papua, Cleland also organized the flow of information throughout the territories, exchanging messages with the district officers in the different regions of the territory, who would themselves liaise with the patrol officers in the more remote stations.

The usually biannual visiting missions from the Trusteeship Council were coordinated by members of the Department of External Affairs, in consultation with the Department of Territories and the administrator. After their elaborately stage-managed tours of the Trust Territory of New Guinea, the visiting mission delegates would travel to Port Moresby to meet with Cleland and then on to Canberra to meet with Hasluck. Policies about administration were decided in the name of both Cleland and Hasluck, and the visiting mission delegates spoke with them as the policymakers for the territory.

At UN headquarters in New York, the different kinds of documents that were sent to or generated by the Trusteeship Council were debated by delegations from the administering and non-administering authorities. The administering authorities spent months preparing their annual reviews, which had to answer questions posed by Trusteeship Council questionnaires (see chapter 6). Special Representative Jones (or sometimes Forsyth) usually presented the annual report for the Trust Territory of New Guinea, after which he would answer questions from the other delegates. Then a subcommittee of delegates would prepare a report on Australia's report that would include recommendations. The wording of these, and later the recommendations themselves, would be voted on by the council. Similarly, visiting missions would produce a report after each trip to a trust territory, which would then be debated in the council. Again, Jones was usually present to answer questions about the Territory of New Guinea and defend Australia's policy decisions that came up for debate during the presentation of the visiting mission reports about the Territory of New Guinea. The final report of the visiting mission also included recommendations, which would also be voted on by the council. Finally, petitions from residents of the trust territories were admitted into the record and debated. All of the debates regarding these documents were made part of the Trusteeship Council's official record.

In writing this second half of the book, I have relied on documents from these different agencies and departments, using a vast set of records that in themselves testify to the ways in which decolonization happened through the management of information flows. Records from the Department of External Affairs, the Department of Territories, and the administrator are available from the National Archives of Australia and, in some cases, from the National Archives of Papua New Guinea. Each visiting mission produced many massive files: from biographical snapshots of delegates, to itemized bills for charter flights into and out of the trust territory, to detailed debates about the itinerary of the visit, to summary analyses evaluating how the trip went. Annual reports likewise produced archival material that can be measured by the cubic foot, as different departments of the Territory of New Guinea administration tried to organize the enormous amount of statistical and narrative material requested. Finally, there are extensive collections of cables sent among diplomats and politicians in Canberra, New York, Washington, and London, in which broader questions of policy, diplomacy, and administration get discussed in detail. UN documents, including the reports, recommendations, and verbatim records of debates, are largely available through the online UN archives or at physical UN depository libraries. In addition, draft versions of some documents appear in records from the Department of Territories or Department of External Affairs. These various primary documents formed the basis for my analysis in the next two chapters.

In many of these documents, especially those that focus on how to communicate with the Trusteeship Council, authors of memos and cables speak in the voice of their national delegation: "Australia" has a position, objection, or comment that needs to be transmitted to the council (see Riles 2000). The materials from Cleland as administrator of Papua New Guinea, or from Hasluck as minister for territories, obviously have a more individualized sense of authorship and authority. But these are not documents that tend to offer deep insights into their authors or their contexts of utterance. I sometimes follow the convention of speaking about "Australia's" position on a given topic, even as I recognize that this assumes a coherence of both the state and the position that is not necessarily evident.

CONCLUSION

While there was significant disagreement between the anticolonial non-administering authorities and Australia as the administering authority, both sides shared a number of fundamental perspectives on the Trust Territory of New Guinea, as I will show in the following chapters. First, they agreed that it had to be decolonized in and through English rather than Tok Pisin. Second, they agreed that it was a space in which a kind of circulatory primitivity governed all considerations of its "advancement." But whereas Australia had produced the problem of fragmentation in response to that imaginary of noncirculation, the anticolonial Trusteeship Council delegations tried to stitch those fragments together into a national consciousness through the implementation of a bureaucratic order. As was true of the chapters in part 1, the next two chapters will focus on language and infrastructure together to understand how the Trusteeship Council organized a project of decolonization.

5

English and the Channels
of Decolonization

In 1953, representatives of the UN Trusteeship Council traveled to the Territory of New Guinea on a visiting mission in order to inspect the area, observe Australia's management of the territory, and speak with Papua New Guinean people about how the UN could help them one day achieve self-government. During similar visiting missions to territories like Togo or Tanganyika, local people would present to council representatives lengthy written and oral petitions, in English or French, regarding the unification of the territory, their political future, and their desire for independence. In those territories, local people not only were already participating in various levels of self-governance, but were demanding more.

In the Territory of New Guinea, the presentations to the visiting delegates were rather different. In 1953, there was only one small region of the territory—just outside the old German colonial capital of Rabaul on the island of New Britain—in which people engaged in any kind of self-governance. Local government councils there, the first experiments in self-governance, collected a small tax from each family and used the money to build schoolhouses, medical aid posts, and structures where people could process copra from their coconut trees. But even there, in the most politically, economically, and educationally "advanced" part of the Territory of New Guinea, the delegates were stunned by the kinds of presentations local people gave them. Not only was the level of "advancement" low compared to the other trust territories in Africa and the Pacific, but far more concerning was the fact that the local people did not seem to be demanding self-government at all. In some cases, they seemed to be doing the opposite, as was the case with a petition presented to the delegation by leaders of Tavuiliu Village.

The original petition is not included in the files I examined, but a typewritten copy of it is. A handwritten comment—"allow"—next to a grammatically incorrect sentence suggests that someone wanted to keep all the typos and errors that were in the original. Below, I have reproduced the document's formatting as much as possible, including all errors, which are not marked with *sic*:

Wednesday   18th March 1953

Tavuiliu Committee
Welcome by the U.N.O. Missionaries

We are very pleased to see you today, and we are very happy too, because you visited this Territory of Papua and New Guines.

Today is the day for usto tell you that we are not in the Village Council. The three important things that we are not to have a village council, "is"

(1) We are foolish. We haven't got enough sense for this Council.

(2) We need to give the help to each of us.

(3) Most of our people are very poor. They have no money at all.

These three things are very important in our minds.

Now we wish to tell you that we are very anxous to stay under the control of the Administration.

We have a small quantity of money, so we ready for the Co-operative. And we wish too, to give a Tax for the Administration, if he is allowed.

Now the Village Council closed the schools, hospitals and every thing for the Administration. If he allows usto buy another school in some other places, we wish to follow that the Administration say.

Wisky is very dangerous.

1. It fills the man and makes his brand foolish.

2. It makes man poor and kills his wife with their children.

Thank you very much for those reations.

We give them to you.[1]

This document is officially registered as UN document T/PET.8/7.

This is a complicated, multi-voiced communication, with various implied as well as overtly identified audiences, claims to its authors' foolishness notwithstanding. One addressee of the petition is the neighboring local government council. The Tavuiliuans were upset that this council had cut off their access to certain schools and medical posts because they had not agreed to join with and pay taxes to the council. That is to say, the petition is about how the Tavuiliuans want to *retain* their autonomy and not be under the thumb of the neighboring village's leadership. The second addressee is the Australian administration. The petition is a demand that the administration help the Tavuiliuans deal with their dispute with the neighboring local government council, to help them regain access to these services. They are also claiming that they do not have enough money for the tax that the local government council is charging, although they do have a smaller amount that they could give to the administration if necessary. In addition, the self-deprecating opening (a common way to start speeches across Papua New Guinea) about being foolish can be read as a complaint to the Australian administration that the Australians have not done enough to prepare them for managing funds and resources. The third and perhaps least important addressee is the explicitly identified one, the delegates of the UN visiting mission (note that they are referred to as "missionaries," something that the delegates continually bristled at).[2] While the delegates are recognized as important visitors, the Tavuiliuan leaders mostly seem to opportunistically take this high-profile moment to direct a very overt and effective complaint at more local targets.

The agenda of the Tavuiliu Committee can partly be read from the letter itself, especially if a reader has some familiarity with the way complaints tend to be lodged in Papua New Guinean contexts. Some of the context of the local dispute is spelled out more fully in accompanying documents, so there is evidence that it was clear to some members of the Australian administration at the time. But what is also clear from those documents is that this sort of local contextualization was not at all visible to the UN delegates. In fact, the discussion of this petition in the Trusteeship Council chambers in New York begins, "Although the meaning of this petition is not clear. . . ."[3] The Tavuiliuans' refusal to join one of the only organs of self-governance then in the territory, and their claims about their own foolishness, became a recurring issue brought up during subsequent discussions of the Territory of New Guinea (in later reports the group seems to be referred to by the name "Raluana"). Over the next few years in Trusteeship Council debates, the (nationalist) Chinese, Syrian, Soviet, Belgian, and other delegations continued to inquire about the Tavuiliuans' refusal, although they eventually grasped some of the local dynamics involved. During subsequent visiting missions, the status of Tavuiliu's relationship to the neighboring local government council was on the official agenda and delegations were constantly on the lookout for any other groups that might be refusing to join councils. Tavuiliu's refusal to join a project of self-governance was so surprising, and such a contrast with the petitions from Togoans, Cameroonians, or Tanganyikans, that many delegates on the council argued that this could only be read as a damning portrait of the failures of the Australian administration. Papua New Guineans didn't even know what they should be asking for.

While it sometimes seems like the council's debates about these visiting mission reports meandered from topic to topic, we can read the flow of questions as a way to give us a sense of the causal links delegates made. For example, in the course of a few questions about this petition, the Chinese delegation goes from asking about why Tavuiliuans refused to join the self-governing local government councils, to asking about the state of education in the territory, to asking how the Australians planned on solving the "language problem," to asking about the status of Tok Pisin.[4] In making this link between a refusal of self-governance and Tok

Pisin, the Chinese delegation's questions exemplify a particular way of viewing the connection between self-determination and English that will be the primary topic of this chapter.

The contemporary dominance of global English is often connected to either earlier colonial education policies or twenty-first-century conditions of neoliberal labor (e.g., Cutts 1953, wa Thiong'o 1986, Cohn 1996, Pennycook 2009, Heller 2010, Cameron 2012). By contrast, the postwar twentieth century is seen as the highwater mark for ethnolinguistic nationalism and the near universalization of the nation-state (Fishman 1968, Anderson 1991, Kelly and Kaplan 2001). But some of the architects of decolonization were interested in creating an international order that would counter empire rather than just universalize the nation-state form. The creation of institutions of decolonization had an important role in the development of global English as well. But while there is considerable scholarship on the use of French in the anticolonial Negritude movements of West Africa and the Caribbean (e.g., Wilder 2009, Warner 2019), less has been said about the role of English in decolonization (but see Mazrui 2004).

For some of the colonial territories like Papua and New Guinea that were not actively engaged in large-scale nationalist independence movements, anticolonial delegations on the Fourth Committee on Non-Self-Governing Peoples and the Trusteeship Council tried to bring them into the UN bureaucratic order first, with an eventual goal of self-determination through a nationalist project coming later. This meant that decolonization in these cases was a matter of developing an informational infrastructure that might eventually lead to nationalist movements for self-determination. In the Territory of New Guinea specifically, this meant creating a communicative network in English, the only official UN language that some Papua New Guineans had even a passing familiarity with. English would be the channel linking would-be Papua New Guinean nationalists with external anticolonial activists and structures. The anticolonial delegations of the UN promoted not a national language, but the colonial language as the engine of decolonization that Papua New Guineans and outside anticolonials would share. Because of that, language could sometimes be one of the few things that both the colonial and anticolonial sides of the UN could agree on. In the Trust Territory of New Guinea, a surprising coalition of delegations and groups all agreed that whatever needed to be done in the colony, one of the first orders of business was the eradication of Tok Pisin.

The irony of the UN interventions in the territory is that while the UN representatives recognized circulation and communication as the base of the problem, they also demanded the eradication of the only language that seemed on its way to potentially solving one part of it. They demanded the eradication of Tok Pisin because they thought it was inhibiting democratic politics by not creating the proper channels of connection among Papua New Guineans or between Papua

New Guineans and external anticolonial actors. How the UN decolonizers came to blame the lack of democratic communication on Tok Pisin, the most likely solution to at least part of that problem, is what I turn to next. In doing so, I hope to show how circulation structured the antipathy to Tok Pisin, blinding the UN delegates to its ability to create a proto-national entity.

THE "HUMAN AND GEOGRAPHICAL FACTORS" OF THE TERRITORY OF NEW GUINEA

For many members of the Trusteeship Council, the problem of independence in the Territory of New Guinea was a problem of creating channels of information. This is especially clear in a 1956 visiting mission report on Australia's challenges as the administering authority:

> The Mission believes that human and geographical factors must always be kept in mind in considering any aspect of development in the Territory, whether it concerns what has taken place or is envisaged in the future. These form a serious obstacle in many areas in the way of administration and the general advancement of the people. The first consists of an undeveloped population divided by a multitude of cultural and linguistic differences, scattered over an extensive area in village units which generally contain no more than one to three hundred inhabitants, with a substantial number who have not yet been brought completely under administrative control. The second concerns communication difficulties. The Mission realizes that these have been annually stressed and that the Trusteeship Council is aware of the difficult terrain, the lack of roads and similar features of the Territory; nevertheless it is useful to recall what this signifies in concrete terms. For example, Administrative contact with many village groups is brief and infrequent since it has to be maintained by patrol officers traveling for days and weeks on foot with carriers. Administrative officers, other than patrol officers, visit villages for specific purposes, but frequently the patrol officer in the main represents the Administration and as such has many functions.[5]

Note that both of the issues mentioned here—the small populations divided by languages and the communication problems that come from having lots of mountains—are essentially one issue of circulation: in the Territory of New Guinea, it is hard to get messages in and out. That has kept the people isolated from one another and, the implication seems to be, from learning from one another or the wider world. Without communications, there is no cultural development. With improved communications—especially those fostered by UN intervention—this development can be accelerated.[6]

Cultural primitivity either was not an issue for the Trusteeship Council or was fobbed off onto missionaries as a process of changing "native" mentality. But both the council and the Australian administration agreed that circulatory primitivity was important and in some ways the harder problem to solve. It would take roads and the introduction of a proper lingua franca, things the administration never had enough money or men to actually implement. Council discussions, with the Australians trying to defend their record of enlightened governance and the anti-colonial states trying to demand a faster timetable to independence, are filled with examples in which the circulatory primitivity of the Territory of New Guinea takes a prominent role. Even when it was mentioned only in passing, it was usually mentioned early on, as the context that governed all comments about the territory. By 1956, it had become so standard to begin discussions of the territory with an invocation of mountains and languages that the authors of the visiting mission reports felt they needed to draw special attention to these factors, to shake Trusteeship Council readers out of a feeling of complacency toward the scale of the problem so that they could really grasp the extraordinary impact of the geographic and linguistic fragmentation.

One of the primary heroes of the 1956 visiting mission's report is thus the airplane, and the "pioneering use" that the Australian administration had made of it in the territory. With the ability to construct roads extremely limited by the mountains, the best alternative was simply flying over the terrain, dropping in from above on the discrete local communities. The challenges of the Territory of New Guinea that were "without parallel" could be mitigated by airplanes:

> The fact that these people emerging from stone age conditions are living in areas which are extremely rugged and have remained unpenetrated until quite recently and that they are isolated from each other by mountains and ravines, language differences, fear of each other and a readiness to kill as the only way of self-preservation, make the task a formidable one. But positive factors also exist which throw a new and encouraging light on the situation. One of them is the existence of methods of penetration which were not available in earlier times. The intelligent and pioneering use of small aircraft by Australians is one of them.[7]

In the face of mountains, languages, and "a readiness to kill," airplanes literally swoop in to save the colonial administration. But airplanes can play this heroic role only if the challenges of the Territory of New Guinea are mostly communication challenges, if colonization and subsequent decolonization are about the circulation of information.

The UN delegates were voicing a vision of modernity focused on the cultural and infrastructural ability to move in productive ways (Edwards 2003, Urry 2007). Georg Simmel (1997), for example, notes that "primitive peoples" in general are extremely mobile hunter-gatherers, whereas the communities he considered culturally stagnant, like those in the European Middle Ages, were too immobile. For him, only the moderns get the proportions just right. Mobility has likewise been discussed in terms of class and capital, with laborers usually considered too mobile (see Thompson 1974, Scott 2018: 2). Both Australian and UN documents depict the Territory of New Guinea as an outlier from any of these perspectives, its population suffering from an off-the-charts immobility that had to be dislodged before the wheels of history could even start to turn.

THE PROBLEM WITH TOK PISIN

Even the most utopian anticolonial members of the Trusteeship Council saw limits to Australia's ability to bring together what they thought the mountains and languages were keeping apart. But without the capacity to flatten the landscape and eliminate all vernacular languages, what exactly could the council suggest? In addition to demands for roads and airplanes, one of the most controversial demands that the council made was for the elimination of Tok Pisin. This is particularly strange given that Tok Pisin would seem to offer a potential solution to the linguistic side of the communication problem by serving as a lingua franca for an increasingly large percentage of the population. Yet Tok Pisin was identified as a force antithetical to independence very quickly. From 1953, it was a special subject of consideration during discussions of the Territory of New Guinea's political and economic development. In particular, the use or abandonment of Tok Pisin seemed to council members to imply something important about the kind of movement and circulation in which Papua New Guineans were participating.

The final page of the 1953 visiting mission report contains a few paragraphs on language and on the dissemination of information about the UN. In a relatively short paragraph, the visiting mission makes a recommendation that would become the most controversial element of the document for Australian readers:

> The Mission is strongly of the opinion that pidgin is not only not a suitable language for instruction, but that it has characteristics derived from the circumstances in which it was invented which reflect now outmoded concepts of the relationship between indigenous inhabitants and immigrant groups [e.g., administrators, missionaries, plantation owners, and shopkeepers]. Therefore, it believes that the most energetic steps should be taken to eradicate this jargon from all instruction given within the Territory, and that plans be urgently developed to eliminate it from the Territory completely.[8]

Aside from the slightly tortured prose about "characteristics derived from the circumstances in which it was invented," which I address below, no reason was given for the demand that "pidgin" be eliminated. What makes the recommendation even stranger is the fact that a paragraph on the same page seems to prove Tok Pisin's value in the territory. After lamenting that most people seem to know nothing about the UN *except what they learned through Tok Pisin radio and newspapers*, the report concludes that "the preparation of special material on the UN in a medium which the people could readily understand would go a long way toward remedying this situation."[9] In other words, the language acting as a lingua franca for a wide swath of the population, Tok Pisin, should be eliminated, but isn't it a shame that there is no way to communicate with a wide swath of the people of

Papua New Guinea? Why, if Tok Pisin is clearly serving a purpose that the UN itself recognizes, do they still demand that it be eliminated?

The following comment from the 1956 visiting mission report on the Territory of New Guinea provides one of the clearest elaborations, and makes the link to questions of circulation explicit. Across several pages, the report provides an elaborate defense of the 1953 demand for the elimination of Tok Pisin. After listing a number of tentative steps Australia was taking to encourage Papua New Guinean participation in governance (creating local government councils or an auxiliary civil service, for example), the report continues:

> Each step of this nature which the people take into wider spheres of activity diminishes whatever value Melanesian Pidgin once possessed for them. As has been noted, it had been a practical expedient when little or no participation was expected of the people in the direction of their affairs, and when the development of a national consciousness among them or their advancement on a territory-wide scale was scarcely envisaged. Today, however, a new goal has been set for the people: their progressive development toward self-government or independence. The Mission is therefore convinced that, regardless of how satisfactory Pidgin may have been for the purposes it served in the past, it is now inadequate and completely unsatisfactory as a means of communication for any people who expect to take their place in the modern world in the future. It believes that some advocates of Melanesian Pidgin are unaware of the goal which has been established for the Territory or do not approve of it and, as the 1953 Visiting Mission said, Pidgin reflects now outmoded concepts of the relationship between indigenous inhabitants and immigrant groups.[10]

The report's authors are arguing that while Tok Pisin is a lingua franca and has facilitated communication, it doesn't facilitate the right kind. The right kind of language would enable the literal and figurative mobility of speakers to move around the nation-in-waiting and move up a political ladder, to embark on what Benedict Anderson (1991) would later call the "creole pilgrimage." The right kind of language would produce political demands for self-government. The authors seem to argue that Papua New Guineans cannot make such demands for self-government while they are speaking Tok Pisin. For them, it seems to have something to do with Tok Pisin speakers' ability to circulate around the territory and the kinds of interactions they have when doing so.

The Trusteeship Council members take the mountains and the diverse languages of the Territory of New Guinea as barriers to interaction and the cultivation of a national consciousness, but they seem at least to think of these as natural barriers. Tok Pisin, by contrast, is a dishonest barrier in their view—pretending to enable interaction but not fixing the problem of communication, insofar as it has not produced a national consciousness. From the perspective of the UN, it is worse than the other barriers because the only movement it has enabled is movement for colonial labor. As a language of command in Cohn's (1996) sense of the term, it has facilitated only Australian colonizers' barking of orders to Papua New Guinean laborers. Thus, the only thing a Papua New Guinean can voice in Tok Pisin—a language in which the term for white man is *masta* (from Eng. *master*)—is subordination. It is, in the words of one Australian commenter, a "slave language . . . a caste tongue, a lingo for lesser-breeds, inferiority made half-articulate."[11]

When the Australian colonizers or Trusteeship Council members talk about the isolation of Papua New Guineans divided by mountains and languages, they ignore the significant movement of men for various forms of colonial labor. When the 1953 report makes reference to the "circumstances" in which Tok Pisin was invented, they mean the blackbirding system of coerced Melanesian labor on sugarcane plantations on Samoa and coastal New Guinea where Tok Pisin was stabilized and developed (Mühlhäusler 1978). Stewart Firth (1976) says that roughly one hundred thousand Pacific Islanders were recruited to work on plantations across the Pacific between 1867 and 1914, in addition to roughly another hundred thousand recruited in German New Guinea alone during that time frame (see also Jolly 1987). In 1956, roughly forty-five thousand New Guinean laborers were employed in the territory, about ten thousand of them working in service to the colonial government and the rest working for private or missionary enterprises.[12] These mostly male laborers were all speakers, to one extent or another, of Tok Pisin.[13]

Even when small groups of laborers kept to themselves in monolingual ethnic units (what were called labor lines, or *lains* in Tok Pisin), they had to have some Tok Pisin knowledge in order to understand the commands of white overseers and of indigenous workers who had been promoted to *bos boi* (from Eng. *boss boy*) status, since neither overseers nor *bos bois* would likely have any knowledge of a laborer's vernacular language.[14] Margaret Mead's (1931) short paper on Tok Pisin even refers to the language as "talk boy" (*tok boi*, or "laborer language"). As Kulick (1992) wrote, knowledge of Tok Pisin was considered one of the Western valuables a laborer would come home with (see also Wedgwood 1953: 106).

But for the Trusteeship Council members, whether they were administering authorities hoping to stall the move toward independence or non-administering authorities demanding a faster timetable to independence, Tok Pisin was a deficient language capable of fostering only the movement of labor but not, say, a labor movement. Even if there was a paranoid belief among colonizers that Tok Pisin was being used to communicate secret messages of rebellion (see chapter 3), the UN members worried that Tok Pisin had so far not been able to produce any kind of consciousness among the laborers as a larger group. When the 1956 visiting mission report on the Territory of New Guinea says that some "advocates of Melanesian Tok Pisin are unaware of the goal which has been established for the Territory or do not approve of it," the authors are referring to Australian colonials who the UN delegates assume are interested in Papua New Guineans only as cheap labor. In this view, Tok Pisin is the linguistic channel for moving to and from the plantation only as a "boy" rather than as a potential citizen.

More than this, the members of the visiting mission in 1956 used Tok Pisin as a scapegoat for their frustrations that Papua New Guineans were not demanding independence. The council members assumed that if messages about forms of democratic governance could come "in" from the "outside," then Papua New Guineans would have a natural desire for it. Tok Pisin's apparent deficiencies with regard to expressing concepts of proto-national and global governance—and its facility for plantation-based, racist forms of address—shouldered the blame for the strange way that the visiting mission interacted with local Papua New Guinean groups. So how did the Trusteeship Council's visiting missions want colonized peoples to interact with the UN? A pamphlet that the Trusteeship Council Secretariat produced (but never distributed, for reasons I outline below) offers a good look at the council's model of proper bureaucratic decolonization.

HOW TO MAKE POLITICAL DEMANDS

In 1953, the Trusteeship Council produced a short pamphlet, explaining the role and functions of the UN as a whole and the trusteeship system in particular, that was supposed to be distributed directly to peoples in trust territories. Written as a fictional account of a young teacher conversing with a colonial officer in an unnamed African trust territory, "The Story of Aman and the United Nations" was written in what they hoped was a simplified English accessible to as many of the trust territory residents as possible (French translations were planned at one point as well). It was written as an Everyman story—perhaps that is why "Aman," a man, was the protagonist—of a simple rural resident engaging in direct communications with a friendly global bureaucracy.

In "The Story of Aman and the United Nations," the description of the petition system presents the UN Secretariat's ideal narrative of political participation and communicative flow for trust territory indigenous peoples. In the story, Aman writes a petition to the Trusteeship Council to ask for more supplies and teachers for the school at which he works. He gives it to delegates of the council during the visiting mission's inspection of Aman's trust territory. Several months later, Aman receives a letter from the council in the mail:

> The men of the council, the letter said, had read Aman's paper in their meeting and had talked and given much thought to this matter. They were all in agreement that all of the people in Aman's village who wanted to learn to read and write should be able to do so. Education was a very important work because in this way people got the learning to help themselves. Some way should be found, the council said, to get for Aman's village the needed teacher and books. Now the representative of the big nation which watched over Aman's country was a member of the council and took part in the talking over of Aman's paper. He said his government was in agreement with all the council had said. (United Nations 1952: 27)

This pamphlet was never distributed to the peoples of the trust territories. In 1952, the administering authorities of the Trusteeship Council raised strong objections to it. Some of the criticism concerned the pseudo-simplified version of English, which the British, French, and Belgian delegates all argued would be offensive to educated people in the trust territories.[15] The pamphlet is filled with grammatically complex nominalizations and circumlocutions that only seem to make the processes and events discussed more abstract (e.g., "Education was a very important work because in this way people got the learning to help themselves").

More importantly, the administering authorities denounced the pamphlet for presenting a version of the trusteeship system that considerably downplayed the role of the colonial states and considerably overplayed the role of the UN in providing state services.[16] They thought that the pamphlet promoted the belief of the UN Secretariat and the anticolonial non-administering delegations that "the inhabitants of Trust territories should be encouraged to look in the first place to the United Nations as the source of responsibility for their progress and welfare and only secondly to the Administering Authorities."[17] The critics denounced in particular the story's depiction of direct communication between the UN and local peoples. Indeed, they considered the pamphlet's production itself to be a version of this, since no input from the administering authorities had been sought as the story was written. For Australia, the UK, or France, such direct communication undermined the administering nations' authority and prestige in the eyes of the trust territories' inhabitants. Although five thousand copies had been printed by the time it came up for debate in the Trusteeship Council, all the other planned copies and translations were canceled because the administering authorities refused to distribute them (thereby proving that the UN could not, in fact, have unrestricted communicative access to trust territory peoples).

Particularly given this denunciation by the administering authorities, we can read "The Story of Aman and the United Nations" as a relatively undiluted version of the UN Secretariat's and the anticolonial delegations' perspective on the trusteeship system: the council shepherds the non-self-governing indigenous peoples of the world toward greater political control while overseeing the administering authorities' efforts to usher that independence along, to the point that eventually the administering authorities should retreat completely. This is largely described in terms of a flow of communication in which the UN gives indigenous peoples knowledge of UN services, the people petition the UN for them, and the UN sends in its representatives while browbeating the administering authorities into helping. As part of this information flow, the visiting missions collect new petitions while checking on the progress of programs that were developed in response to earlier petitions. The narrative roughly follows what Margaret Keck and Kathryn Sikkink (2014) have called a "boomerang pattern" of international advocacy.

Even though the administering authorities did not share this ideal of the UN's role in trust territories—indeed, delegates from administering authority states would strongly dispute this version of the trusteeship system—all delegates on visiting missions to the Trust Territory of New Guinea assumed that they would engage in interactions that were recognizably about the voicing of political demands. But aside from some of their visits to Tolai communities on New Britain island, which had had the longest and most intense contacts with the colonial administration, the UN delegates were usually very disappointed, if not bewildered, by their interactions with Papua New Guineans from the highlands and interior. Even visits to New Britain—like the visit to the Tavuiliuans discussed at the beginning of this chapter—could cause UN confusion.

As I discuss more in the next chapter, during UN visits to the highland and interior regions of the Territory of New Guinea, interactions with local groups were often less about democratic talk and more about visual presentation and performance. Papua New Guineans, who may have only been told by colonial officers that a group of important people were coming and to gather at an administrative center on a given day, usually presented dances of welcome. These were, of course, political events for Papua New Guineans, ways of recognizing important outsiders that should be reciprocated. But as political events they did not necessarily involve the enunciation of demands or desires as would be expected by the delegates hoping to find citizens-in-training like the fictional Aman.[18] As mentioned at the outset, this contrasts sharply with the delegations' experiences in other trust territories, like Somaliland or Togo, where local peoples submitted hundreds of petitions during visiting missions that were carried back to UN headquarters. From 1946 to 1966, the Trusteeship Council received only twenty-seven petitions from people in the Territory of New Guinea, and many of these were from the Chinese community rather than from indigenous Papua New Guineans (Tomasetti 1970: 49).

In this context, knowledge of the UN's functions (discussed in trusteeship documents as the problem of "dissemination of information about the United Nations") was an important index for the delegates of the political development of the indigenous peoples in a territory. Because the UN Secretariat envisioned itself as the driver of progress toward development, it considered it essential that colonized people know about the UN's services and its work on those peoples' behalf. The Australian administration was well aware of this by 1953, and worried that the visiting mission would take this lack of dissemination of information about the UN as a synecdoche of Australia's overall neglect of Papua New Guineans.[19] Not only did Papua New Guineans often dance and sing rather than petition or demand, but they seemed to have no idea that the UN delegates were there in order to be the addressees of such speech acts. The blame for this was laid at Tok Pisin's feet. The 1956 visiting mission report says:

> The Mission's arrival had also been publicized via radio, the press, including a Melanesian Tok Pisin news-sheet, and by the Administration. In most of the Territory,

however, it was apparent that the people did not know what the Mission represented. In the least advanced areas large numbers attended public meetings at the request of the Administration. But at these it was exceedingly difficult to convey information concerning the United Nations that had much significance for them. The most concrete definition that could be given was that the United Nations was a "big fella kivung" (large council) whose aim was to try to prevent wars. The Mission was identified as a "good fella too much" which had come to "lookim dispela place", meaning that the Mission had come to inspect the place. The people, nevertheless, understood that they were free to speak on matters of concern to them, and they did so, freely.[20]

The description of the UN as a large council with the aim of preventing war seems like a perfectly adequate one, as does the claim that it was a very good ("good fella too much," what would now be written as "gutpela tumas") group that came to inspect the area ("lookim dispela place"/"lukim dispela ples").[21] For "the least advanced" Papua New Guineans who had only been "pacified" (i.e., had regular interactions with the Australian administration) for five years or so, it is unclear how the UN's system of international oversight and global bureaucracy ought to have been described, since this description seems if anything to mimic the language used in "The Story of Aman and the United Nations." Indeed, the UN had to explain its role to peoples in the so-called developed as well as underdeveloped nations regularly throughout the 1950s. Here Tok Pisin's etymological relationship to standard English is used to highlight the disparity between the UN's high-minded ideals of information flows leading to independence and the realities of trying to move through the process of colonization and decolonization for communities with such shallow histories of interaction with the administration. What the audiences at these gatherings lacked was an extended experience of colonial education and the emerging postwar global order, but what the UN report emphasized instead was Tok Pisin's inability to either voice liberal political demands for self-government or facilitate the flow of information to and from a global bureaucracy. Yet note the optimism of the final sentence: even with the limited language of Tok Pisin, New Guineans still managed to "speak on matters of concern to them," proof that the UN's model of communication leading to independence worked even with a deficient medium of communication.

INFORMATION FLOWS

The Trusteeship Council insisted upon standard (Australian) English as the only language that could produce the proper flow of information and political development that the UN was trying to create (often against the wishes of the administering authorities). Tok Pisin kept Papua New Guineans out of the flow of information: messages from the UN to the trust territory peoples, petitions and complaints from those peoples to the UN, the reports on compliance with petition-based issues, and the administering authorities' responses. Visiting mission delegates thought that Tok Pisin circumlocutions, while fine for enabling labor migration, were inadequate to the task of explaining the intricacies of the council's relations with the General Assembly or the Fourth Committee. Rather than face up to the longer struggle involved in Papua New Guinea's decolonization, the visiting mission held on to its assumptions about the naturalness of people coming together for nationalist struggles and blamed Tok Pisin instead.

The UN's demand to eradicate Tok Pisin was met with disdain and anger from members of the Australian public and officialdom, although the people who usually spent their time talking about how ridiculous and un-language-like Tok Pisin was did not suddenly shift into making a defense of it. Instead, they argued that the UN had no right to demand anything in regard to it: "Pidgin is an established language, and was established long before the United Nations Trusteeship Council came into existence."[22] Minister for Territories Paul Hasluck, who wanted to "slay the dragon of Pidgin," brought out the familiar specter of communism that so often seemed to accompany discussion of Tok Pisin, stating to the Australian press that to "say that [Tok Pisin] should be abolished immediately is as ridiculous as to suggest that all Europeans should begin speaking nothing but Russian next week."[23]

Robert A. Hall Jr., the American linguist focused on pidgins and creoles who was mentioned in earlier chapters, took great offense at what he dismissively called the UN's "pronunciamento." He rushed to print a short book in response, *Hands Off Pidgin English!* (1955), and he traveled to Papua New Guinea to investigate conditions in person soon thereafter. His rejoinder focused in large part on proving that Tok Pisin was a "real" language with a grammar and a lexicon that reflected "Melanesian" influences and an ability to expand and grow as the territory itself did. Hall worked with W. C. Groves, the longtime director of education in the Territory of New Guinea, and both men argued in as many places as possible for the linguistic complexity of Tok Pisin, as if getting Tok Pisin into the category of grammatical "language" would be the thing that would make its critics disappear.[24] Even UNESCO's (1953) *Use of Vernacular Languages in Education*, in which Camilla Wedgwood's section on Tok Pisin (pp. 103–15) specifically claims it as a vernacular language that should be used in education in the Territory of New Guinea, was not enough to get the Trusteeship Council to reverse its opinion. Other commenters at the time offered alternative suggestions to replace Tok Pisin's deficiencies— English written phonemically, or Ogden and Richards's Basic English, or, in one of the more far-fetched suggestions, Charles Bliss's invented iconographic language known as Semantography.[25]

None of those arguments ever convinced the members of the Trusteeship Council, although it is worth noting that files in the National Archives of Australia show that the government took the suggestion of using Basic English seriously for a brief period in the 1950s, particularly given Winston Churchill's endorsement of it. Aside from a certain prejudice against pidgin and creole languages that speakers of the pidgin or creole's lexifier language almost always express, these arguments failed in part because they did not get at the primary issue that many members of the Trusteeship Council had with Tok Pisin. For Soviet, Indian, and other anticolonial council members who made the most aggressive demands for the Territory of New Guinea's near-term independence, the integrity of the Queen's English was not a concern. For these delegates, it was not just that Tok Pisin didn't seem to fit the mold of a proper language as a code, but that Tok Pisin seemed to be incapable of producing either the speaker mobility needed for proto-national "creole pilgrimages" or the message mobility needed for the UN's direct communications with Papua New Guineans as a channel. Tok Pisin, they thought, had only supported the issuing of unidirectional commands in a plantation environment. It did not allow for the circuit of information flow that the Trusteeship Council and the UN Secretariat in particular envisaged for a progressive path to self-government.

The UN Secretariat's concern about the crucial role of the dissemination of information about the UN was not just a form of organizational self-importance. The secretariat and some of the more vocal members of the anticolonial bloc of nations required that territories have the informational and linguistic infrastructure needed to develop an international institution capable of squaring off against the colonial empires of Europe. Self-determination for members of this bloc did not have to mean, first and foremost, a national consciousness and desire for independence. Self-determination could exist, at least for a time, as an informational flow between the UN and the non-self-governing territories. But like the unpaved roads that get washed away every year in the rainy season, Tok Pisin seemed to them to be an infrastructural mirage. It could not help foster the kind of communication that would produce lasting change.

CONCLUSION

The prior routes of Tok Pisin–speaking laborers, to plantations and back again, had not produced the kinds of consciousness raising that delegates from the newer nations in the UN hoped were universal. Indeed, the entire framing of the naturalness of a desire for self-government depended on a story of material constraints on circulation to explain the conditions in the territory at all. If it was only a matter of getting the good news about democracy out to the people, then the UN only had to worry about the ease with which information flowed. When the Chinese delegation meandered from interrogating the Tavuiliuan refusal to set up a local government council to discussing education, language policy, and the problem of Tok Pisin, it followed a chain of connection that established Tok Pisin as a "slave language," even if it was one that many men spoke and even if it was the only immediate medium for the wide dissemination of information.

Pidgin languages have always occupied a marginal position, both in popular discourses and in specialist discussions within disciplines like linguistics. Pidgins even have a marginal position within pidgin and creole studies. Creoles have canonically been considered native and "full" languages, whereas pidgins were usually considered a "reduced" second language, a stepping-stone to creoles within what was once called the pidgin-creole life cycle (Hall 1962).[26] Creoles were supposed to offer privileged insights into linguistic genesis or linguistic prehistory (however misguided that idea was), while pidgins at best showed how languages became simplified or reduced. Michel DeGraff's (2003) discipline-transforming critique of creole exceptionalism has nothing to say about pidgin languages. Salikoko Mufwene (2020) discusses pidgin languages to the extent that he argues that pidgins are not the precursors to creoles, but otherwise he has relatively little to say critically about theories of pidgin genesis, in contrast to his primary focus on criticizing theories of creole genesis.

Within anthropology, pidgins have not been the basis for metaphors of cultural transformation and efflorescence, whereas creoles and creolization have been very rich and productive sources of metaphor in regard to cultural forms that emerged in the colonial and postcolonial Atlantic context. Even if these creolization metaphors can be criticized as overly broad and circular (see Palmié 2006), they have nonetheless been extremely powerful and productive for describing cultures from New Orleans to São Paulo. Pidgins, in the rare cases when they are theorized, are discussed as forms of simplification and reduction (see Mühlhäusler 1974), which are not usually the kinds of concepts that anthropologists use to talk about cultures. That is to say, if creoles and creolization have been reframed from their original, pejorative linguistic meaning of "impure mixture" to being seen as objects and processes of creativity and adaptive survival, pidgins remain much more tied to the colonial sense of simplistic bastardization.

One of the most significant features of pidgins is their capacity to act as the linguistic infrastructure for a mobile colonial labor force. If the model of creole formation is based on the permanent forced relocation of Africans to plantations in the Americas and the radical cultural and linguistic transformations that this violent dislocation created, pidgins have instead been linguistic platforms enabling ongoing labor mobility. The use of Tok Pisin in colonial Papua New Guinea allowed men to travel to plantations and back home again, where those experienced laborers taught it to younger men who subsequently participated in similar forced and temporary migrations of their own.

In that sense, the partiality of Tok Pisin was a problem. It suggested that between primitivity and modernity was some kind of ambiguous state of semi-transformation and only partial speakerhood of the language of the new order. Tok Pisin was testament to circulation in its disordered and coerced form. It contrasted with English as the global language of empire or post-empire it was on its way to becoming. At certain points, the criticisms of Tok Pisin are organized around the question of whether it had a code at all (as the Lutherans sometimes claimed; see chapter 2)—whether it was a structured system of relations, as Saussurean linguistics would demand. Here the kinds of defenses of Tok

Pisin that linguists made were most apropos and effective. Robert Hall, Stephan Wurm, Peter Mühlhäusler, and the Catholic priest Francis Mihalic, among others, all worked to prove that Tok Pisin was independent of English and had a stable, structured core. They defended it as a code. At other points, however, the criticisms of Tok Pisin that various administrators, missionaries, or UN observers made focused on Tok Pisin as a channel for unwanted information or unwanted interactions. Here, the linguists' pleas to consider Tok Pisin a "real" language largely missed the point.

The UN observers did not necessarily care about the structural integrity of the grammar of Tok Pisin or English, or about the productivity of Tok Pisin's morphological system. They were concerned with the routes that Tok Pisin had enabled and those that it was blamed for foreclosing. Tok Pisin seemed to be the infrastructure of indentured labor, without creating a creolized language for uniting workers or for uniting subjects in opposition to colonizers. For many Australian administrators, Tok Pisin was an embarrassing reminder of how little had been done in the colony, a reminder that whatever had been done was in support of the circulation of labor rather than the "advancement" of the community. In an important moment of alignment, Australian administrators, anticolonial delegations from the UN, and even colonizer delegations from the UN all agreed that the modes of circulation and forms of knowledge enabled by Tok Pisin needed to be radically restructured, and that the only language in which positive change was possible was English.

Tok Pisin, especially in the era during which it was more often referred to as "Pidgin," was a language that most colonizers hoped would remain on the road, as it were, moving laborers from their fully culturalized village homes (where indigenous languages would be spoken) to temporary contract work on plantations or in towns. Lutheran missionaries, Australian colonizers, and even the well-meaning UN delegates hoping to usher in decolonization tried to limit the growth and spread of Tok Pisin and the extent to which its speakers could be considered cultural subjects. Histories of pidgins and creoles often rush to make the necessary counterclaim—that these languages that begin in contexts of extractive colonial labor schemes flourish into becoming full-fledged languages. But in trying to understand colonial spaces as communicative networks of control, it is important to examine the processes that marginalize languages. The UN architects of a hoped-for decolonization of the Territory of New Guinea saw that process as a matter of bureaucratic management, one that required the elevation of English first. An ethnolinguistic nationalism, if there ever was to be one, could come later on.

6

Defying Predictions

*Global Bureaucracy and the Art of Not Making Guesses
about the Future of New Guinea*

For the Lutheran Mission, circulatory primitivity was an experiential problem: feelings of remoteness, isolation, and disconnection when working within a space that seemed to be nothing but impenetrable mountains with their forests of trees and languages. The romance of remoteness was also present in patrol reports, like the one I quoted from at the beginning of this book's introduction. When it came time for Australia to present its governance over the Trust Territory of New Guinea to the UN Trusteeship Council, however, its representatives usually did not lean on those tropes. At one presentation, Australia's special representative to the council, J. H. Jones, tried to use his previous experience as a patrol officer to give an evocative account of a lonely patrol, but this was unusual. Instead, circulatory primitivity took a different form when Australia confronted the bureaucracy of the UN. Rather than an experience of remoteness, Australia presented an image of fragmentation—of a space in which no abstractions, predictions, or generalizations were possible. But the Trusteeship Council, through its practice of bureaucratic management, required that even this image of unpredictable fragmentation be presented in a bureaucratic form. Australian diplomats and politicians who liaised with the council thus became experts at routinizing the unpredictability of the trust territory—of offering an organized presentation of fragmented disorganization. In this chapter, I show how this bureaucratic presentation of unpredictability came to be the response to UN oversight of the decolonization process.

It is rather odd to have a colonial administration argue that predictions are impossible, since bureaucratic control over any territory or people depends on a certain amount of prediction. One has to predict likely tax revenues or population growth or business prospects in order to engage in even the most basic state functioning. And when pushed, the Australian bureaucrats admitted that of course they had short-term plans covering one year or two. But they in essence made an argument that James Scott (2009) would make a few decades on: certain spaces, like Papua New Guinea, are good for evading governance. That is, Australia engaged in the art of not being governed by the UN. While state bureaucracy is usually thought of as creating order, bureaucratic expressions of disorder and unpredictability are sometimes just as much the outcome of careful work (Feldman 2008, Matthews 2008). In this chapter, I look at how Australia steadfastly refused to make predictions about the future of the Territory of New Guinea, and why this became one of the central tensions in the relationship between Australia and the Trusteeship Council.

A prediction depends on being able to abstract from concrete instances in order to identify variables that determine changing outcomes. Australian claims against being able to predict the future of the Territory of New Guinea depended on being able to present the territory and Papua New Guineans themselves as containing too many variables—or, rather, too much variation—to make prediction possible. Without the kinds of standardization and homogenization that mass society produces, Australia suggested that each part of the Territory of New Guinea, each village, each linguistic group, had to grapple with its particularities. No routinization of information would be possible. As I have argued throughout this book, the circulatory primitivity of Papua New Guinea was the key issue for all those involved with its colonization and decolonization.

In the sections that follow, I examine the questionnaire that the Trusteeship Council developed to guide Australia's annual reports on the Territory of New Guinea, and I look at how Australia pushed back against the central request for information in the questionnaire: the target date or prediction for the future development of the territory. I then look at how Australia planned the Trusteeship Council's biennial visiting missions to the territory to be a demonstration of the unpredictability of Papua New Guinea and Papua New Guineans.

THE TRUSTEESHIP COUNCIL QUESTIONNAIRE

In April 1947, the Trusteeship Council agreed to a provisional questionnaire that would be used by each of the administering authorities to develop a report for every trust territory.[1] This would help fulfill one of the information oversight powers of the council—to receive and examine annual reports from the administering authorities. The format and much of the specific wording of the provisional questionnaire seem to have come largely from drafts put together independently by the Trusteeship Council Secretariat and the US delegation, with the US draft's wording featuring especially heavily in the provisional questionnaire's sections on political and economic aspects of trust territory administration.[2] Two other Great Power nations that were administering authorities, the UK and France, also submitted draft suggestions, but theirs were not featured in many places in the approved provisional questionnaire. The UK was initially so reluctant to be constrained by the questionnaire that their draft was simply a skeleton outline of topics to be covered in a report, rather than a detailed list of questions.[3] Some of the wording from France's draft questionnaire was taken up in the final version, although primarily in questions on a rather French set of topics: policing, prostitution, and alcohol production and consumption.[4] The League of Nations Permanent Mandates Commission Questionnaire was also discussed as a model for the Trusteeship Council's provisional form.

Initially, Australian diplomats did not have strong objections to the provisional questionnaire. They were members of the subcommittee assigned to create it, along with the UK, the US, and a non-administering authority, Mexico. Upon submitting the provisional questionnaire, the subcommittee suggested that it be used for a few years on an experimental basis: "The Committee believes that the [administering authorities] themselves will be able to advise upon the most satisfactory means of presenting the desired information, and to suggest alternative questions which may prove to be of a greater value in relation to local conditions."[5] The provisional questionnaire was at least initially devised with administering authorities, and the kinds of information they would want to pass along, very much in mind.

But after a few years of membership on the now up-and-running Trusteeship Council, the Australian delegation argued against a suggested revision of the questionnaire. By 1952, it was clear that the non-administering authorities, and especially the Soviet Union, were taking a hostile position toward the administering authorities, and that the Trusteeship Council Secretariat was often supportive of their stance. Australia worried that revisions to the provisional questionnaire would be based not on the guidance of the administering authorities, but most likely on that of the non-administering authorities, a group whom the Australians were starting to refer to as the "anti-colonials." An undated memo on Department of Territories letterhead gives an overview of Australia's position on the 1952–53 revision of the provisional questionnaire: "When the revision of the questionnaire was under consideration Australia expressed the view that its form was not suitable as a basis for the annual reports, and that the Administering Authority should be free to submit an annual report in the form it considered most convenient."[6] Australia wanted to maintain the freedom to submit the kind of information it felt was most relevant and, as important, the kind of information it felt was most able to show Australian efforts at administration in a positive light. It did not want to have to respond to specific questions about the pace of change or proof of advancement that were becoming more important to Trusteeship Council discussions.

In 1952, a revised Questionnaire (hereafter capitalized; no longer bearing the "provisional" characterization) was approved by the council.[7] It included a more expansive set of questions, had a long list of statistical appendices to be completed, and was formatted to create a set of standard terms and measures so that each trust territory could be judged in relation to the others. In a preface, the Questionnaire defines some of the terms specific to the council that I have already used many times in this book (e.g., *administering authority, indigenous inhabitants*). It defines *general hospitals* as opposed to *health centers, nurses* as opposed to *nurse auxiliaries, pre-primary* as opposed to *primary education*. It gives statistical standards and classifications, like the "International Standard Industrial Classification of All Economic Activities" and the "Standard International Trade Classification, Revised." These standards and classifications were devised by the UN and related bodies like the International Labor Organization, and their use in the annual reports was intended to place the trust territories within the family of nations that the UN supervised.

The question of standardization extended beyond just the prefaced list of terms and classifications and into the genre of the response that the questionnaire was meant to elicit. Many of the administering authorities had been submitting annual reports in "narrative" form, meaning that the report tried to have a certain amount of flow and coherence, or as much of it as a dry annual report could. In addition to the narrative, administering authorities submitted an index that indicated where, within the prose narrative, the answers to specific questions from the provisional questionnaire could be found. During the debate about the 1952 revised Questionnaire, a primary sticking point for the administering authorities was the ability to respond to it with a "narrative" rather than what was referred to in Trusteeship Council debate as a "catechism" (that is, a report that was organized solely as a set of questions and answers).

All the delegations from administering authorities that were present at the debate argued that they needed to respond in narrative form for readability, to ensure usefulness for other agencies, and to provide a complete picture of the trust territory. The Belgian delegate "recognized that it was the Council's duty to ask questions; nevertheless it was not sufficient for the Administering Authorities merely to answer questions; their duty was to furnish a report, i.e., a general picture of conditions in the Territories for which they were responsible. It was impossible for one questionnaire to apply equally in all respects to all the Trust Territories."[8] In this case, the nature of the administering authority's obligations to the UN is defined as a problem of the genre of information to be transmitted.

Some of the delegations from non-administering authorities (El Salvador, the Dominican Republic, and especially the Soviet Union) argued instead that to not return a report in catechetical question-and-answer form was to shirk the duties of the Trusteeship Council. The Soviet delegation "could see no justification for the reservations expressed by the representatives of the United Kingdom and Belgium, the obvious purpose of which was to reduce the amount of information to be submitted by the Administering Authorities."[9] The Soviet delegation demanded "complete and exhaustive answers to all the questions in the questionnaire, without exception," and insisted that the narrative form would only allow administering authorities the chance to obscure their nonresponses to various queries. For the representative of El Salvador, question-and-answer-based "uniformity in drafting would also facilitate the study and discussion of the reports by the Trusteeship Council."[10] The catechism format would allow for proper comparative discussion, pitting French as opposed to British as opposed to Australian administrative progress toward decolonization of their trust territories.

From all angles, the genre of response to the Questionnaire seemed to transform the duties and obligations of the Trusteeship Council. Were trust territories primarily dominions of their administering authorities or of the council? If the former, then they were individual states demanding responses unique to the conditions of each territory. If the latter, then they were eleven comparable nations-in-the-making, all on the same path to self-government or independence. Administrative control was argued as a matter of how best to fill out a form (see Merry 2011, Cowan 2013, Niezen and Sapignoli 2017).

In the end, the revised Questionnaire was approved by the Trusteeship Council, but with the reservations expressed during the June 6, 1952, debate officially noted. Australia's report for 1953/1954 used the new Questionnaire. The administering authorities were able to respond to the Questionnaire in narrative rather than catechetical format, although the narrative was largely organized by the questions and the order in which they appeared in the Questionnaire. The genre of the report remained a source of contention for several years. Still, the revised Questionnaire succeeded in eliciting more information from Australia.[11]

With 190 main questions (and many more sub-questions), the Questionnaire covers the primary areas of Trusteeship Council interest: the political, economic, social, and educational advancement of the indigenous inhabitants of each trust territory. While Part V, "Political Advancement," was relatively short (covering questions 14–28), it was the most important section in terms of Trusteeship Council debate. Even in 1952, the end goal of self-government or independence was very much on the minds of the non-administering authorities, and debate during council meetings was focused especially on the conditions of political advancement. The questions in this section asked for the overall structure of—as well as the extent of the participation of the indigenous inhabitants in—territorial and local government, the civil service, and the judiciary. It also asked about voting rights, political organizations, and other aspects of the legal system. All of these questions were, to a large extent, further specifications of one of the first questions in the Political Advancement section: "Explain the policy by which the Territory is to be brought to self-government or independence and state briefly the principle problems which remain to be overcome before the objectives can be attained."[12] In fact, in the original debate about the revised Questionnaire, the representative of Belgium objected to this question, saying that it "was pointless as the whole annual report was the answer to it."[13]

Almost as soon as the Questionnaire was approved in 1952, the Trusteeship Council agreed to consider the question of whether each trust territory should in fact have its own individualized questionnaire. Australia's delegation opposed this move "on the grounds that separate questionnaires could be framed in such a manner as to embarrass the Administering Authorities by emphasizing less favorable aspects of administration and restricting questions on which favorable information was available."[14] So even though the administering authorities objected to the catechetical format as being too standardized, they also objected to territory-specific questionnaires as being too potentially embarrassing. Given that the Trusteeship Council's sanctioning force was in essence just embarrassment in the court of world opinion, this complaint amounted to a suggestion that Special Questionnaires (as the country-specific questionnaires came to be known) were punitive. More generally, demands for the transmission of information were received by administering authorities as infringing on their governing power in the trust territories. Given the way that topics recurred in debates about particular trust territories year after year, the administering authorities saw that demands for certain kinds of information would, in essence, require administrative policies in response to those demands to demonstrate some sense of "development" from one report to the next.

As I demonstrate in the next section tracking the development of the Special Questionnaire for the Territory of New Guinea, the demands for information coming from the non-administering authorities on the Trusteeship Council in fact attempted to push policies in the territory in specific directions. Specifically, the Special Questionnaire was geared toward eliciting a particular form of information in return: the long-range plan. In response, Australia had to try to present in bureaucratic form a demonstration of the fragmentation of the territory that would nullify the purpose of any long-range plans.

THE MAKING OF THE SPECIAL QUESTIONNAIRE

The Trusteeship Council debated whether to create territory-specific Special Questionnaires for several years after the 1952 approval of the primary Questionnaire. For the Trust Territory of New Guinea, they debated this issue most intensively from 1956 to 1957, with a final version being approved in 1959.[15] The territory-specific Special Questionnaires were initially going to be quite different from one another and from the revised Questionnaire that was approved in 1952. For example, instead of a standard 190 questions, the draft New Guinea Special Questionnaire had 174—it deleted or radically transformed questions from the 1952 revised Questionnaire and added others. But the desire for standardization won out. After debate in 1956, the Trusteeship Council decided that Special Questionnaires would not delete any of the standard questions, although they could add parts to those questions or add entirely new questions. New questions would be inserted as additions—for example, a question added after question 20 would be called 20A. In this way, every Special Questionnaire still had 190 questions. All questions on politics still came in Part V and included questions 14–28. Anyone could go to question 181 in any Special Questionnaire to get information about the languages spoken in a territory, although only the New Guinea Special Questionnaire had additional queries regarding the elimination of Tok Pisin (as discussed in chapter 5).

Administering authorities were given the opportunity to examine and comment on Special Questionnaire drafts. A draft Special Questionnaire is included in the archives, along with comments on it from members of the Department of Territories in Canberra and from the administrator of New Guinea in Port Moresby. In certain cases, members of the Department of Territories commented on the comments of the administrator, so that we can see a relatively lively set of intertextual reactions in these pages. I also discuss the official comments on the draft that were presented by the Australian delegation to the Trusteeship Council. The final version of the Special Questionnaire gives us a last source of comparison.

Here, I track the comments on two draft questions from the Introductory and Political Advancement sections. If we think of the Special Questionnaire as a means of extracting policy through the demand for information, we can see the comments and responses of various functionaries in Australia as different ways of deflecting those demands and those policies. Comments from readers in the Department of Territories usually respond to the draft questionnaire in terms of the political consequences of questions or the consequences of implementing the policies the questions are demanding. Closer to the territory government itself, the administrator talked about whether a question could be answered given the data available to the administration, in addition to whether it *should* be answered. Across these discussions, we also see how the Special Questionnaire anticipated Australia's common defense about the unpredictability of fragmented New Guinea, through a demand for an accounting of that fragmentation.

Question 2: Organized Diversity

As discussed throughout this book, the overarching characterization of Papua New Guinea was that it was a space of radical difference and fragmentation on ethnic, linguistic, and geographic levels. While the Trusteeship Council often made comments about the difficulty of creating transportation infrastructures—including roads, air services, and (somewhat improbably) railways—their more frequent target for discussion was the ethnic and linguistic differences that made mass communication seemingly impossible. The Special Questionnaire takes this topic on by trying to enforce some order on Australia's account of New Guinean difference through a major overhaul of question 2.

Questions 1–6 are part of the "Introductory Descriptive Section" that asks for a general overview of the geography, people, and history of any trust territory, a kind of encyclopedia entry to orient readers new to the area. This section rarely changed from one annual report to the next. But now the drafting committee on the Special Questionnaire was asking for a significant change to the question on the peoples of the territory. In the 1952 revised Questionnaire, the question is relatively straightforward:

> Q2: Give a general account of each section of the population of the Territory and its ethnic, linguistic, religious and social structure.[16]

While not an insignificant request for basic ethnographic descriptions of the indigenous inhabitants of any territory, the generality of the question meant that it did not elicit extended discussion. The question assumes a certain amount of ethnic homogeneity of the indigenous inhabitants of the eleven trust territories. But the draft Special Questionnaire demands a wildly increased level of detail in response:

> Q2: Describe the structure of tribal societies in detail taking into account the following:
> a. The source of power, the delegation of authority, the nature of leadership, etc.;
> b. The character of society viz. patrilineal, matrilineal, feudal, autocratic, co-operative etc.;
> c. The ideals, aims and norms of society;
> d. The sources of livelihood (hunting, fishing, cultivation etc.);
> e. The location of the tribes (mountain, lake, river, or plain dwellers);
> f. The role of women in society;
> g. The position of old people;
> h. The role of youth and education of children;
> i. Nature of social security;
> j. Religious or quasi-religious beliefs;
> k. Ownership of land, houses, properties, etc.;
> l. Customary administration of justice;
> m. Customs and usages which are contrary to the Universal Declaration of Human Rights.[17]

In comparison with the 1952 Questionnaire that was to be used for all Trust Territories, Question 2 of this draft of the Special Questionnaire for New Guinea has gone from a request for a generalized description of major ethnographic categories to an extraordinary demand for a wide range of sociological particulars. The assortment of topics in items (a) through (m) looks something like the contents of "a certain Chinese encyclopaedia entitled 'Celestial Empire of benevolent Knowledge'" from Jorge Luis Borges's (1964) essay on the impossibilities of universal classification. It suggests that the drafters of the Special Questionnaire had a rather unstructured imagination of human social diversity, largely predicated on which areas of social life had become institutionally organized areas of concern for the other major organs of the UN (e.g., women, elderly, and youth for the Economic and Social Council; human rights and justice for the Security Council).

Nevertheless, the demand here is for exhaustive information about each individual "tribal society" in the Trust Territory of New Guinea. The Trusteeship Council was going to create a bit of order out of the chaos of fragmentation that they kept hearing about each year.

Note that at this point the council was aware of at least three hundred different "tribal societies" in the territory.[18] The revised question 2 is asking for an exhaustive accounting of one group, but in this case that must be multiplied by several hundred. Any kind of answer to this question that would be minimally responsive would also be dizzyingly complex. Regardless of whether there was an expectation of answering the question for all three hundred tribal societies, the demand for information here acts as a classificatory schema, the Trusteeship Council inventing on the spot its own disorganized and abbreviated version of *Notes and Queries on Anthropology* (Royal Anthropological Institute 1951), the text that acted as the comparative framework for so much British social anthropology. This question (which was not included on the Special Questionnaires for Tanganyika or Nauru) recognizes the enduring claim to the Territory of New Guinea's unique fragmentation and demands order in return, even if that order comes in the form of, say, a nonsensical list of possible "characters of society" (question 2b) into which these groups would have to be fit.

The absurdity of the question is apparent to most of the Australian readers of the draft Special Questionnaire whose comments are recorded in the archival documents. An initial response from someone marking up the draft with marginal notes reads, "No objective, best elsewhere."[19] This is crossed out, and "Impracticable" is written underneath. If the first response is that the question seems pointless, the more enduring comment is that it is simply impossible to respond to. The comments from the Department of Territories that are compiled and sent for review from the administrator continue in this vein: "Consider question generally impracticable to answer in detail in view of complexities of tribal societies in New Guinea. Some parts particularly impracticable (e.g., part c). Much of information sought is given in relation to indigenous inhabitants generally in specific chapters of report."[20] To this the administrator adds: "Agree with your view. To answer the question would mean continuous full scale and intensive anthropological investigations which would be quite beyond the resources of the Administration."[21] Sometimes the fragmentation of Papua New Guinean communities into so many different groups actually seemed to minimize the differences among them: all Papua New Guineans were homogenized into just being primitive in a way that did not require an army of anthropologists to prove. The handwritten marginal comment on the administrator's comments is simply a surprised "Anthropology! Add." That is to say, the idea of a military-like mobilization of anthropologists seems ridiculous, and the administrator's comments need to be added to the comments that will get sent to the Australian delegation at the UN.

Each of these points—the impracticability of trying to answer question 2, and especially part c; the redundancy in relation to other sections of the report; and the need for large-scale anthropological mobilization to answer the question—get listed together in the Department of Territories' comments to the UN delegation. As was common for Australia's UN delegation, these negative comments from Canberra and Port Moresby were translated into slightly more positive and diplomatic proposals to the Trusteeship Council for what could be included in a revised question 2: "In view of the complexities of tribal society in New Guinea it would be generally impracticable to answer the question as modified. Elements of sections (f) (g) (i) (k) and (m) in particular are already and might continue to be answered more appropriately in other sections of the report."[22] In addition to a global complaint about the impracticability of the question, the delegation suggests that at least the sections on women, the elderly, the nature of social security, land and property, and customs contrary to the UN Declaration on Human Rights could be omitted as redundant with other questions on the Questionnaire.

The drafting committee was partially responsive to these comments, making at least a nod toward "practicability" and removing a few of the subsections of the question that the Australian delegation objected to, although they left in both the subsection on land and property and the one on human rights.[23] Throughout the negotiations over the question, we see the Trusteeship Council attempting to force Australia into a more definitive enumeration of the chaotic difference and fragmentation that they always refer to whenever deferring questions of independence or self-government (and which I discuss more in later sections of this chapter). Faced with claims of fragmentation, the council wants that fragmentation organized. More broadly, we see the council again assuming that the properly worded elicitation of information can produce a properly organized transition to decolonization.

Question 21: Creating "National Consciousness"

In the 1952 revised Questionnaire, question 21 asks about the integration of local indigenous institutions of government with the territorial government:

21. Explain the methods of local government with particular reference to the utilization of indigenous institutions, authorities and customs and the development of other forms of local self-government. Enumerate and describe such types of local government as exist. In respect of each type, state and explain the statutory and other basis upon which it functions and the provisions thereof; in particular describe, as to both law and practice:
a. Its relationships with the central territorial government;
b. Its relationship with any executive, legislative or advisory councils or other organs;
c. The composition of the local government, the methods of election or appointment of members and extent of administrative control thereof, the qualifications

(including literacy) required of them, the duration of their terms of office, the source and kind of the remuneration;

d. If chiefs or other traditional rulers are used as a basis for local government purposes, the methods of their appointment, recognition and revocation, and the extent of any administrative control;

e. The extent to which the area of local government coincides with tribal or similar divisions, and the extent of any amalgamation or federation of local authorities;

f. The functions and powers of local authorities, in particular financial powers, with an account of their use in the year under review;

g. Any changes made or proposed during the year under review in the organization of local government.[24]

Answers to this question in the 1950s often focused on indigenous local government councils, which had the power to levy taxes, run schools, and otherwise manage local administrative affairs (this was the form of self-government the Tavuiliuans demanded to *not* have, as discussed at the start of chapter 5). In 1956, there were only six of these local government councils in the whole territory, covering just a few thousand indigenous inhabitants, and the Trusteeship Council regularly prodded the Australians to hurry the process of establishing more of them. In part to elicit more information on these, question 21 was modified slightly in the draft Special Questionnaire: "Add to the end of 21: State whether any steps have been taken to promote the establishment of new local government councils and to foster national consciousness."[25]

This gets to the heart of this question in terms specific to the Trust Territory of New Guinea: is the administering authority speeding up the process of creating local government councils and have the indigenous inhabitants been informed that they are part of the same collective entity? In other words, what is being done to counter the experience of political fragmentation?

This question sparked comments from a number of readers at the Department of Territories. The first comment is the most blunt: just a handwritten "X" next to the question (questions deemed acceptable by this reader have a check mark next to them).[26] A typed memo providing commentary on the draft questions simply says to "delete all reference to 'national consciousness.'" On this typed memo, another reader has offered a rather improbable interpretation of the question in a handwritten marginal comment: "What does reference to 'national consciousness' mean? If it means development of pride in own traditions as people, ok."[27]

From the administrator's more practically minded perspective, the question elicited two comments on the draft: "The reference should be to 'Native Local Government Councils' and that part of the question can be answered.[28] It is agreed that reference to 'national consciousness' should be deleted."[29] Australia had been accustomed to answering questions about the slow pace of implementing local government councils, so this first part of the question was not particularly provocative. However, the demand for national consciousness had to be opposed.

The memo that the Department of Territories gave to the Australian delegation to the Trusteeship Council combined these various comments into one unified voice of dissent: "The question should be amended to refer to 'native local government councils'. The meaning of 'national consciousness' is questioned and we would prefer to see the words deleted. It would be acceptable to refer to 'development of pride in own traditions as a people.'"[30] This last diversion from what was the intended direction of the question about national consciousness toward something like ethnic pride was, it would seem, too much for the Australian delegation to try to present before the council. In the official comments from the Australian delegation, their suggested wording for this amendment of question 21 is "State what steps have been taken to promote the establishment of new local government councils and to foster territorial consciousness."[31] The drafting committee does not accept even this minor suggestion, and the final wording of the question remains the same as in the draft. Australia must respond to what has been done to foster "national consciousness."[32]

Both question 2 and question 21 show that the Trusteeship Council and Australia viewed fragmentation as the primary concern for the territory's political advancement. The council attempted to counter some of the problems of fragmentation first by extracting information from the administering authority that could cultivate organized knowledge of the fragmented parts in an upward flow toward the council, and second by cultivating the transmission of knowledge of self-government in a downward flow toward Papua New Guineans.

The response to both of these moves from the Department of Territories (and, more distantly, the administrator) was to insist that such flows of information were either "impracticable" or unacceptable. The fragmentation of the Trust Territory of New Guinea would not be cured or mollified by an army of anthropologists, and the road to self-conscious political unity was simply refused. Australia would not be hurried into the process of telling Papua New Guineans about self-government any time soon.

Across this major difference, we see that both the Trusteeship Council and the administering authority use the upward and downward flows of information about the fragmentation of the territory as modes of administration. The council recognizes its demands for upward flows of information as part of its UN Charter–given right to supervise, and the administering authority recognizes its own autonomy in the administrative process through the attempted refusal to provide certain kinds of information.

There were significant differences in how Australian government departments responded to the Trusteeship Council's attempts to manage through information requests. The Administrator in the Territory of New Guinea often focused on practicalities, arguing that the UN was being unreasonable or misguided and that the Trusteeship Council did not understand life on the ground in New Guinea. The members of the Department of Territories were more principled in their opposition to Trusteeship Council demands, seeing in the requests for information limits to Australia's sovereignty. Finally, the people working at the Australian delegation to the UN tended to be the most conciliatory to the Trusteeship Council and assumed that more information was going to have to be forthcoming from Australia eventually. They pushed those in the Administration in Port Moresby or in the Department of Territories in Canberra towards greater elaboration, even if they recognized that nobody in either locale was willing to articulate intermediate or final target dates for the attainment of self-government.

One of the few times when members of the administration of the Territory of New Guinea came face to face with the Trusteeship Council were during the Council's biannual visiting missions. In the next section I look at the visiting missions to see how people on the ground responded to the council's demands for more information. In many cases, the radical fragmentation of the Territory of New Guinea's landscape and people was held up as a defense against control by information management.

THE UNPREDICTABLE PAPUA NEW GUINEAN

If, in some sense, the endgame of independence was built into the trusteeship system from the beginning, the demand for future-oriented plans still seemed to surprise the Australian delegation time and time again. From the Australian perspective, UN-monitored administration of the Trust Territory of New Guinea meant that annual reviews could examine whether it was yet at the point where independence could be discussed. But it did not seem to include the idea of predicting when such a state would be reached. The reason for this, given so often as to be a cliché of Australian reports, was that the territory defied predictive capacities. In particular, Australians claimed that the fragmentation and diversity of the territory made any predictions impossible. Whether this was just a near-to-hand excuse for holding on to their own administrative autonomy or a clear-eyed assessment of the situation, the relationship between Australian bureaucrats and UN functionaries was organized around the problem of prediction under conditions of fragmentation. With Papua New Guinea's actual independence still two decades away (and as yet unforeseen by almost any person involved), the question of independence in the Trust Territory of New Guinea got whittled down instead to the question of Australia's forecasting ability. And like almost everything else in the territory, the the lack of forecasting was blamed on fragmentation.

Predictions are based on an ability to abstract from the concrete conditions of any situation and examine trends, regularities, or norms. To predict is to reduce the amount of information at hand. Modernist authors (e.g., Simmel 1997: 153) have argued that people with "primitive" mentalities are unable to abstract from the immediacy of co-presence to imagine long-distance bonds, and Australian administrators turned this into a more generalizable statement of the condition of the Trust Territory of New Guinea broadly. For the administrators in the trust territory and the civil servants in Canberra, it was a space of circulatory primitivity that made abstractions impossible. No abstraction from the concrete situatedness of a given group or its geographic locale would be possible. Its micro-level forms of diversity meant that seemingly any piece of information might be necessary to describe the difference between one village and the next. The linguists and anthropologists then starting to do research in Papua New Guinea only exacerbated this sensibility among the administration staff. To that extent, Australia used the territory's fragmentation to resist any imagination of the future that deviated from the present. The only future that Australia could predict was one that was more or less identical to the present, a predictive map as big as the territory it was trying to depict.

Members of the Trusteeship Council, especially the more adamantly anticolonial ones, instead imagined "progress" toward independence and self-government as an essentially homogenizing project. Civilization was a matter of becoming enough alike that all people could approach a universal, if not fully realized, human capacity for self-determination. Not only did the UN depend on universal declarations of human nature and human rights, but in the case of the Trusteeship Council it was actively engaged in trying to make indigenous inhabitants of trust territories as uniform as possible: indigenous people who would all be oriented toward the prominent goal of freedom and autonomy in a way that may not have been true of those peoples in the past. In that sense, the council members were both engaged in projects of massive cultural change and unwilling to admit as much (see Steffek 2021) given that they saw a universal yearning for freedom as simply less realized in certain communities than in others. Thus, progress toward independence would be progress toward a reduction in diversity as various peoples started to take up the reins of democratic self-control. But as Australian representatives to the UN claimed, in the Territory of New Guinea progress only seemed to add to diversity and fragmentation.

Australia's attitude toward predictions and fragmentation is stated clearly in the debate on the Trusteeship Council's 1956 visiting mission report: "Due to the enormous and important differences existing in the Territory and among the people the Administration could not predict the rate of territorial development and believed that a target date for a territory-wide Legislative Assembly based on direct universal adult suffrage could have little value, and the establishment of such a date could only introduce a dangerous element of irresponsibility into the situation."[33] These claims about geographic and linguistic fragmentation sometimes came with statistics about the numbers of languages spoken, the size of the mountains, or the size of the territory (sometimes measured in comparison with countries represented on the Trusteeship Council, e.g., "seven times as big as El Salvador," "nine times as big as Haiti"). The small gains in transportation infrastructure were always heralded in terms of the "severe natural difficulties" that the administration faced.

Australia gave various reasons for their lack of forecasting. In some cases, the inability to predict was said to be based on a sense of cultural primitivity, because "backward" peoples seemed to be unknowable—according to J. H. Jones, "the political development of a backward people is not easy to predict."[34] Sometimes policy recommendations from other members of the Trusteeship Council are just too complex, as Jones says about a Burmese recommendation to set a date for direct elections to a territory-wide legislative assembly: "the attainment of this objective is conditioned by so many incalculable factors as to make such predictions valueless."[35]

At other times, the variable rate of change is used as a reason to avoid predictions. In the debate about the 1956 visiting mission report, the representative from Australia, Ronald Walker, chastised other members of the Trusteeship Council who were demanding predictions and timetables. He was especially critical of a prediction from Syria that New Guinea would be independent in twenty to thirty years given the optimism of the 1956 visiting mission report (an optimism that contrasted sharply with the council's more pessimistic sensibilities after debate on the 1954/1955 annual report): "Had [Australia] last year submitted to the Council target dates, which members of the Council would have accepted without serious question, there would have been loud cries today for their drastic revision. [Australia] has no means of ascertaining whether the prediction offered by the representative of Syria is correct or not, or whether, if incorrect, it envisages too long or too short a time."[36] Walker argued that the rate of change in the territory fluctuated so radically as to make any target-date predictions out-of-date almost as soon as they were announced. His disparaging attitude toward target dates is especially clear in a seemingly sarcastic hypothetical that perhaps the territory could be ready for independence in *less than* twenty years, an idea so far outside then-current thinking in Australia as to be absurd.

The most concise and yet thorough statement of Australian opposition to timetables for independence comes in J. H. Jones's Final Statement on July 17, 1956. It is worth quoting at length:

> It must be remembered, moreover, that this territory reveals already, at this very early stage of its progress, enormous and important variations in the conditions of development. There is little in common between the conditions of the more sophisticated coastal peoples of the Gazelle Peninsula, for instance, and the primitive highlanders of the mainland, while members will not have forgotten that more than twelve per cent of the population of the Territory still have had no contact with the administration or with their neighbors. Tremendous variations of geography, climate, local resources, as well as the physical isolation of so many areas, add to the difficulties of predicting the course or speed of the future development of the Territory. The conditions of terrain have led to an almost unparalleled fragmentation of society, as a result of which each step that we take to promote total progress must be taken within the limits of very small separate communities, whose reactions are not only unpredictable but do not even follow a common pattern. We therefore cannot predict the rate of territorial political development any more than we could predict the response of the people of Raluana [i.e., the Tavuiliuans] to establishment of a local

government council. In these circumstances, a target date could have little value, and we believe that establishment of one could only introduce a dangerous element of irresponsibility into the situation.[37]

While one important problem from Australia's or the UN's perspective is the primitiveness of the people of the territory, we can see here that cultural primitiveness is in many ways overshadowed by the sort of circulatory primitivity qua fragmentation that renders bureaucratic management and predictive capacities all but powerless. The variations in geography have led to an "unparalleled fragmentation of society" that refuses organization. In the Australian version of New Guinea's natural and social history, geographic boundaries created linguistic boundaries, which in turn created diverse and seemingly stochastic responses to colonial administrative interventions. Even in the supposedly more "advanced" parts of New Britain around Rabaul, the Tavuiliuan group was a major focus of Trusteeship Council debate for refusing to create a local government council (see chapter 5). As was the case with Christian missionary interventions, the original diversity of the territory and its people produced colonial interventions that seemed to exacerbate diversity rather than tamp it down.

At the end of the lengthy quote from Jones above, he mentions a "dangerous element of irresponsibility" that target dates would introduce. This short statement (which is repeated at other moments by Jones) is a small hint of a larger discourse within the Australian administrative records about the potential "confusion" that would be caused by target dates. In response to the United States proving its determination to vote with the non-administering authorities on the issue of intermediate target dates, a memo written by staff of the Department of External Affairs from July 1956 lays out an almost apocalyptic future set in motion by the US decision. The analysis begins with a basic claim of confusion on the part of Papua New Guinean people if a target date for independence were to pass without any political change:

> The danger of the "time-limit" or "target date" approach is precisely that it courts confusion, disruption and undermining of confidence. Political development, depending as it does on moral and psychological factors primarily . . . is very unpredictable in any community. More especially is it unpredictable in primitive and fragmented communities of which New Guinea consists today. Setting target dates and time limits for stages of development however demands that predictions be made.

This moment of confusion would lead to larger problems of all-out revolt:

> If a hitherto trusted government committed itself to a schedule of target dates there would inevitably be disappointments for all or many of the people affected. Loss of confidence in the administering authority would ensue. Authority in general would very soon be mistrusted. Thus would be destroyed the asset on which the future good of the people most depends. Worse than this, as faith in the administering authority dissolved, demagogues would seize their opportunity; subversive agents would take

their share. Weak measures would not cure such a situation; strong measures would inevitably call for easily-misrepresented forms of action; effects on political development would be incalculable, but can scarcely be imagined to be beneficent. The state of confusion thus brought about would quite possibly involve a collapse of authority in wide areas. Damage would be done to the whole development of the territory, not only political, but economic, social, educational technical and so on.[38]

The demand for timetables, it is argued, would lead to a total societal collapse in which all authority would be distrusted, Soviet or other communist "subversive agents" would sow discord, and violent counter-revolutionary measures would need to be taken. And a collapse of the Trust Territory of New Guinea would be more than the collapse of the territory, since Australia saw (and still sees) Papua New Guinea as a strategically essential buffer between it and its regional rivals. In fact, the memo begins by setting this geopolitical context: "The vital importance of New Guinea to Australia does not seem to have influenced the American representative on the Trusteeship Council. . . . One is led to ponder whether the US Administration or at any rate the relevant section of the State Department is sufficiently aware of the stark realities of the New Guinea-Australia relationship in world politics and in Australian security."[39] The demand for target dates was thus an imminent threat to the national security of Australia in this worst-case scenario. The fragmentation of the Territory of New Guinea that made predictions impossible would lead to a much worse (albeit imagined) fragmentation of the Australian nation-state. If Weber (1978: 989) argued that bureaucratization made revolutions impossible, here we have a strangely flipped argument from Australia: the imposition of bureaucratic information structures will themselves lead to revolutions that have to be avoided at all costs.

Australia's response to the Trusteeship Council's demands for target dates after the US switched to voting with the non-administering authorities on this issue depended on keeping the circulatory primitivity of the Territory of New Guinea—in its bureaucratic guise of "fragmentation"—in view in all Trusteeship Council matters. This was particularly important during the biennial visiting missions to New Guinea. In the next section, I examine some of the ways in which both Australian administrators and the UN diplomats staged and perceived this sense of fragmentation in their tours of the territory.

VISITING MISSIONS:
MAKING FRAGMENTATION VISIBLE

During the biennial visiting missions to the Territory of New Guinea that happened throughout the 1950s and 1960s, a delegation of three or four representatives from Trusteeship Council member delegations would inspect the territory and write up a lengthy report for discussion and approval by the rest of the council. While the administering authority had to present an annual report, the visiting mission reports were given much greater weight and credibility. In fact, at one point J. H. Jones, the special representative for the Territory of New Guinea, complained to the council that they were only debating the 1956 visiting mission report and completely ignoring the 1955/1956 report that the Department of Territories had just spent months putting together.[40] The visiting missions were heavily staged and orchestrated affairs whose itineraries were developed largely by the administering authority itself and were meant to showcase the administration's rule in the most positive light possible. In the Trust Territory of New Guinea, this meant that the mission was escorted from technical schools to native hospitals to administrative headquarters, with occasional visits to a select set of pre-vetted villages in more remote areas. Personnel from the Department of Territories or External Affairs accompanied the mission and kept notes on it, tracking what the mission representatives were asking about or were interested in, what they seemed to find disagreeable, and any unexpected events that occurred during the course of the trip. These notes were typed and sent to Canberra in time to forewarn staff in the Department of Territories ahead of the meetings that the mission arranged with members of that department at the end of their tour of the territory.

Each visiting mission produced several very thick files related to the itinerary, including background information on the representatives chosen to carry out the mission, transcripts of meetings held in Port Moresby with the administrator or in Canberra with the minister for territories, and reports from Australian staff monitoring the movements of the mission. The visiting missions produced significant reports that were presented to and debated by the Trusteeship Council, and transcripts of those debates are also available. The archival record for each visiting mission is thus significant, and I'll be able to address only a few of their features here.

We can see the highly orchestrated visiting missions as moments when Australia is trying to impress upon the council the idea of the unpredictability of the Territory of New Guinea. If the territory is as much of a jumble as Australia says, if it is a space that defies any attempts at prediction and abstraction from the individual case, then the best way to highlight this is through a practice of ostensive reference: drag the visiting mission to as many isolated outposts of diversity over as many mountain passes as possible, in order to give the delegates the best indication of the administrative problems of the territory.

The administration always had to delicately navigate between blaming the circulatory and cultural primitivity of the territory for the lack of administrative progress and defending itself against claims from the non-administering authorities that the primitivity was proof of Australia's bad job. The visiting missions had to be tightly constructed narrative adventures through the Territory of New Guinea that would allow Australia to use circulatory and cultural primitivity as an excuse while not drawing condemnation for it. How does one neatly and quickly demonstrate the impossibility of administering certain spaces and peoples without the

FIGURE 8. United Nations publicity photo documenting the preparations for the 1956 Trustee-ship Council visiting mission tour of the Pacific. From left to right, the delegates for the visiting mission are Sir John MacPherson, of the United Kingdom, chairman of the mission; José Rolz Bennett, of Guatemala; Daniel Massonet, of Belgium; and E. Chacko, of India. (UN Photo/MB, UN7487304)

organization and speed of the demonstration becoming evidence of the opposite? In other words, how do you present chaotic fragmentation in an organized way?

The confidential report on the 1956 visiting mission by J. D. Petherbridge, the official observer of the mission for the Department of External Affairs, is an important source for understanding how Australia viewed the UN's observations.[41] Petherbridge provided an overview of the attitudes and tendencies of the delegates individually: the Belgian delegate was "the weak link" and a bit of a mystery; the UK delegate and mission leader was the reason for the success of the trip; the Indian delegate was fair and well prepared but might compose sections of the report under the influence of the very anticolonial Indian delegation in New York, which would "present further difficulties"; the Guatemalan delegate was particularly interested in education issues (see figure 8). But his most interesting comments are found in his detailed descriptions of the individual stops on the mission's tour. Here we see some sense of Australia's orchestration of primitivity and fragmentation.

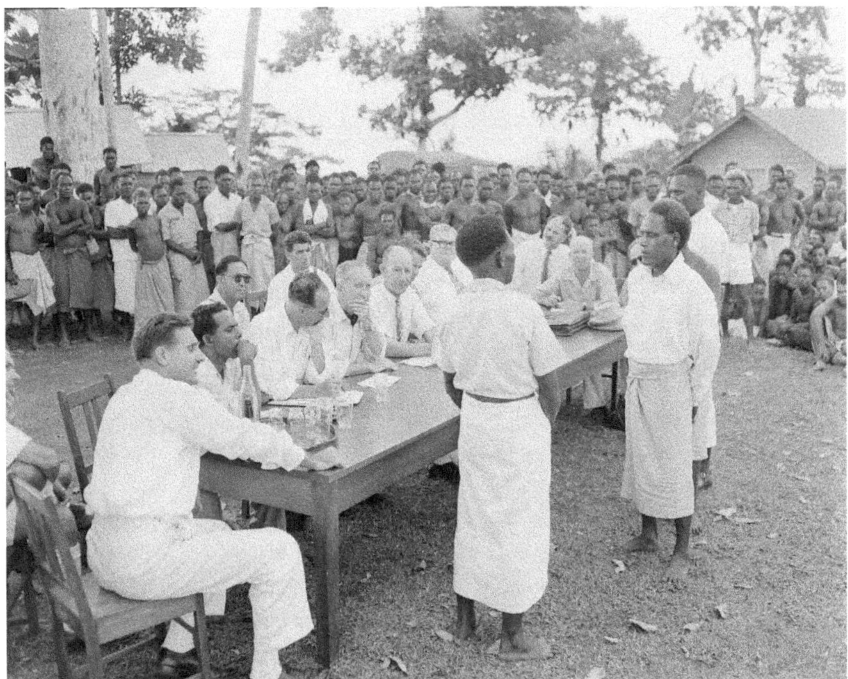

FIGURE 9. Members of the UN Trusteeship Council's 1956 visiting mission to the Pacific, listening to councillors at Vunadidir, near Rabaul. (National Archives of Australia, A1200, L20052)

The tour began on a high note, as Petherbridge points out: "By commencing its tour in Rabaul the Mission saw first the most advanced district in the territory and, perhaps, in the Tolais, the most sophisticated of its peoples."[42] Not only could the administration present one of the more intensely developed areas—with technical schools, hospitals, and five of the six local government councils in the territory—but it could also present a set of people with specific demands and questions for the mission. Petherbridge goes into detail summarizing the individual statements and speeches of Tolai leaders demanding more schools, better hospitals, and fairer tax policies. While these represent complaints about the Australian administration, they are nevertheless perfect demonstrations of exactly what the visiting mission hopes to find: indigenous inhabitants clearly expressing a set of political, social, and educational goals and demanding better governance (figure 9). This was as close as the Territory of New Guinea got to matching Trusteeship Council expectations for people on the path to independence, and the visiting mission spent several days in the Rabaul area so that this first impression could sink in. Yet even here, Papua New Guineans were not voicing demands for representation with the speed or urgency that the visiting mission clearly wanted to see. Using a passive construction that leaves the speaker of the question unclear,

Petherbridge notes that "the question was asked as to whether the growth of the Village Council system had reflected itself in any request for more representation in the Legislative Council."[43] It had not.

After a quick visit to Bougainville, the mission next traveled to Morobe District on the New Guinea mainland. Finschhafen was one of the first sites of colonization and missionization in German New Guinea, briefly the seat of the German administration (before it was transferred to Rabaul) and for many years the headquarters of the Neuendettelsau Lutheran Mission. Finschhafen presented as positive an image as the administration could muster on the mainland. Again, indigenous inhabitants were called together for an outdoor meeting with the visiting mission, and a number of senior men eloquently voiced their demands for the kinds of state interventions that could bring about rapid political or social transformation: more schools, a canning factory, assistance with road building.[44] While a step down from the Tolais in Rabaul, Finschhafen could serve as proof of the administration's effectiveness on the mainland.

For the administration, Rabaul and Finschhafen established that hospitals could be built, training centers could produce skilled workers, and self-determination could even be enacted in a limited way. More importantly, the open-air meetings demonstrated that local people were sometimes articulating a set of demands. So far, so good. But at this point the mission turned inland, and the tenor of open-air meetings with the visiting mission started to change. The complaints became less about Papua New Guineans demanding freedom and more about them proving their "primitive" state: a man at Butibum village near Lae complained that the coastal people were doing better than they were doing in the hills. "To illustrate his point, he produced six of the villagers who had dressed up as the most primitive of hill people. He said the hill people would do better if they had roads."[45] As the tour turned inland, the visiting mission got its first presentation of primitivity, connected as always to questions of circulation (in the form of a desire for roads in this case). The visiting mission may have considered Rabaul or Finschhafen primitive, of course, but this was the first time that someone presented himself (or rather his six traditionally dressed family members) as primitive due to a lack of transportation infrastructure.

Things only got worse when the tour boarded a small plane to head into the mountains. As Petherbridge notes, the quick move from Finschhafen and Lae into the mountains was an orchestrated play of contrasts: "On the flight from Lae to Bulolo, the Mission stopped at a highland village called Menyamya for about two hours. This was of interest in providing the contrast to the people of the lowlands. It was met by a mob of hillsmen who yelled and waved their shields and spears. The Mission inspected a small school that had recently commenced."[46] No longer could the mission have meetings as such. Instead they met mobs. There were no questions asked or answered, just the brandishing of spears and shields. The idea that even here a school might be started could be proof of the administration's dogged determination: Australia does not forsake these inarticulate people.

The same scheduling strategy—moving from a more developed coastal town to a less developed hinterland—was repeated in the Madang District. The mission flew from Madang Town's neat streets and its large Native Hospital to Aiome, "which gave [the mission] a second glimpse of the more primitive people of the hills. As the Chairman [of the visiting mission, the UK's Sir John Macpherson] said, this was designed to help them keep their ideas in proper perspective."[47] Here Sir John, former administrator of Nigeria and a sympathetic ear for Australia, helped do some of the work of framing the contrast between the more manageable coastal areas and the less manageable mountainous interior that had been built into the itinerary. The nadir of fragmentation and primitivity was not necessarily in the more recently "pacified" areas of the Western Highlands that they visited after this, but rather in the remote outposts of the Sepik. "The Mission held several other meetings in the Wewak District, but in most cases they were with very backward people who staged performances in their ceremonial dresses rather than asked questions. Such was the case at Telefolmin, Green River and Lumie and especially at Maprik, where a crowd of some 15,000 people met the Mission."[48]

Rather than meet in order to exchange questions and answers—that is, hold events in which indigenous inhabitants of trust territories affirmed their humanity by demanding self-governance or otherwise lived up to the vision of politics in the "Universal Declaration on Human Rights"—here the men and women of the Wewak District enacted a different mode of polity making. For local people, the act of being a host for such an arriving group (as indexed by the dance/presentation performance) was part of a claim of mutual political recognition, one that would ideally initiate a series of exchanges between local communities and the UN (figure 10). But this mode of doing politics was visible to the mission only as backwardness, as Petherbridge notes—a discursive silence that was amplified by the volume of the welcome songs sung during the time that the UN mission had reserved exclusively for demands for self-determination. Maprik's fifteen thousand singing "natives" was the exact image of the primitive grouping that Australia wanted the mission to remember: a jumble of many different groups incapable of identifying themselves as such and opting to dance and sing instead. This is not how local people would describe the event, but it was the framing Australian officials constructed through their stage management of the visiting mission.

In a draft of the visiting mission's report, the meetings at Menyamya and Telefomin receive special comment as perfect exemplars of fully primitive persons. Menyamya's "mob" is described by the visiting mission as a band of happy children. The Anga people (identified with what is now considered a disparaging ethnonym) "could scarcely have comprehended what they were told concerning their visitors, but this did not appear to diminish their pleasure or dampen the happy reception they extended [the mission]."[49] The group at Telefomin was likewise unable to communicate with the mission or be communicated to by the mission: "Due to the small degree of contact which they have had with the outside world, here as in similar areas, it was completely impossible to apprise the people who had

FIGURE 10. The head of the UN Trusteeship Council's 1956 visiting mission, Sir John Macpherson (center), chats with a patrol officer (right) from the Aiome Patrol Post as both stand in front of the Papua New Guineans who have been "lined" in order to welcome the visiting mission. During the colonial era, Papua New Guineans would be ordered to line up in their home villages in this same way so that patrol officers could take a census or collect taxes. (National Archives of Australia, A1200, L20128)

gathered what the Mission was or its object in visiting them. The most that could be done was to enquire into local conditions and assure them of its interest in their progress and welfare."[50] A sort of bureaucratic first contact, the UN visiting mission could only smile and be smiled at, and hope that discussions of self-determination would happen on a subsequent trip.

When the mission made its final stops in the Western and Eastern Highlands for the segment of the tour focused on indigenous inhabitants, the mission (and Petherbridge) were in many ways impressed by the speed with which the Highlanders seemed to be picking up the terms and principles of democratic governance, especially since these were the people who had most recently been "pacified." On the one hand, the Western Highlanders were considered incapable of local government councils. They lived in scattered hamlets and had no hereditary chiefs, so the future looked dim. On the other hand, "the Mission was interested in one innovation in [the Western] District, namely an unofficial 'parliament' which consists of the leaders of all groups in the sub-district and which has been convened at Mount Hagen to arrive at decisions of importance. One such decision recently was the fixing of the bride price which had risen to such a degree that it made it difficult for men to obtain wives."[51] The Western Highlands region had both the greatest number of still "uncontacted" people and some of the brightest possibilities for parliamentarians.

The visiting mission's itinerary was a planned play of contrasts—from the Tolai's "advanced" status of incipient self-government to the "mobs" in Menyamya and Maprik brandishing spears and performing dances. And that plan was not lost on the delegates of the visiting mission, who specifically drafted a report organized by this diversity. Noting that their report comes in two parts—first a district-by-district account and second a discussion of the territory as a whole or in terms of specific industries or areas—they write that this is important

> because the people in such areas as the Gazelle Peninsula [e.g., Tolais], the Sepik River [e.g., the groups at Maprik] and the Highlands, to mention a few, are worlds apart and no proper understanding of their problems is possible unless these differences are apprehended. It must also be noted that general problems which affect the whole Territory frequently have a different emphasis in different places. . . . In Chimbu [Eastern Highlands District], emerging from the stone age, one already can find school boys with enough discernment to want a school for girls so that they may find wives who are on their own level of attainment. At Menyamya on the other hand, also emerging from the stone age, the people requested nothing and appeared to be unaware of the need for anything.[52]

Seemingly acceding to Australian claims, the visiting mission report is organized around the idea that the diversity of the Territory of New Guinea defies organization. As with Australian claims about the impossibility of prediction given such a fragmented set of communities, there are no variables that can be used to abstract away from the concrete experience of dizzying diversity. As the draft says a few pages on, "The great diversity of physical types and linguistic groups among the New Guineans precludes any general description of them which would be applicable to the Territory as a whole."[53]

Although the visiting mission report for 1956 admits to the dizzying diversity of the Territory of New Guinea and of Papua New Guineans themselves, and points to it as a globally unique situation, it does not argue that this makes prediction impossible. The report in fact calls for an increased emphasis on plans and target dates, and an increased rate of speed in the political development of the territory's people. One of the recommendations of the visiting mission was that Australia ought to ask for help from other international organizations or other nations, a recommendation that was almost universally received in Australia as a grave insult (see Handman 2024). But note that this is the same response to the territory's diversity that Australia itself took in its attitude toward Christian missions: an all-hands-on-deck acceptance of help from whichever corner is willing to provide it. Diversity begets diversity, and if Australia had accepted this help, both it and the

Trusteeship Council would, no doubt, have quickly cursed the lack of standardization that comes when different groups all try to do the same thing.

CONCLUSION

The Trusteeship Council's approach to the Territory of New Guinea was to demand different forms of information: either information to be sent upward from Australia or information to be sent downward. The council hoped to enact decolonization through bureaucratic information transfers. When Australia refused to engage in a game of prediction, a different question of information flow became important: the ways in which information flowed (or didn't flow) through Papua New Guinea itself. The fragmentation of the territory into a set of seemingly discrete, enclosed units—each guarded by imposing mountain ranges, deep river valleys, and/or linguistic boundaries—became Australia's signal excuse for evading the bureaucratic ties of prediction. Not only were the peoples of the territory diverse, and not only were they grouped into small, out-of-the-way places, but their responses to any developmentalist action were also diverse. There was no mass media that could reach each of these groupings, and even if there had been, Australia argued, there was no way to guess how any mass-mediated news might be received. This argument assumed not just fragmentation and isolation, but a lack of standardization. In response to the Trusteeship Council's misguided attempt to impose order on the territory's diverse peoples through the revision of question 2 of the Special Questionnaire, Australia balked: only an army of anthropologists could allow us to answer that question (and they aren't very good at fitting things into discrete categories). The visiting missions became a stage for demonstrating this diversity, as Australian hosts flew the council dignitaries into and out of the mountains, from written Tolai petitions for more education to Maprik sing-sings and the smiling "mobs" of Menyamya.

Bowker and Star (2000) emphasize the fundamental role of classification in bureaucratic information flows. Classifications privilege certain distinctions and erase others. Australia's refusal to classify, its refusal to try to create a set of variables, privileged not one thing over another but one time over another. It privileged the status quo of Australian colonial rule by claiming that no amount of information would be sufficient for a prediction of the Territory of New Guinea's future. For all of Australia's evolutionary talk of backwards and advanced societies, they maintained a version of colonial administration stuck in an unending present swallowed up by the diversity and fragments that loomed so large in their visions of the territory. With a modernist culture of horizontal communications in mass society as their background, the Trust Territory of New Guinea could be nothing but mountains and linguistic boundaries.

Conclusion

In 1960, the UN General Assembly passed Resolution 1514 (XV), the "Declaration on the Granting of Independence to Colonial Countries and Peoples." Although there were no votes against the resolution, Australia and the main colonizer countries abstained, a vote that was meant to signal their disapproval of at least aspects of the resolution. But the tide had turned at that point, and even Australian politicians and civil servants started to realize that the colonial era was going to be coming to an end in the near future. Increasingly, in the following years, Port Moresby became a center of more overt anticolonial expression, particularly after the University of Papua New Guinea opened in 1965 and students started to envision and organize for an independent country. After several Australian governments had dragged their feet, finally the Labor government headed by Prime Minister Gough Whitlam started to work with the emerging Papua New Guinean elite to prepare for independence on September 17, 1975 (for more of the history leading up to independence, see Denoon 2012). Although members of the Australian delegation to the Trusteeship Council like Ronald Walker had thought it was absurd in 1956, Papua New Guinea did in fact gain independence in twenty years.

Concerns about circulation as a problem for Papua New Guinea's postcolonial experience often focused on the role that English would play in the future nation-state. As the members of the Trusteeship Council had hoped, English did become the official language of the country. For the anticolonial council delegates, English would enable the downward flow of information about political advancement from the UN to the people of Papua New Guinea. English would in that way act as a channel for the emergence of a national identity, as the UN-sponsored networks would ideally produce a desire for nationalist self-determination.

Yet things didn't pan out as some at the Trusteeship Council had envisaged. There were political movements, but these tended to be at the regional rather than the territorial scale (see May 1982). The largest may have been Papua Besena, led by Josephine Abaijah (see Wu 2024), a movement advocating for the autonomy of Papua from the former Territory of New Guinea rather than from Australia. In fact, Abaijah wanted Papua to be incorporated fully into Australia, so that Papuans would have the same rights as Australians. Nationalist movements in Papua New Guinea have not been the dominant political forces that they are in other post-colonies. Scholars have talked about Papua New Guineans as having a form of "negative nationalism" (Robbins 1998), as if the common feeling of being developmentally behind the rest of the world has been the only thing uniting people in the country.

Things also didn't pan out as the Trusteeship Council had hoped in regard to Tok Pisin, which never was "eradicated." Instead, it has flourished, even spreading into Papua and taking over much of the role that Hiri Motu played as that territory's colonial lingua franca. If, in the colonial period, it was mostly adult men who had been on labor contracts who knew the language, now most people in Papua New Guinea use or at least passively understand Tok Pisin. And yet this incredible expansion of the reach of Tok Pisin has not produced an expansion in the esteem in which it is held.

As I mentioned at the start of chapter 2, the first prime minister of the country, Sir Michael Somare, once argued in Parliament that Tok Pisin should not be an official language—while speaking Tok Pisin! Things have not improved much since then, as colonial nostalgia colors a lot of contemporary discussions about the country. Discourses of colonial nostalgia in Papua New Guinea often center on language, and especially on the quality of English-language education. There are regular complaints in the letters to the editor of the national newspapers that kids these days are learning only their vernacular languages or Tok Pisin, and not English as they had under Australian rule (Slotta and Handman 2024). The Tok Pisin Bible remains the best-selling book in the country, and yet many people who command only minimal English skills often save up to buy an English-language Bible. Tok Pisin has become the most commonly used language in two domains that are usually thought of as producing affective connections to the speaker—politics and religion—but seemingly without becoming a beloved language at all.

It is worth contrasting the case of Tok Pisin briefly with that of Malay in the neighboring Dutch East Indies. In analyses of the history of Malay (the precursor to Bahasa Indonesia), many scholars suggest that the Dutch colonial forces wanted to have nothing to do with the language (Maier 1993, Siegel 1997, Errington 2003). Comparable to the history of Tok Pisin, they neglected Malay, focusing more attention on either the promulgation of Dutch or the study and use of some of the languages with large numbers of speakers. It was partly out of the colonizers' neglect that Malay was able to transform into a language of an incipient

Indonesian nationalist identity: without the elaborate honorific registers required in Balinese or Javanese, or the deference required in speaking to a colonial officer, speaking Malay to other inhabitants of the Dutch East Indies felt like one was speaking outside of the existing and extremely hierarchical social order into a space of nationalist horizontality.

But in Papua New Guinea, speakers have tended to focus less on finding the language of horizontal nationalist identity and more on finding the linguistic channels through which their social networks can expand. Multilingualism has long been one of the communicative tools for doing so. For a while, Tok Pisin seemed to offer access to wider communicative networks for Papua New Guineans, but many speakers now feel that Tok Pisin is most notable because of its limited communicative capacities compared to English. Instead of being oriented toward the affective connections and horizontalities of linguistic nationalism, many Papua New Guinean speakers focus instead on questions of communicative rather than linguistic equity (Slotta and Handman 2024). That is, many focus on a form of equity that emphasizes communicative channels to others rather than the equal treatment of their own vernacular language on the national stage or in educational settings. With this orientation toward connection to others, many Papua New Guineans focus on how English seems to offer the widest networks and they lament the loss of English language comprehension among contemporary school kids. Concerns about English tie into colonial nostalgia in Papua New Guinea, which are often keyed to a sense of remoteness and dislocation. For many, the era of independence marks the era of severed connections to others around the world (Demian 2021).

In that sense, the way that circulatory concerns defined the colonial and decolonial attitudes toward English may be one of the most enduring influences on local ideologies of language. Multilingualism has long been a Papua New Guinean strategy for cultivating wider social networks. However, the zero-sum approach to the language of schooling, in which more time spent on one language is necessarily less time spent on another, has meant that many parents and older students now try to calculate which languages can create the widest networks and enable the widest forms of circulation. There are vocal groups of parents and teachers who value English above all other languages as the channel for these wider networks.

The legacies of circulatory primitivity can be seen in Papua New Guinean infrastructure as well. In present-day Papua New Guinea, a frequent comment is that it is the "last place," as in the last place to get connected up to the rest of the world (Kulick 1992). In other words, a sense of attenuated or absent circulation still seems to characterize the ways that people, now primarily Papua New Guineans themselves, tend to talk about the country. Many scholars have written about the problems of and discourses about roads and transportation in Papua New Guinea (Hayano 1990, Lipset 2014, Handman 2017b, Beer and Church 2019, Dwyer and Minnegal 2023). It still seems like a country formed by a series of discrete spaces disconnected from one another. As Peter Dwyer and Monica Minnegal (2023) note, airstrips are relatively quick and easy to construct, and much of the country has been connected through the aviation network. But if airstrips are easy to make for local communities, the money and logistics needed to get a plane to fly to one's area and then to purchase a ticket are usually well beyond the means of rural, mostly subsistence farmers who populate the areas connected by these strips. In fact, passenger air travel in Papua New Guinea is some of the most expensive in the world on a per kilometer basis. Roads are much more expensive to build and to maintain, and thus remain relatively rare outside of urban centers, yet actually getting a ride on one is much cheaper and easier for the individual rider.

The "pioneering use of airplanes" that the UN commented on so approvingly has remained the main form of transportation infrastructure for much of the country. It worked, to an extent, to connect those discrete outposts of colonial administration, like Lutheran Mission stations or administrative stations. But because of that enduring sense of circulatory primitivity—the idea that getting anything over and across Papua New Guinea was a feat—the use of aviation networks has maintained that sense that the country is just a set of lightly connected islands of sociality surrounded by mountains and languages that make deeper intercalation impossible. Now mobile cellular phone networks similarly work to connect communities, yet these often remain communities that are extremely difficult to travel to or from (Foster and Horst 2018, Foster 2023).

. . .

On my most recent trip to Papua New Guinea, I was reminded of how difficult moving around the country can be. During the North American summer of 2023, my husband and I went there with our daughter, who we wanted to introduce to people in Titio village in Morobe Province, where I had done my earlier research. Our daughter has a middle name—Etai—that we gave her in honor of a good friend from that original fieldwork, and we needed to introduce her to her namesake now that she was old enough to manage the travel and appreciate the experience. Knowing the vagaries of travel in Papua New Guinea, we left about ten days open in our schedule just to make sure that we would be able to fly with the small aviation company that services the Waria Valley. They had long flown on Tuesdays and Thursdays, and we assumed that a similar sort of schedule was still in operation.

When we got to Lae, though, it seemed that we would not be able to go at all. Over the past few years, the aviation company had crashed several of their planes, sometimes with fatalities and sometimes not. They were at this point operating only one plane, and it was unexpectedly making runs up in the Central Highlands that week. At the last minute, though, after we had started to come to terms with the fact that the primary purpose of what had been a long and expensive trip might not be fulfilled, we received a phone call. They would be flying to the Waria Valley that week. We could take the flight in on Tuesday and come out again on Thursday.

Two and half days was not what we had been hoping for, but just minutes before it had seemed that the trip was not going to happen at all, so two and half days felt like a gift. We bought three extremely expensive tickets that afternoon and started to get supplies together to take to friends in the village.

We had a wonderful visit, and there was a very meaningful ceremony in which the namesake relationship between the older Etai and our daughter was made official (*kamap ples klia*, in Tok Pisin). On Thursday we hiked forty-five minutes back to the Garasa airstrip from Titio, and waited all day for the plane. As had been true of every day I had spent waiting for planes at that airstrip, people passed time by telling stories of plane crashes they had witnessed or heard about, always my least favorite form of sociality as I contemplated my imminent travel. But stories of travel—difficult, dangerous, surprising, expensive—are frequently told. The troubles of circulation have remained a constant preoccupation.

As usual, there were many people waiting to get on the plane. With so many relatives living in town, there is a constant demand for seats on the plane to take people and goods in and out. We saw the workmen loading an extraordinary amount of cargo onto a ten-seater plane that was starting to look smaller with each bag packed into the hold. And when they finally loaded passengers, we had to crawl over the cargo that was stacked two feet high in the skinny aisle that ran between the seats. Taxiing on the grass airstrip, we bumped over the slightly uneven terrain. As we gained speed, we waved goodbye through the airplane's small windows to friends who had gathered to see us off. My husband and I shot nervous glances at each other as we quickly approached the end of the runway and didn't seem to be gaining elevation. At the last minute, the plane lifted off the ground, just clearing the barbed wire that marked the boundary of the airstrip.

Having entrusted our lives to a company that had suffered multiple crashes, we were sitting in a plane overloaded with cargo that had seemingly only just managed to get off the ground. About to climb over an eight-thousand-foot mountain range—passing a peak where a World War II fighter plane was still visible where it had crashed, nose first, straight into the ground—I somehow felt quite lucky. Unlike many others, we had the money to travel by plane.

. . .

Modernist imaginaries of circulation assume that more circulation produces more progress, or more health, or more wealth. When colonizers confronted the challenges of having to move across the many mountains and languages of Papua New Guinea, they did so with these modernist imaginaries firmly in place. Circulatory problems became the overarching framework for the missionaries and administrators trying to navigate the territory. And yet as much as they constantly lamented the lack of circulation and the difficulties of movement, they just as often were suspicious of many forms of circulation that seemed to make the territory too easy to move around in. The contradictions and conflicts among different colonial projects could be seen in how different actors worked to channel the flows of people and goods and talk in certain ways rather than others. In the colonial period this was a problem of creating communication infrastructures like roads, radios, and aviation networks. In the decolonial era, when problems of circulation were still the predominant framework for understanding Papua New Guinea, the focus was on the development of bureaucratic information flows that the anticolonial members of the Trusteeship Council hoped would encourage Australia's departure and precipitate on-the-ground movements for self-sovereignty.

Papua New Guinea is a difficult place to move around in, as my recent trip reminded me. More than that, it is a place where people have long thought, and continue to think, about the problems of circulation and the ways in which it has deeply affected their lives and the policies and choices their governments have made. But even as some of those problems seem inevitable—mountains are hard to climb, especially when they are so densely forested—I have tried to show that it wasn't just a set of natural boundaries that created the version of Papua New Guinea that exists today. Modernist imaginaries about circulation made the country into a space of fragmentation, in response to which missions, networks, and languages multiplied. The worry over fragmentation produced even more fragments, and responding to fragmentation became the guiding concern, a source of continuity across colonialism and decolonization, a concern that exists to this day in everyday experiences of circulation.

INTRODUCTION

1. I am grateful to the late Peter Dwyer for pointing me to this text.

2. Nomad No. 3 of 1972/73 Patrol Report, Appendix no. 7, p. 66, National Archives of Papua New Guinea.

3. Pidgin languages emerge in contexts in which speakers of many languages share only restricted access to another language and then use a simplified version of that other language as a basis for communication. Most of the languages that are referred to as pidgins came out of contexts of temporary forced labor, where speakers of many different languages used a European colonizer's language to communicate with one another while working terms of indenture. However, some pidgins developed in the context of precolonial and colonial-era trading networks, including the pidginized version of the Motu language, spoken on the south coast of Papua New Guinea during their *hiri* voyages, and Chinook Jargon (or Chinook Wawa), spoken along the Columbia River in the Pacific Northwest region of the United States, among others. In general, pidgins were spoken as second languages and tended to be somewhat restricted in their contexts of use. Colonizers often had to learn pidgin languages from their workers, but the fact that the languages involved simplifications of European linguistic forms allowed Euro-American observers to initially think that pidgins were the product of European colonizers using (and colonized peoples imitating) "baby talk" versions of their languages. I discuss critiques of pidgin and creole as categories of language in the conclusion to chapter 5.

4. In British/Australian Papua, a different lingua franca, known as Hiri Motu or Police Motu, became the more prominent language of the colonial state, although a form of pidgin English was used in Papua early on as well (Dutton 1985).

5. Overseas Broadcasting Service, ABC Radio Australia, International Report, Progress in New Guinea by EWP Chinnery, for broadcast 14–15 June 1955, National Archives of Australia (NAA), A1838, 893/2/2 part 5, p. 2.

6. Interested readers are directed to several important histories of the Lutheran missions in New Guinea: Winter (2012) provides an important critical reading of the political context of the Neuendettelsau Mission, focusing on its connections to rising nationalist movements in Germany and the specific Nazi connections of some of the missionaries. Midena (2014) examines the early missionaries' overlapping religious and scientific orientations that influenced their ethnographic output and evangelistic approaches. Wagner and Reiner (1986) collect essays and remembrances from many of the people involved in the original events, providing an insider's perspective on the Lutheran mission field.

7. This problem of institutional fragmentation became especially noticeable for the UN Trusteeship Council in the years before Papua New Guinea's independence. See Observations by UN Trusteeship Council on Multiplicity of Religious Missions in New Guinea, NAA, A452, 1959/5433, 1959.

8. Missions-Administration Conference, 1959, p. 3.

9. Missions-Administration Conference, 1961, p. 103.

10. Communications—New Guinea and Papua—Use of aerial ropeways in New Guinea as a means of transport, NAA, A518, BD808/1, 1947; Basic English—Use of in Territory, NAA, A452, 1957/2339, 1957.

1. REMOTE NETWORKS: AIRPLANES, RADIOS, AND THE MAKING OF COMMUNICATIVE DISTANCE IN LUTHERAN NEW GUINEA

1. Minutes, Annual Conference, 1955, Lutheran Mission New Guinea, p. 15, Archives of the Evangelical Lutheran Church in America.

2. The Catholics created their own missionary radio network because the CRMF leadership did not allow the Catholics to join theirs.

3. Radio and Electrical Workshop, Annual Conference Report, 1968, p. 5, Archives of the Evangelical Lutheran Church of Papua New Guinea.

4. Radio and Electrical Workshop, Annual Conference Report, 1970, p. 1, Archives of the Evangelical Lutheran Church of Papua New Guinea.

5. The Lutheran language policies are discussed in the next chapter.

6. "The Secular Involvement," unpublished typescript manuscript, p. 17, John Kuder Papers, Archives of the Evangelical Lutheran Church in America.

7. Ibid.

8. Ibid., p. 15.

9. "A Miracle before Our Eyes," unpublished and undated typescript manuscript, Rev. Otto F. Theile, Addresses, n.d., p. 6, Archives of the Evangelical Lutheran Church in America. Much of the early history of civil aviation took place in Papua New Guinea, particularly in the Wau and Bulolo gold fields (Sinclair 1978). The figures from the larger airplanes working out of Wau and Bulolo are even more astounding: "When the plant for the AWA's first wireless station was transported from Salamaua [at the coast] to Wau we started with 300 native boys carrying the gear over trackless country on a journey which occupied six weeks. Recently a large dredge weighing 4000 tons [sic—should say "4000 pounds"] was carried in sections over the same country by air. The trip occupied 35 minutes" (see *The Age*, "The 'Reach' of Teleradio," September 16, 1938). Air travel seemed to erase the mountains and forests that had been, until this point, among the most consequential features of working in Papua New Guinea, whether as a missionary or a gold miner.

10. "The Secular Involvement," p. 28.

11. The Lutherans had great experience dealing with drainage and water tables through their extensive road-building projects along the coast.

12. "A Miracle before Our Eyes," p. 1.

13. "A Glimpse at Transportation in Lutheran Mission New Guinea," undated pamphlet prepared by the Board of Foreign Mission, American Lutheran Church, Archives of the Evangelical Lutheran Church in America.

14. According to Sinclair (1978), Loose was a pilot and engineer with the Junkers aviation company after World War I, but he ran afoul of the Nazi Party and was happy to take the opportunity to leave Germany to fly for the Lutherans in 1935. As I discuss below, the relationship of the Lutherans to Nazism became an important part of their aviation history.

15. Huber (1988: 77) talks about the use of boats as a "defining technology" for the neighboring Roman Catholic mission in earlier decades (see also Allen 1976). Clearly, aviation was a defining technology for the Lutherans in the 1930s and after (and for the Catholics too—they started using planes just after the Lutherans did).

16. Seventh-day Adventists also participated in this race to the highlands, although as a smaller mission they were not quite the existential threat to the Lutherans that the large Roman Catholic mission was.

17. Johannes Flierl, Report from Senior Joh. Flierl for 1927, trans. Wera Wilhelm, LMF 51-10, Archives of the Evangelical Lutheran Church in America, 1928.

18. Board of Foreign Missions, minutes, December 6–7, 1927, p. 1, Archives of the Evangelical Lutheran Church in America. The translation from German is mine.

19. I will discuss the radio network more in the second half of this chapter. I focus here only on how the radio network supported the aviation system.

20. *Northern Star* (Australia), "Radio Telephony for Planes," January 5, 1938. Radios became an important part of patrols. In Philip Fitzpatrick's memoir of his time as a patrol officer, using, maintaining, worrying about, and sometimes trying to ignore his radio is a running theme (Fitzpatrick 2005: 63–64, 94–95, 117–18, 164–65, 195).

21. "The Secular Involvement," p. 43.

22. For the missionaries who had worked or continued to work along the coast, this regimentation to clock and calendar happened through the scheduled, monthly visits of the Lutheran ship *Simbang*, for "her trips represent the inevitable passing of time; something which so often we tend to minimize here where work is generally made to conform to conditions of the weather, rather than by a predetermined schedule" ("A Glimpse at Transportation in Lutheran Mission New Guinea," p. 2). The aviation-related radio schedules meant that this regimentation to the time of the "outside world" happened on a daily basis. For more on missionary reformulations of time in colonial Papua New Guinea, see Schieffelin (2002).

23. *Queensland Times*, "Aeroplanes in Mission Work," August 2, 1939. Pilots did not always wait for return correspondence; sometimes they did not even land. Bergmann (n.d.: 52–61) describes dropping mailbags down to waiting missionaries from the window of the low-flying *Papua*.

24. "A Miracle before Our Eyes."

25. UECLA-NG General–Personal Donations for Aircraft 1934–1935, Archives of the Evangelical Lutheran Church of Papua New Guinea.

26. "Transportation," R. R. Hanselmann, LMM 55-20, Archives of the Evangelical Lutheran Church in America.

27. "The Secular Involvement."

28. *Pacific Islands Monthly* vol. 12, no. 8, National Library of Australia, nla.obj-310 385031.

29. We can turn a bit farther from the Pacific to see an even more explicit use of technology to make God accessible. At roughly the same time that the Lutherans were making history in the use of aviation to spread the gospel, agit-prop air squadrons were criss-crossing the rural Soviet countryside in order to prove to Russian peasants that God did not exist (Palmer 2006). In what were called "aerial baptisms," peasants were taken up in Soviet planes in order to prove to them that neither God nor angels were visible in the skies as the priests had told them. These baptisms into atheist technological progress both depended upon and subverted the Christian association of skies with God. Peasants were even presented with Stalin-centric Soviet postcards after their atheist baptisms by air, in lieu of the miniature icons that Orthodox priests would give those recently baptized by water (Palmer 2006: 242).

30. *The Mercury*, "Clash Likely, Japanese Advance in New Guinea," March 21, 1942.

31. F. C. Folkard, "Clash Soon in New Guinea," *The Sun*, March 20, 1942.

32. *The Advertiser*, "New Guinea Missions," October 28, 1939.

33. Translation of enclosure in letter no. 40/1073, dated 23 April 1940, from O. Theile, Brisbane, to the Superintendent, Lutheran Mission, Finschhafen, Lutheran Mission Aircraft—New Guinea, National Archives of Australia (NAA), MP508/1, 31/701/37.

34. For a contrastive context in which the speed of circulation is at issue, see Yeh (2017).

35. The devastation of the war years for the Lutheran missions in Papua New Guinea has been discussed in a number of other places (Fricke 1947, Wagner and Reiner 1986).

36. Kuder letters to Board of Foreign Mission, 1945, John Kuder Papers, Archives of the Evangelical Lutheran Church in America.

37. Radio and Electrical Workshop, Annual Conference Report, 1968.

38. The privacy of the missionary teleradio network stands in stark contrast to the way that teleradio worked in New Caledonia according to Bolton (1999), who says (336–38) that there was only one network used for the whole colony and that when broadcasting began, it used this frequency as well. So, while only some people could transmit on the single network, it functioned (and was listened to) much like a broadcast station.

39. Base stations had to be strict in their control over the sked and radio traffic. In a memoir of his time volunteering with the Catholic missions in the Sepik region, Michael Courage writes about how he feared the woman who ran the traffic on the radio network he used in Simbai: "I had imagined her, when talking over the radio from Simbai, to be rather a dragon, very precise and standing no nonsense, as indeed she had to be to keep all the pilots and stations in ordered contact. Of course she wasn't a bit like that [when I met her], being quite charming and I thoroughly enjoyed my conversations with her in between the almost ceaseless voices saying 'Madang, Simbai . . . Madang, Simbai. Are you receiving me?'" (Courage and Wright 1967: 98).

40. List of stations, Christian Radio Missionary Fellowship: 1949–1965 Correspondence, Archives of the Evangelical Lutheran Church of Papua New Guinea.

41. For example, Claude D'Evelynes to John Kuder letter, 30 October 1953; Kuder to D'Evelynes letter, 1 December 1953; D'Evelynes to Kuder letter, 9 December 1953; Kuder

to D'Evelynes letter, 10 December 1953, Christian Radio Missionary Fellowship: 1949–1965 Correspondence, Archives of the Evangelical Lutheran Church of Papua New Guinea.

42. Statement of the CRMF, undated but possibly 1 April 1954, Christian Radio Missionary Fellowship: 1949–1965 Correspondence, Archives of the Evangelical Lutheran Church of Papua New Guinea.

43. For example, Conlon to Johnson letter, 16 August 1962, Christian Radio Missionary Fellowship: 1949–1965 Correspondence, Archives of the Evangelical Lutheran Church of Papua New Guinea. See also Radio and Electrical Workshop, Annual Conference Report, 1967, in which the author applauds missionaries for finally being better about sticking to skeds during the evenings, but now implores people to do so during the day too. The 1968 Radio and Electrical Workshop Report to Conference also urges missionaries to stick to their skeds.

44. Radio and Electrical Workshop, Annual Conference Report, 1968.

45. Claude D'Evelyns to John Kuder letter, 7 May 1957, Christian Radio Missionary Fellowship: 1949–1965 Correspondence, Archives of the Evangelical Lutheran Church of Papua New Guinea.

46. This kind of system contrasts with the privacy afforded to radio users that Lucas Bessire (2012) discusses. In the Ayoreo indigenous community, which uses two-way radios today, contemporary transistor radio technology no longer requires individual crystals to tune into specific frequencies. One can pick any frequency one wants within a wide kilohertz band. There are set frequencies that everyone in the Ayoreo community knows about and uses, and these frequencies have the same privacy problems that the missionaries had. But since the radios Ayoreos use now allow one to transmit on any frequency within the shortwave band, specific pairs of people can secretly arrange to use frequencies that are not used by others, which vastly increases the likelihood of privacy. Someone would have to be slowly scanning through all the frequencies at exactly the right time to catch the conversation. Because radios in the early part of the twentieth century could only transmit on the frequencies for which they had crystals, the kind of privacy that Bessire discusses was not possible. The missionary radio networks were thus extremely public from the perspective of other missionaries in the field who could tune in to an endless supply of gossip and chatter.

47. Carl Spehr to John Kuder letter, 23 March 1957, Christian Radio Missionary Fellowship: 1949–1965 Correspondence, Archives of the Evangelical Lutheran Church of Papua New Guinea.

48. Administrators in the Department of Posts and Telegraphs were "fighting hard to get the equipment and the men to make a big thing of their . . . networks. He told me so and I have seen the advertisements for the technical personnel. It is his avowed ambition to swallow up all these private networks." Claude D'Evelynes to John Kuder letter, 7 May 1957, Christian Radio Missionary Fellowship: 1949–1965 Correspondence, Archives of the Evangelical Lutheran Church of Papua New Guinea.

2. TOK PISIN AND THE LINGUISTIC INFRASTRUCTURE OF THE LUTHERAN MISSION

1. Information Handbook, Visit of the United Nations Visiting Mission to the Trust Territory of New Guinea, 13 March 1953 to 15 April 1953, typescript manuscript, Visiting Mission 1953—New Guinea, National Archives of Australia (NAA), A518, 103/1/40 part 1, p. 14.

2. As reported by the Tok Pisin–language newspaper, *Wantok* (July 10, 1976, p. 15), under the headline "Somare no laikim tok pisin" (Somare does not like Tok Pisin). After quoting Mr. Somare's comments against Tok Pisin, the final line of the short article is "Na taim em i mekim dispela tok, em i yusim tok pisin yet" (And when he said this, he used Tok Pisin itself). See also Romaine (2013: 247–48).

3. The Problem of Language: Paper No. 1, Pidgin, Department of Education, January 1955, NAA, A518, 1/103/1/45, pp. 11–12.

4. Ibid., p. 12.

5. "Transportation," ALC NG LMM 55-20, 156.1934.12, Archives of the Evangelical Lutheran Church in America.

6. Austronesian languages are present across the island Pacific, from indigenous communities of Taiwan to the Rapa Nui language spoken on Easter Island. Austronesian languages share a number of phonological and morphological traits, and the historical relationships among the languages are well known. By contrast, Papuan languages are found only on New Guinea and some nearby islands. The languages within this family vary widely in terms of their typological traits, and the family is now better known as Non-Austronesian to signal that these languages only seem to share the characteristic of not being related to Austronesian ones.

7. John Kuder to Paul Hasluck letter, 22 October 1959, Lutheran Mission New Guinea: Educational Questions 1956–60, p. 8, Archives of the Evangelical Lutheran Church of Papua New Guinea.

8. "This Is for Your Information," undated, ALC 29/8/8/1, Archives of the Evangelical Lutheran Church in America.

9. Record of Discussions at Private Sessions, p. 3, Missions-Administration Conference 1959, Archives of the Evangelical Lutheran Church of Papua New Guinea.

10. Winter (2012: 109–22) has a full discussion of the ways that national socialist ideologies inflected this debate. Briefly, early (ca. 1929) support for the church lingua francas was an extension of German nationalist ideologies then ascendant in the Weimar Republic. Yet even a missionary like Georg Pilhofer, who was most vocal about wanting to create a Papuan "*volk*" through the spread of Kâte, realized that this required a steady project of inculcating a church lingua franca so that it could later become a nation-forging entity for speakers of other languages.

11. I thank John Barker for pointing out this connection.

12. Flierl is referring here to a comment cited earlier in his essay, from another colonial administrator who had called Tok Pisin that "horror of horrors" (see Flierl 1936: 13).

13. "Missionary Methods," undated, Rev. Otto Theile, ALC 29/8/8/1, p. 10, Archives of the Evangelical Lutheran Church in America.

14. Record of Discussions at Private Sessions, p. 3, Missions-Administration Conference 1959, Archives of the Evangelical Lutheran Church of Papua New Guinea.

15. John Kuder to Paul Hasluck letter, 22 October 1959, Lutheran Mission New Guinea: Educational Questions 1956–60, Archives of the Evangelical Lutheran Church of Papua New Guinea.

16. Note again the connection in the colonial mind (more likely the Australian's than the Papua New Guinean's) between aviation and Christianity, as discussed in chapter 1.

17. This is indeed how the Tok Pisin version of the proclamation was written; it is intended to say something like "The British are the new colonial power, they care for black people just like they care for their own children." See Copy of proclamation in "Pidgin" English by Australian Military Government to natives of German New Guinea, Australian War Memorial 33 [28].

18. "What Should Be the Attitude towards the Pidjin Language in Mission Work," 1930, by Stephen Lehner, ALC NG LMF 55/10, Archives of the Evangelical Lutheran Church in America.

19. Ibid.

20. "About My Visit to the Inland Stations," 1938, by Georg Pilhofer, ALC NG LMF 51/10, Archives of the Evangelical Lutheran Church in America.

21. The fact that Ilaoa uses a Latinate term here suggests that this is a very early attempt at using Tok Pisin within a Lutheran context when the theological vocabulary would have been extremely small and in flux. It may also be important that Ilaoa, as a Samoan missionary who did not share the Euro-American history of long-standing Catholic-Protestant conflict, was less inclined to the kind of deep-seated antipathy toward Catholics that his fellow German, Australian, and American Lutheran missionaries felt, and thus would have been more open to incorporating Catholic usage.

22. Undated and unattributed. A similar version of the prayer is found in "What Should Be the Attitude towards the Pidjin Language in Mission Work," 1930, by Stephen Lehner, ALC NG LMF 55/10, Archives of the Evangelical Lutheran Church in America.

23. In contemporary Tok Pisin versions of the "Our Father" prayer, only the exclusive first-person plural pronoun *mipela* is used.

24. Ralph Sutton, "One-Teach-One, the Laubach System," *Pacific Islands Monthly* vol. 21, no. 2, September 1, 1950, pp. 81–83.

25. John Kuder to Translations Secretary letter, 9 January 1950, Correspondence with British & Foreign Bible Society, Archives of the Evangelical Lutheran Church of Papua New Guinea.

26. Ibid.

27. Lae Wampar, Annual Conference Reports, 1952, Archives of the Evangelical Lutheran Church of Papua New Guinea.

28. See Mumeng and Lae, Annual Conference Reports, 1953, Archives of the Evangelical Lutheran Church of Papua New Guinea.

29. "The Native Labor Program of the Mission," by Theodore G. Braun, p. 5, Conference Papers, 1953, Archives of the Evangelical Lutheran Church of Papua New Guinea.

30. Ibid., p. 5.

31. Ibid.

32. Ibid., p. 6.

33. President's Report for 1954, Reports 1936–1976, p. 9, John Kuder Papers, Archives of the Evangelical Lutheran Church in America.

34. This is from a written transcript of Kuder's responses to Sievert's written questions that Kuder recorded by audiotape. I have added material in square brackets to help correct for the disfluencies of his off-the-cuff remarks. "Dr. John Kuder Interviewed by Rev. John Sievert," 1983, John Sievert's Correspondence and Manuscript of Questions Answered by

John Kuder, 1971, 1983, pp. 38–39, John Kuder Papers, Archives of the Evangelical Lutheran Church in America.

3. TELEPATHY TALES: TOK PISIN, COMMUNIST RADIO, AND OTHER CHANNELS OF ILLEGITIMATE CIRCULATION

1. F. M. Ashfield, "Telepathy?," *Smith's Weekly*, November 2, 1946, p. 18.

2. Luckhurst (2002: 157) points to a very similar kind of story from nineteenth-century Canada, in which the forensic accounting of distance crossed by telepathic communication was one of the most prominent features of the tale: a marchioness, and wife of the governor, "confirmed the story of a drowned footman whose sweetheart dreamt the exact details of his death 'more than 500 miles distant in Ottawa', knowledge received quicker than the speed of the available telegraph."

3. The quoted text is from Archibald Rutledge (1883–1973), an American Christian writer who focused on stories of southern hunting and outdoor life that were published in magazines like *Field & Stream*. The original quotation appears in Rutledge's book *It Will Be Daybreak Soon* (1938), where it refers to African Americans in particular and does not contain the phrase "to the negro"—Henkelmann seems to have inserted this phrase himself in order to generalize Rutledge's comment to a wider, pan-Black racial context. "Receptivity of the Soul of the Melanesians," 1939, by Frederick Henkelmann, ALC 29.8.7.2, p. 5, Archives of the Evangelical Lutheran Church in America.

4. I thank Rupert Stasch for pointing me to Taylor (2016).

5. Henry Dexter, "Bush Telegraph, Telepathy—or What?," *Pacific Islands Monthly* vol. 2, no. 12, July 19, 1933, p. 13.

6. Periti, "How Did Mina Know!," *Pacific Islands Monthly* vol. 24, no. 11, June 1, 1954, p. 83.

7. Luckhurst (2002: 150) notes that colonial reports of telepathy often involved domestic servants, whose ambivalent position—within the household but not within the family—made them seem somewhat threatening and disruptive.

8. L. Poole, "'Black Magic': How Do Islanders Communicate?," *Pacific Islands Monthly* vol. 24, no. 4, November 1, 1953, p. 55.

9. N. W. Macdonald, "Can Anyone Explain This Queer Case? (Letter to the Editor)," *Pacific Islands Monthly* vol. 23, no. 11, June 1, 1953, p. 41.

10. A Google ngram count of instances of the phrase *bush telegraph* in its English-language corpus shows a rapid rise from the 1920s to a peak in 1960, and then a drop in usage in the following decades. The terms *coconut radio* and *coconut wireless* are in use in much smaller numbers starting in the 1920s. See https://books.google.com/ngrams/graph?content=bush+telegraph%2Ccoconut+radio%2Ccoconut+wireless&year_start=1800&year_end=2000&corpus=en-2019&smoothing=3 (accessed July 11, 2024). I thank Robin Hide for pointing me to these figures.

11. For similar reports of colonial laborers knowing faraway events before the colonizers did, see Julius Scott's (2018) discussion of communication networks among enslaved people in the Caribbean prior to the Haitian Revolution. Likewise, C. A. Bayly (1996: 214) discusses reports that in colonial India international news circulated in local markets "long before official reports arrived on British ships."

12. *The Age*, "The 'Bush Telegraph' in Many Lands: Primitive Methods of Communication," February 16, 1952, p. 9.

13. George H. Johnston, "Tribes in Turmoil: How the 'Bush Telegraph' Works in New Guinea," *Sydney Morning Herald*, March 21, 1942, p. 7.

14. Ibid.

15. *Pacific Islands Monthly*, "Calling Rarotonga?," vol. 17, no. 12, July 18, 1947, p. 28.

16. Even the antiwar movement in the United States could sometimes depend on special mental powers, as when Abbie Hoffman and others led a protest to try to telekinetically levitate the Pentagon. For a brief account, see https://www.smithsonianmag.com/smithsonian -institution/how-rag-tag-group-acid-dropping-activists-tried-levitate-pentagon-180965338/ (accessed September 20, 2021). I thank Matt Tomlinson for pointing me to this story.

17. Report on Mass Communications to His Honour the Administrator and the Public Service Commissioner from Committee of Enquiry, headed by L. F. Butler, July 9, 1959, p. 23, Territory of Papua and New Guinea: Miscellaneous Typescripts Reports, 1952–1959, Pacific Manuscripts Bureau 608.

18. Christian Radio Missionary Fellowship Proposals for Christian Broadcasting Station in New Guinea, March 1954, NAA, A452/1, 1965/6099.

19. A full account of these ambitions is outside the scope of this discussion, but see, for example, Louis (1978) and Waters (2013, 2016). Although Australia seems, from certain perspectives, like an accidental imperialist, Australian politicians had contemplated a Pacific empire at various points, starting in the nineteenth century (Waters 2016). The Japanese invasion of the Territory of New Guinea during World War II was seen as an existential threat to Australia. In the postwar era, Australian politicians and military leaders saw Papua New Guinea as one of the most strategically important areas for national defense. The Australian military installations on Manus, the most northerly island in Papua New Guinea, were considered the first line of defense against the northern "Asian Powers." As Louis (1978: 305) details, the most fantastic versions of this imagined Australian empire stretched across most of the island Pacific. Concrete proposals were drawn up in the 1950s for a unified Melanesia that would involve Australian control over Dutch New Guinea, Australian Papua, the Trust Territory of New Guinea, the British Solomon Islands Protectorate, the New Hebrides, and the Gilbert and Ellice Islands (Waters 2016). Paul Hasluck, the minister for territories during most of the 1950s, was strongly in support of trying to create a wider Australian sphere of influence. However, the Menzies government in 1960 definitively put aside any plans for expanded colonial control in Australia. This was the same year that the UN General Assembly passed Resolution 1514 (XV), the "Declaration on the Granting of Independence to Colonial Countries and Peoples." Territorial control over the Pacific stopped being an Australian ambition at that point, although of course politicians continued to use other forms of influence.

20. Claude D'Evelynes to C. R. Lambert letter, 16 October 1962, Christian Radio Missionary Fellowship: 1949–1965 Correspondence, Archives of the Evangelical Lutheran Church of Papua New Guinea.

21. The administration began an inquiry into whether they could jam these foreign signals in return, although the Australian foreign intelligence service declined to do this (Foreign Propaganda Broadcasts—Monitoring of in Papua and New Guinea, NAA A518/2/ V926/1/6). Australia was likely following the policies in place in the US and UK: as the leaders of "the free world," they would not normally engage in jamming. Of course, the UK made exceptions to this policy during moments of crisis, for example in Cyprus and Egypt in 1956 (Nelson 1997: 21).

22. President's Report for 1961, p. 1, Reports 1936–1973, John Kuder Papers, Archives of the Evangelical Lutheran Church in America.

23. Missions-Administration Conference 1961, p. 94, Archives of the Evangelical Lutheran Church of Papua New Guinea. In both colonial and contemporary discourse, if someone wants to delegitimize a Papua New Guinean's political claim, they do so by referring to it as a cargo cult or as an example of irrational "cargo cult thinking."

24. *South Pacific Post*, July 6, 1956, p. 2.

25. It's not clear whether he was, in fact, advocating this. See *Pacific Islands Monthly*, "P-NG Man Gaoled for Sedition," February 1961, p. 20.

26. Missions-Administration Conference 1959, pp. 75–80, Archives of the Evangelical Lutheran Church of Papua New Guinea.

27. Tolala, "Territories Talk-Talk," *Pacific Islands Monthly* vol. 26, no. 11, June 1, 1956, p. 31.

28. The fears about Tok Pisin revealed in Aufinger's or Lawrence's works turn the language from a simple jargon for commands into a version of Herman Melville's short story "Benito Cereno," which plays on the dialectic of master-slave relations (Melville 2014 [1855]). In this story [spoiler alert for a 170-year-old text], the slaves on a ship called the *San Dominick* have revolted and taken charge. Having been adrift for days with dwindling supplies, the *San Dominick* comes into a deserted natural harbor. However, another ship is there, and the narrator of the story, that ship's Captain Delano, comes aboard the *San Dominick* to help out. On the *San Dominick*, the actually-in-charge slaves and the now deposed Captain Don Benito Cereno put on a pantomime of normal order that is difficult to discern through Delano's unreliable narration. Only at the very end of a long day of playing at master-servant relationships that are, in fact, reversed is the truth revealed. The ending draws the reader to go back through the scenes and read them again for their hidden meanings: Benito Cereno's servant Babo, who is in fact the leader of the slave revolt, is not just shaving him, but putting a knife to his throat; the older African men cleaning tools and picking oakum to an "Ashante" rhythm are not just working but keeping open channels of communication with the other slaves on board so that they can be alerted in case of trouble; Babo's words of support and care are in fact threats on Don Benito's life. The positions of master and slave can be reversed even as a seemingly normal set of operations on a slave ship continue.

29. Hall published books and articles about Haitian Creole, Tok Pisin, and what became known as the pidgin-creole life cycle (Hall 1953, 1955, 1958, 1962). His early familiarity with Tok Pisin largely came from interviewing anthropologists after their fieldwork, most notably Margaret Mead and Gregory Bateson. He visited Papua New Guinea to work with Tok Pisin speakers for the first time in 1956, after many of his Tok Pisin–related publications had already appeared.

30. The Problem of Language: Paper No. 1, Pidgin, Department of Education, January 1955, NAA, A518/1, 103/1/45.

31. R. W. Robson, "From Notes Made in New Guinea," *Pacific Islands Monthly* vol. 24, no. 2, September 1, 1953, p. 20 (emphasis in original).

4. DEMANDING INDEPENDENCE ON BEHALF OF OTHERS: THE TRUSTEESHIP COUNCIL AND THE TRUST TERRITORY OF NEW GUINEA

1. There has been a call to revive the Trusteeship Council as a UN organ for managing climate change, in which the "trust territory" in this case would be the Earth as a whole (see Desai 2021).

2. For example, in Trusteeship Council—Use of Pidgin English in Trust Territory of New Guinea, National Archives of Australia (NAA), A518/1, 103/1/45.

3. Eighteenth Session of Trusteeship Council—July/August, 1956; Examination of 1954–55 New Guinea Report, Conclusions and Recommendations Adopted by the Council on New Guinea, Trusteeship Council—Examination of New Guinea Report 1954/55, NAA, A518/1, 103/4/16.

4. Report of the Department of External Affairs Observer Accompanying the United Nations Visiting Mission to the Trust Territory of New Guinea, 1956, NAA, A452, 1957/91 part 2.

5. Ibid., p. 77.

6. Ibid.

7. Comments on the State Department Note of 11 October 1956, Trusteeship Council Eighteenth Session, NAA, A1838, 891/2/18 part 4.

8. Department of External Affairs, Inward Cablegram 480, from the Australian Mission to the United Nations, 31 July 1956, Trusteeship Council Eighteenth Session, NAA, A1838, 891/2/18 part 3.

9. Department of External Affairs, Inward Cablegram 486, from the Australian Mission to the United Nations, 2 August 1956, Trusteeship Council Eighteenth Session, NAA, A1838, 891/2/18 part 3.

10. Comments on the State Department Note of 11 October 1956, Trusteeship Council Eighteenth Session, NAA, A1838, 891/2/18 part 4.

11. Eighteenth Session of Trusteeship Council—July/August, 1956, Examination of 1954–55 New Guinea Report, Conclusions and Recommendations Adopted by the Council on New Guinea, Trusteeship Council—Examination of New Guinea Report 1954/55, NAA, A518/1, 103/4/16.

12. Memo from Department of Territories (first page missing), NAA, A1838, 891/2/18 part 4, pp. 4–5. The memo was added to the file after another document dated 15 February 1957, so it is likely that this document was produced in late February 1957.

5. ENGLISH AND THE CHANNELS OF DECOLONIZATION

1. Visiting mission—1953—New Guinea, National Archives of Australia (NAA), A518, 103/1/40 part 1.

2. For example, the delegate from Syria in a 1953 session expresses his concern and annoyance that Papua New Guineans are not distinguishing the UN mission from the Christian missions. See United Nations, Trusteeship Council 12th Session Official Records 472nd Meeting, Wednesday, 1 July 1953 at 2 p.m. New York, T_PV-472-July-1–1953, p. 206.

3. United Nations, Petitions concerning New Guinea: 45th Report of the Standing Committee on Petitions, T/L.377.

4. United Nations, Trusteeship Council 12th Session Official Records 472nd Meeting, Wednesday, 1 July 1953 at 2 p.m., New York, T_PV-472-July-1–1953, p. 186. Soviet questions moments later about what Australia was doing to prepare New Guineans for self-government (ibid., p. 190) could also be read as part of an extended discussion of the Tavuiliu petition, although the Soviet delegation does not make that link overtly.

5. Draft of Visiting Mission report, Trusteeship Council—Visiting Mission to New Guinea 1956, NAA, A452, 1957/91 part 2, p. 8.

6. This sort of development-by-information was a common approach, seen for example in David Lerner's (1958) discussion of modernization in Turkey and the Middle East.

7. Draft of Visiting Mission report, Trusteeship Council—Visiting Mission to New Guinea 1956, NAA, A452, 1957/91 part 2, p. 84.

8. United Nations Visiting Mission to Trust Territories in the Pacific, 1953, Report on New Guinea, T/1078, p. 25.

9. Ibid.

10. United Nations Visiting Mission to Trust Territories in the Pacific, 1956, Report on New Guinea, T/1280, p. 40.

11. Colin Simpson, letter to the editor, *Sydney Morning Herald*, 25 July 1953, included in "Basic English—Use of in Territory," NAA, A452, 1957/2339. Simpson was the author of several widely read books about Papua New Guinea. In the Australian National Archives, relevant letters to the editors of newspapers from prominent figures were frequently clipped and made part of the permanent files on the administration of Papua and New Guinea.

12. Appendix XVII: Composition of the total economically active indigenous population classified for each major group of industry at 31st March, 1956, Report on the Trust Territory of New Guinea 1955/56, Australia Commonwealth Parliament 1957, p. 185.

13. Women were about 1 percent of the labor force in the mid-1950s. Appendix XVII: Number of indigenous workers employed at 31st March, 1956, showing sex, marital status, and age groups classified according to each major group of industry, Report on the Trust Territory of New Guinea 1955/56, Australia Commonwealth Parliament 1957, p. 186. For more on the gender dynamics of labor recruitment, see Jolly (1987).

14. The Lutheran missionary Reverend Freund complained to the Australian administration that it was in fact unethical to send New Guineans out on labor contracts if they did not know Tok Pisin. Missions-Administration Conference, 1954, p. 5, Archives of the Evangelical Lutheran Church of Papua New Guinea.

15. See United Nations, Trusteeship Council Official Records, Tenth Session, 389th Meeting, 3 March 1952 at 2.30 p.m. New York, T/SR.389. Note that a version of this pamphlet that is listed in the WorldCat database identifies it as material for juvenile readers, although at the time the UN Secretariat did not think of it as something aimed only at children.

16. This would have been particularly galling to Australia, which was always trying to promote its work to both the United Nations and the Australian public (see Landman 2010).

17. Undated memo from the Office of the High Commissioner for United Kingdom containing the views of the British Government on the United Nations plan for the dissemination of information, Dissemination of Information of United Nations in Trust—Territory, NAA, A518, 103/1/22 part 1.

18. Trusteeship Council—Visiting Mission 1956, NAA, A452, 1957/91 part 2.

19. See Copy of personal letter to Trevor Pyman, External Affairs from R. Hamilton, Australian Observer with the Visiting Mission, 5 April 1953, NAA, A518/1, 103/1/40 part 1, p. 6.

20. United Nations Visiting Mission to Trust Territories in the Pacific, 1956, Report on New Guinea, T/1280, paragraph 300.

21. Note that the visiting mission report misidentifies "good fella too much" as a noun phrase, rather than as an adjective (*gutpela*) with adverbial intensifier (*tumas*).

22. The Problem of Language: Paper No. 1, Pidgin, Department of Education, January 1955, NAA, A518/1, 103/1/45, p. 2.

23. *Adelaide Advertiser*, "UN Opposition to 'Pidgin' Unreal," July 21, 1953. Articles about the UN demand and Hasluck's comments in response appeared in several different newspapers across Australia.

24. Apparently there were some calls to use Tok Pisin in Dutch New Guinea for the same sort of reasons that Groves and Hall articulated: it was a real language that used "Melanesian" categories and is thus easy to learn for Melanesian people. "Pidgin Niet Ideaal," *de TIFA: Weekblad voor Nieuw-Guinea* vol. 4, no. 186, November 21, 1959, p. 2. Thanks to Rupert Stasch for locating and translating this article.

25. "Basic English—Use of in Territory," NAA, A452, 1957/2339.

26. The pidgin-creole life cycle mapped out an evolutionary progression from an unstable jargon used for the most basic moments of contact and trade, to a grammatically more stable pidgin that had reduced phonologies, morphologies, syntax, and lexicons compared to "normal" languages and was only spoken as a second language, to a creole that had the grammatical and lexical complexity of a "normal" language. Creoles were thought to emerge when pidgin speakers started to have children and the children innovated on the language as they grew up. While there have been some cases of pidgins becoming expanded and used as first languages (Tok Pisin being one of them), most Atlantic creoles have no attested pidgin phase and are better understood as being the outcome of language change as enslaved people learned non-standardized forms of French or English from other laborers or overseers. See DeGraff (2003) and Mufwene (2020) for a fuller critique of this model.

6. DEFYING PREDICTIONS: GLOBAL BUREAUCRACY AND THE ART OF NOT MAKING GUESSES ABOUT THE FUTURE OF NEW GUINEA

1. United Nations, Trusteeship Council: Provisional Questionnaire: As Approved by the Trusteeship Council at the Twenty-Fifth Meeting of Its First Session on 25 April 1947, T/44.

2. United Nations, Compilation of Questions in the Formulation of Questionnaires: Memorandum, Prepared by the Secretariat, 25 March 1947, T/9; United Nations, Delegation of the United States: Draft of a Model Questionnaire for Trust Territories, Item 8 of the Agenda for the First Session of the Trusteeship Council, 8 April 1947, T/24.

3. United Nations, Working Paper on Formulation of Questionnaires, Delegation of the United Kingdom, 18 March 1947, T/6.

4. United Nations, Draft of a Sample Questionnaire, Delegation of France, 27 March 1947, T/11.

5. United Nations, Trusteeship Council Provisional Questionnaire: As Approved by the Trusteeship Council at the Twenty-Fifth Meeting of its First Session on 25 April 1947, T/44, p. 3.

6. Trusteeship Council Questionnaire, undated, Trusteeship Council—Special Questionnaire on New Guinea, National Archives of Australia (NAA), A518, 103/1/72.

7. United Nations, Questionnaire: As Approved by the Trusteeship Council at the 414th Meeting of the 11th Session, 6 June 1952, T/1010.

8. United Nations, Official Record of the 414th Meeting of the Eleventh Session, 6 June 1952, T/PV.414, p. 2.

9. Ibid.

10. Ibid.

11. In the 1950/1951 report, the main text is 82 pages long with an additional 90 pages of appendices. There is a jump, starting with the use of the new questionnaire in 1952/1953, to having about 100 pages of text and another 100 pages of appendices. By 1958/1959, with

the special questionnaire that I discuss below, the report text is 132 pages with 107 pages of appendices.

12. United Nations, Questionnaire: As Approved by the Trusteeship Council at the 414th Meeting of the 11th Session, 6 June 1952, T/1010, p. 6.

13. United Nations, Official Record of the 414th Meeting of the Eleventh Session, 6 June 1952, T/PV.414, p. 2.

14. Trusteeship Council Questionnaire, undated, NAA, A518, 103/1/72.

15. United Nations, Special Questionnaire for the Trust Territory of New Guinea, Approved by the Trusteeship Council at Its 22nd Session, 1959, T/1010/Add.1.

16. United Nations, Questionnaire: As Approved by the Trusteeship Council at the 414th Meeting of the 11th Session, 6 June 1952, T/1010.

17. United Nations, Revision of the Questionnaire Relating to the Trust Territories, 5 July 1956, T/1267, p. 3.

18. Trusteeship Council—16th Session, Opening Statement on the Trust Territory of New Guinea by the Special Representative (Mr. JH Jones), 20 June 1955, Australian Reports on New Guinea, NAA, A1838, 893/2/2 part 5, p. 10. As I have mentioned already, the current estimate is that in the nation-state of Papua New Guinea there are roughly eight hundred languages.

19. Memo from Australian Mission to United Nations, 27 July 1956, Trusteeship Council—Special Questionnaire on New Guinea, NAA, A518, 103/1/72.

20. Comments on Proposed Additions and Revisions of Questionnaire in Respect of New Guinea, 6 July 1956, Trusteeship Council—Special Questionnaire on New Guinea, NAA, A518, 103/1/72.

21. Memo from D. M. Cleland to Secretary, Department of Territories, 7 March 1957, Trusteeship Council—Special Questionnaire on New Guinea, NAA, A518, 103/1/72.

22. United Nations, Revision of Questionnaire Relating to Trust Territories, Working Paper Submitted by Australia Concerning the Third Progress Report of the Sub-committee on the Questionnaire (T/1267), 25 June 1957, T/L.785.

23. United Nations, Special Questionnaire for the Trust Territory of New Guinea, Approved by the Trusteeship Council at Its 22nd Session, 1959, T/1010/Add.1.

24. Questionnaire: As Approved by the Trusteeship Council at the 414th Meeting of the 11th Session, 6 June 1952, T/1010.

25. Memo from Australian Mission to United Nations, 27 June 1956, Trusteeship Council—Special Questionnaire on New Guinea, NAA, A518, 103/1/72.

26. Memo from D. M. Cleland to Secretary, Department of Territories, 7 March 1957, Trusteeship Council—Special Questionnaire on New Guinea, NAA, A518, 103/1/72.

27. Trusteeship Council—19th Session, 4 March 1957, Trusteeship Council—Special Questionnaire on New Guinea, NAA, A518, 103/1/72.

28. The specifically *native* local government councils differed from the town councils that white Australians ran in the urban centers of the territory.

29. Memo from D. M. Cleland to Secretary, Department of Territories, 7 March 1957, Trusteeship Council—Special Questionnaire on New Guinea, NAA, A518, 103/1/72.

30. Memo from Department of Territories, 7 May 1957, Trusteeship Council—Special Questionnaire on New Guinea, NAA, A518, 103/1/72.

31. United Nations, Revision of Questionnaire Relating to Trust Territories, Working Paper Submitted by Australia Concerning the Third Progress Report of the Sub-committee on the Questionnaire (T/1267), 25 June 1957, T/L.785.

32. United Nations, Special Questionnaire for the Trust Territory of New Guinea, Approved by the Trusteeship Council at Its 22nd Session, 1959, T/1010/Add.1.

33. United Nations, Conditions in the Trust Territory of New Guinea, Summary of Observations Made by Individual Members of the Council during the General Discussion and of the Comments of the Representative and Special Representative of the Administering Authority, 8 August 1956, T/L.729, p. 9.

34. Trusteeship Council, Eighteenth Session, Final Statement on New Guinea by the Special Representative, JH Jones, 17 July 1956, NAA, A1838, 893/2/2 part 5, p. 7.

35. Ibid., p. 8.

36. Statement by the Representative of Australia, H.E. Dr. E. Ronald Walker, CBE, 17 July 1956, Trusteeship Council 18th Session: Examination of Developments in the Trust Territory of New Guinea under Australian Administration, Trusteeship Council—Eighteenth Session (Report of Australian Delegation only), NAA, A518, 103/3/20 part 2.

37. Trusteeship Council—Eighteenth Session (Report of Australian Delegation only), NAA, A518, 103/3/20 part 2.

38. New Guinea: "Attainment of Self-Government," 11 July 1956, Trusteeship Council—Eighteenth Session, NAA, A1838891/2/18 part 3.

39. Ibid.

40. Report of the Australian Representative, 27 August 1956, Trusteeship Council—Eighteenth Session (Report of the Australian Delegation only), NAA, A518, 103/3/20 part 2, p. 7.

41. Report of the Department of External Affairs Observer Accompanying the United Nations Visiting Mission to the Trust Territory of New Guinea, 1956, Trusteeship Council—Visiting Mission to New Guinea 1956, Part 2, NAA, A452, 1957/91 part 2.

42. Ibid., p. 17.

43. Ibid., p. 26.

44. Ibid., p. 30.

45. Ibid., p. 32.

46. Ibid.

47. Ibid., p. 35.

48. Ibid., p. 40.

49. Draft of Visiting Mission Report, Trusteeship Council—Visiting Mission to New Guinea 1956, NAA, A452, 1957/91 part 2, p. 40. There were even more descriptions of the Menyamya overexcitement: "When a demonstration of the efficacy of their black palm bows and wooden shields was requested, half a dozen shields were riddled by bowmen who then in an excess of exuberance attacked the shields with axes and clubs and reduced them to splinters, in scarcely more time than it takes to relate the incident" (p. 39).

50. Ibid.

51. Ibid., p. 42.

52. Ibid., p. 3.

53. Ibid., p. xx.

BIBLIOGRAPHY

ARCHIVAL SOURCES

Archives of the Evangelical Lutheran Church in America, Elk Grove Village, Illinois

"About My Visit to the Inland Stations." 1938. By Georg Pilhofer. ALC NG LMF 51/10.

Board of Foreign Missions. Minutes, December 6–7, 1927.

"Dr. John Kuder Interviewed by Rev. John Sievert." 1983. John Sievert's Correspondence and Manuscript of Questions Answered by John Kuder, 1971, 1983, John Kuder Papers.

"A Glimpse at Transportation in Lutheran Mission New Guinea." Undated pamphlet prepared by the Board of Foreign Mission, American Lutheran Church.

Kuder letters to Board of Foreign Mission, 1945. John Kuder Papers.

"A Miracle before Our Eyes." Unpublished and undated typescript manuscript. Rev. Otto F. Theile, Addresses.

"Missionary Methods." Undated. Rev. Otto Theile. ALC 29/8/8/1.

President's Report for 1954. Reports 1936–1976, John Kuder Papers.

President's Report for 1961. Reports 1936–1973, John Kuder Papers.

"Receptivity of the Soul of the Melanesians." 1939. By Frederick Henkelmann. ALC 29.8.7.2.

"Receptivity of the Soul of the Melanesians." Unpublished and undated manuscript. By Frederick Henkelmann. ALC NG LMM 55-20.

Report from Senior Joh. Flierl for 1927. Translated by Wera Wilhelm. LMF 51-10.

"The Secular Involvement." Undated. Unpublished typescript manuscript. John Kuder Papers.

"This Is for Your Information." Undated. ALC 29/8/8/1.

"Transportation." 1934. ALC NG LMM 55-20, 156.1934.12.

"Transportation." Undated. R. R. Hanselmann. LMM 55-20.

"What Should Be the Attitude towards the Pidjin Language in Mission Work." 1930. By Stephen Lehner. ALC NG LMF 55/10.

Archives of the Evangelical Lutheran Church of Papua
New Guinea, Ampo, Morobe, PNG

Carl Spehr to John Kuder letter, 23 March 1957. Christian Radio Missionary Fellowship: 1949–1965 Correspondence.

Claude D'Evelynes to C. R. Lambert letter, 16 October 1962. Christian Radio Missionary Fellowship: 1949–1965 Correspondence.

Claude D'Evelynes to John Kuder letter, 30 October 1953. Christian Radio Missionary Fellowship: 1949–1965 Correspondence.

Claude D'Evelynes to John Kuder letter, 9 December 1953. Christian Radio Missionary Fellowship: 1949–1965 Correspondence.

Claude D'Evelyns to John Kuder letter, 7 May 1957. Christian Radio Missionary Fellowship: 1949–1965 Correspondence.

Conlon to Johnson letter, 16 August 1962. Christian Radio Missionary Fellowship: 1949–1965 Correspondence.

John Kuder to Claude D'Evelynes letter, 1 December 1953. Christian Radio Missionary Fellowship: 1949–1965 Correspondence.

John Kuder to Claude D'Evelynes letter, 10 December 1953. Christian Radio Missionary Fellowship: 1949–1965 Correspondence.

John Kuder to Paul Hasluck letter, 22 October 1959. Lutheran Mission New Guinea: Educational Questions 1956–60.

John Kuder to Translations Secretary letter, 9 January 1950. Correspondence with British & Foreign Bible Society.

Lae Wampar, Annual Conference Reports, 1952.

List of stations. Christian Radio Missionary Fellowship: 1949–1965 Correspondence.

Minutes, Annual Conference, 1955.

Missions-Administration Conference, 1954.

Missions-Administration Conference, 1959.

Missions-Administration Conference, 1961.

Mumeng and Lae, Annual Conference Reports, 1953.

"The Native Labor Program of the Mission." By Theodore G. Braun. Conference Papers, 1953.

Radio and Electrical Workshop, Annual Conference Report, 1967.

Radio and Electrical Workshop, Annual Conference Report, 1968.

Radio and Electrical Workshop, Annual Conference Report, 1970.

Statement of the CRMF, undated but possibly 1 April 1954. Christian Radio Missionary Fellowship: 1949–1965 Correspondence.

UECLA-NG General–Personal Donations for Aircraft 1934–1935.

National Archives of Australia, Canberra

Appendix XVII: Composition of the total economically active indigenous population classified for each major group of industry at 31st March, 1956, Report on the Trust Territory of New Guinea 1955/56, Australia Commonwealth Parliament 1957, p. 185.

Appendix XVII: Number of indigenous workers employed at 31st March, 1956, showing sex, marital status, and age groups classified according to each major group of industry, Report on the Trust Territory of New Guinea 1955/56, Australia Commonwealth Parliament 1957, p. 186.

Basic English—Use of in Territory. 1957. NAA, A452, 1957/2339.

Christian Radio Missionary Fellowship Proposals for Christian Broadcasting Station in New Guinea, March, 1954. NAA, A452/1, 1965/6099.

Comments on Proposed Additions and Revisions of Questionnaire in Respect of New Guinea. 6 July 1956. Trusteeship Council—Special Questionnaire on New Guinea. NAA, A518 103/1/72.

Comments on the State Department Note of 11 October 1956. Trusteeship Council Eighteenth Session. NAA, A1838, 891/2/18 part 4.

Communications—New Guinea and Papua—Use of aerial ropeways in New Guinea as a means of transport. 1951. NAA, A518, BD808/1.

Copy of personal letter to Trevor Pyman. External Affairs from R. Hamilton, Australian Observer with the Visiting Mission, 5 April 1953, p. 6. NAA, A518/1, 103/1/40 part 1.

Copy of proclamation in "Pidgin" English by Australian Military Government to natives of German New Guinea. 12 September 1914. Australian War Memorial 33 [28].

Department of External Affairs, Inward Cablegram 480, from the Australian Mission to the United Nations, 31 July 1956. Trusteeship Council Eighteenth Session. NAA, A1838, 891/2/18 part 3.

Department of External Affairs, Inward Cablegram 486, from the Australian Mission to the United Nations, 2 August 1956. Trusteeship Council Eighteenth Session. NAA, A1838, 891/2/18 part 3.

Draft of Visiting Mission Report. Trusteeship Council—Visiting Mission to New Guinea 1956. NAA, A452, 1957/91 part 2.

Eighteenth Session of Trusteeship Council—July/August, 1956; Examination of 1954–55 New Guinea Report. Conclusions and Recommendations Adopted by the Council on New Guinea. Trusteeship Council—Examination of New Guinea Report 1954/55. NAA, A518/1, 103/4/16.

Foreign Propaganda Broadcasts—Monitoring of in Papua and New Guinea. 1952. NAA, A518, 2/V926/1/6.

Information Handbook, Visit of the United Nations Visiting Mission to the Trust Territory of New Guinea, 13 March 1953 to 15 April 1953. Typescript manuscript. Visiting Mission 1953—New Guinea. NAA, A518, 103/1/40 part 1.

Memo from Australian Mission to United Nations. 27 July 1956. Trusteeship Council—Special Questionnaire on New Guinea. NAA, A518, 103/1/72.

Memo from D. M. Cleland to Secretary, Department of Territories. 7 March 1957. Trusteeship Council—Special Questionnaire on New Guinea. NAA, A518, 103/1/72.

Memo from Department of Territories. 7 May 1957. Trusteeship Council—Special Questionnaire on New Guinea. NAA, A518, 103/1/72.

Memo from Department of Territories. Undated [likely February 1957]. NAA, A1838, 891/2/18 part 4.

New Guinea: "Attainment of Self-Government." 11 July 1956. Trusteeship Council—Eighteenth Session. NAA, A1838891/2/18 part 3.

Notes of Conference with Visiting Mission in Canberra on 23 and 24 April 1956. NAA, A518, 1/103/1/45.

Observations by UN Trusteeship Council on Multiplicity of Religious Missions in New Guinea. 1959. NAA, A452, 1959/5433.

Overseas Broadcasting Service, ABC Radio Australia. International Report, Progress in New Guinea by EWP Chinnery. For broadcast 14–15 June 1955. NAA, A1838, 893/2/2 part 5.

The Problem of Language: Paper No. 1, Pidgin. Department of Education, January 1955. NAA, A518, 1/103/1/45.

Report of the Department of External Affairs Observer Accompanying the United Nations Visiting Mission to the Trust Territory of New Guinea, 1956. Trusteeship Council—Visiting Mission to New Guinea 1956, Part 2, NAA, A452, 1957/91 part 2.

Statement by the Representative of Australia, H.E. Dr. E. Ronald Walker, CBE. 17 July 1956. Trusteeship Council 18th Session: Examination of Developments in the Trust Territory of New Guinea under Australian Administration. Trusteeship Council—Eighteenth Session (Report of Australian Delegation only). NAA, A518, 103/3/20 part 2.

Translation of enclosure in letter no. 40/1073, dated 23 April 1940, from O. Theile, Brisbane, to the Superintendent, Lutheran Mission, Finschhafen, Lutheran Mission Aircraft— New Guinea. NAA, MP508/1, 31/701/37.

Trusteeship Council—16th Session. Opening Statement on the Trust Territory of New Guinea by the Special Representative (Mr. JH Jones), 20 June 1955. Australian Reports on New Guinea. NAA, A1838, 893/2/2 part 5.

Trusteeship Council—19th Session. 4 March 1957. Trusteeship Council—Special Questionnaire on New Guinea. NAA, A518, 103/1/72.

Trusteeship Council—Eighteenth Session. Final Statement on New Guinea by the Special Representative, JH Jones, 17 July 1956. NAA, A1838, 893/2/2 part 5.

Trusteeship Council—Eighteenth Session (Report of the Australian Delegation only), 1956. NAA, A518, 103/3/20 part 2.

Trusteeship Council—Use of Pidgin English in Trust Territory of New Guinea. 1956. NAA, A518, 1/103/1/45.

Trusteeship Council—Visiting Mission 1956. NAA, A452, 1957/91 part 2.

Trusteeship Council Questionnaire, undated. NAA, A518, 103/1/72.

Undated memo from the Office of the High Commissioner for United Kingdom containing the views of the British Government on the United Nations plan for the dissemination of information. Dissemination of Information of United Nations in Trust—Territory. NAA, A518, 103/1/22 part 1.

Visiting mission—1953—New Guinea. NAA, A518, 103/1/40/part 1.

National Archives of Papua New Guinea, Port Moresby, PNG

Nomad No. 3 of 1972/73 Patrol Report. Appendix no. 7.

Newspapers

Adelaide Advertiser. UN Opposition to 'Pidgin' Unreal. July 21, 1953.

The Advertiser. New Guinea Missions. October 28, 1939.

The Age. The Bush Telegraph in Many Lands: Primitive Methods of Communication. February 16, 1952, p. 9.

The Age. The 'Reach' of Teleradio. September 16, 1938.

Ashfield, F. M. Telepathy? *Smith's Weekly*, November 2, 1946, p. 18.

de TIFA: Weekblad voor Nieuw-Guinea. Pidgin Niet Ideaal. Vol. 4, no. 186, November 21, 1959, p. 2.

Dexter, Henry. Bush Telegraph, Telepathy—or What? *Pacific Islands Monthly* vol. 2, no. 12, July 19, 1933, p. 13.

Folkard, F. C. Clash Soon in New Guinea. *The Sun*, March 20, 1942.

Johnston, George H. Tribes in Turmoil: How the 'Bush Telegraph' Works in New Guinea. *Sydney Morning Herald*, March 21, 1942, p. 7.

Macdonald, N. W. Can Anyone Explain This Queer Case? (Letter to the Editor). *Pacific Islands Monthly* vol. 23, no. 11, June 1, 1953, p. 41.

The Mercury. Clash Likely, Japanese Advance in New Guinea. March 21, 1942.

Northern Star (Australia). Radio Telephony for Planes. January 5, 1938.

Pacific Islands Monthly. Calling Rarotonga? Vol. 17, no. 12, July 18, 1947, p. 28.

Pacific Islands Monthly. P-NG Man Gaoled for Sedition. February 1961, p. 20.

Periti. How Did Mina Know! *Pacific Islands Monthly* vol. 24, no. 11, June 1, 1954, p. 83.

Poole, L. 'Black Magic': How Do Islanders Communicate? *Pacific Islands Monthly* vol. 24, no. 4, November 1, 1953, p. 55.

Queensland Times. Aeroplanes in Mission Work. August 2, 1939.

Robson, R. W. From Notes Made in New Guinea. *Pacific Islands Monthly* vol. 24, no. 2, September 1, 1953, p. 20.

Sutton, Ralph. One-Teach-One, the Laubach System. *Pacific Islands Monthly* vol. 21, no. 2, September 1, 1950, p. 81–83.

Tolala. Territories Talk-Talk. *Pacific Islands Monthly* vol. 26, no. 11, June 1, 1956, p. 31.

Pacific Manuscripts Bureau

Report on Mass Communications to His Honour the Administrator and the Public Service Commissioner from Committee of Enquiry, headed by L. F. Butler. July 9, 1959. p. 23. Territory of Papua and New Guinea: Miscellaneous Typescripts Reports, 1952–1959. Pacific Manuscripts Bureau 608.

United Nations Documents

Compilation of Questions in the Formulation of Questionnaires: Memorandum, Prepared by the Secretariat. 25 March 1947. T/9.

Conditions in the Trust Territory of New Guinea. Summary of Observations Made by Individual Members of the Council during the General Discussion and of the Comments of the Representative and Special Representative of the Administering Authority, 8 August 1956. T/L.729.

Delegation of the United States: Draft of a Model Questionnaire for Trust Territories. Item 8 of the Agenda for the First Session of the Trusteeship Council. 8 April 1947. T/24.

Draft of a Sample Questionnaire, Delegation of France. 27 March 1947. T/11.

Official Record of the 414th Meeting of the Eleventh Session, 6 June 1952. T/PV.414.

Petitions Concerning New Guinea: 45th Report of the Standing Committee on Petitions. 13 July 1953. T/L.377.

Questionnaire: As Approved by the Trusteeship Council at the 414th Meeting of the 11th Session, 6 June 1952. T/1010.

Revision of Questionnaire Relating to Trust Territories. Working Paper Submitted by Australia Concerning the Third Progress Report of the Sub-committee on the Questionnaire (T/1267). 25 June 1957. T/L.785.

Revision of the Questionnaire Relating to the Trust Territories. 5 July 1956. T/1267.

Special Questionnaire for the Trust Territory of New Guinea. Approved by the Trusteeship Council at Its 22nd Session. 1959. T/1010/Add.1.

Trusteeship Council 12th Session Official Records 472nd Meeting, Wednesday, 1 July 1953 at 2 p.m. New York. T_PV-472-July-1-1953.

Trusteeship Council Official Records, Tenth Session, 389th Meeting, 3 March 1952 at 2.30 p.m. New York. T/SR.389.

Trusteeship Council Provisional Questionnaire: As Approved by the Trusteeship Council at the Twenty-Fifth Meeting of Its First Session on 25 April 1947. T/44.

United Nations Visiting Mission to Trust Territories in the Pacific, 1953, Report on New Guinea. T/1078.

United Nations Visiting Mission to Trust Territories in the Pacific, 1956, Report on New Guinea. T/1280.

Working Paper on Formulation of Questionnaires, Delegation of the United Kingdom. 18 March 1947. T/6.

SECONDARY SOURCES

Agha, Asif. 2011. Commodity registers. *Journal of Linguistic Anthropology* 21(1): 22–53.

Allen, Bryant J. 1976. Information Flow and Innovation Diffusion in the East Sepik District, Papua New Guinea. PhD dissertation, Australian National University.

Anderson, Benedict. 1991. *Imagined Communities: Reflections on the Origin and Spread of Nationalism*. Revised edition. London: Verso.

Ardener, Edwin. 1987. Remote Areas: Some Theoretical Considerations. In *Anthropology at Home*, edited by Anthony Jackson. London: Tavistock. Pp. 38–54.

Aufinger, Albert. 1949. Secret Languages of the Small Islands near Madang. *South Pacific* 3: 90–95, 113–19.

Australian Commonwealth Parliament. 1957. Report to the General Assembly of the United Nations on the Administration of the Territory of New Guinea for Year 1955–56. Canberra: The Parliament of the Commonwealth of Australia. P. 185.

Bakhtin, M. M. 1981. *The Dialogic Imagination: Four Essays*. Edited by Michael Holquist. Translated by Caryl Emerson and Michael Holquist. Austin: University of Texas Press.

Banivanua Mar, Tracey. 2007. *Violence and Colonial Dialogue: The Australian-Pacific Indentured Labor Trade*. Honolulu: University of Hawai'i Press.

———. 2016. *Decolonisation and the Pacific: Indigenous Globalisation and the Ends of Empire*. Cambridge: Cambridge University Press.

Barker, John. 2008. Where the Missionary Ran Ahead of Empire. In *Missions and Empire*, edited by Norman Etherington. New York: Oxford University Press. Pp. 86–106.

Baskett, Geoffrey. 1991. *Islands and Mountains*. Privately published.

Bauman, Richard, and Charles L. Briggs. 1990. Poetics and Performances as Critical Perspectives on Language and Social Life. *Annual Review of Anthropology* 19: 59–88.

———. 2000. Language Philosophy as Language Ideology: John Locke and Johann Gottfried Herder. *Regimes of Language: Ideologies, Polities, and Identities*, edited by Paul V. Kroskrity. Santa Fe, NM: SAR Press. Pp. 139–204.

Bayly, C. A. 1996. *Empire and Information: Intelligence Gathering and Social Communication in India, 1780–1870*. Cambridge: Cambridge University Press.

Beer, Bettina, and Willem Church. 2019. Roads to Inequality: Infrastructure and Historically Grown Regional Differences in the Markham Valley, Papua New Guinea. *Oceania* 89(1): 2–19.

Bergmann, Wilhelm. n.d. *Vierzig Jahre in Neuguinea. Band V.* Typescript manuscript, https://library.ucsd.edu/dc/object/bb18447733.

Bessire, Lucas. 2012. "We Go Above": Media Metaphysics and Making Moral Life on Ayoreo Two-Way Radio. In *Radio Fields: Anthropology and Wireless Sound in the 21st Century*, edited by Lucas Bessire and Daniel Fischer. New York: New York University Press. Pp. 197–214.

Blanton, Anderson. 2012. Appalachian Radio Prayers: The Prosthesis of the Holy Ghost and the Drive to Tactility. In *Radio Fields: Anthropology and Wireless Sound in the 21st Century*, edited by Lucas Bessire and Daniel Fischer. New York: New York University Press. Pp. 215–32.

Blommaert, Jan, and Jef Verschueren. 1995. The Role of Language in European Nationalist Ideologies. In *Language and Peace*, edited by Christina Schäffne and Anita L. Wenden. London: Routledge. Pp. 139–64.

Bolter, J. David, and Richard Grusin. 1999. *Remediation: Understanding New Media*. Cambridge, MA: MIT Press.

Bolton, Lissant. 1999. Radio and the Redefinition of Kastom in Vanuatu. *The Contemporary Pacific* 11(2): 335–60.

Borges, Jorge Luis. 1964. The Analytical Language of John Wilkins. In *Other Inquisitions*. Translated by Ruth L. C. Simms. Austin: University of Texas Press. Pp. 101–5.

Bowker, Geoffrey C., and Susan Leigh Star. 2000. *Sorting Things Out: Classification and Its Consequences*. Cambridge, MA: MIT Press.

Brash, Elton. 1971. Tok Pilai, Tok Piksa, na Tok Bokis: Imaginative Dimensions in Melanesian Pidgin. *Kivung* 4(1): 12–20.

Browne, Bob. 2006. *Grass Roots Guide to Papua New Guinea Pidgin*. Port Moresby: Grass Roots Comic Co.

Burridge, Kenelm. 1995 [1960]. *Mambu: A Melanesian Millennium*. Princeton, NJ: Princeton University Press.

Cameron, Deborah. 2012. English as a Global Commodity. In *The Oxford Handbook of the History of English*, edited by Tettu Nevalainen and Elizabeth Cross Traugott. Oxford: Oxford University Press. Pp. 352–61.

Capell, Arthur. 1955. Review of *Hands Off Pidgin English!* By Robert A. Hall, Jr. *Oceania* 26(1): 72–74.

———. 1959. Review of *Grammar and Dictionary of Neo-Melanesian* by Francis Mihalic, SVD. *Oceania* 29(3): 234–35.

Carey, James W. 1989. Technology and Ideology: The Case of the Telegraph. In *Communication as Culture: Essays on Media and Society*. London: Routledge. Pp. 201–30.

Carpenter, Edmund. 1972. *Oh, What a Blow That Phantom Gave Me!* New York: Holt, Rinehart, and Winston.

Carr, E. Summerson, and Michael Lempert. 2016. Introduction: The Pragmatics of Scale. In *Scale: Discourse and Dimensions of Social Life*. Oakland: University of California Press. Pp. 1–21.

Cass, Philip. 1999. Tok Pisin and Tok Ples as Languages of Identification in Papua New Guinea. *Media Development* 4: 28–33.

Chakrabarty, Dipesh. 2000. *Provincializing Europe: Postcolonial Thought and Historical Difference*. Princeton, NJ: Princeton University Press.

———. 2010. The Legacies of Bandung: Decolonization and the Politics of Culture. In *Making a World After Empire: The Bandung Moment and Its Political Afterlives*, edited by Christopher J. Lee. Athens: Ohio University Press. Pp. 45–68.

Chatterjee, Partha. 1986. *Nationalist Thought and the Colonial World: A Derivative Discourse?* London: Zed Books.

Cohn, B. S. 1996. The Command of Language and the Language of Command. In *Colonialism and Its Forms of Knowledge: The British in India*. Princeton, NJ: Princeton University Press.

Collins, Michael. 2013. Decolonisation and the "Federal Moment." *Diplomacy & Statecraft* 24(1): 21–40.

Connolly, Bob, and Robin Anderson. 1988. *First Contact*. New York: Penguin.

Cooper, Frederick. 2012. Decolonisation and Citizenship: Africa between Empires and a World of Nations. In *Beyond Empire and Nation: Decolonizing Societies in Africa and Asia, 1930–1970s*, edited by Els Bogaerts and Remco Raben. Leiden, The Netherlands: KITLV Press. Pp. 39–68.

Courage, Michael, and Dermot Wright. 1967. *New Guinea Venture*. London: Hale.

Cowan, Jane. 2013. Before Audit Culture: A Genealogy of International Oversight of Rights. In *The Gloss of Harmony: The Politics of Policy Making in Multilateral Organisations*, edited by Birgit Müller. London: Pluto Press. Pp. 103–33.

Cutts, Elmer H. 1953. The Background of Macaulay's Minute. *The American Historical Review* 58(4): 824–53.

Davis, Jenny L. 2018. *Talking Indian: Identity and Language Revitalization in the Chickasaw Renaissance*. Tucson: University of Arizona Press.

Day, Ronald E. 2001. *The Modern Invention of Information: Discourse, History, and Power*. Carbondale: Southern Illinois University Press.

DeGraff, Michel. 2003. Against Creole Exceptionalism. *Language* 79(2): 391–410.

Demian, Melissa. 2021. *In Memory of Times to Come: Ironies of History in Southeastern Papua New Guinea*. New York: Berghahn Books.

Denoon, Donald. 2012. *A Trial Separation: Australia and the Decolonisation of Papua New Guinea*. Canberra: Australian National University Press.

Desai, Bharat H. 2021. A New Mandate for the Revived UN Trusteeship Council. *Environmental Policy and Law* 51(1–2): 97–109.

Dixon, Robert. 2001. *Prosthetic Gods: Travel, Representation and Colonial Governance*. Brisbane: University of Queensland Press.

Dobrin, Lise, and Alex Golub. 2020. The Legacy of Bernard Narakobi and the Melanesian Way. *The Journal of Pacific History* 55(2): 149–64.

Downs, Ian. 1980. *The Australian Trusteeship Papua New Guinea, 1945–1975*. Canberra: Australian Government Publishing Service.

Downs, Troy. 2000. Host of Midian: The Chapati Circulation and the Indian Revolt of 1857–58. *Studies in History* 16(1): 75–107.

Dumont d'Urville, Jules-Sébastien-César. 2003 [1832]. On the Islands of the Great Ocean. *The Journal of Pacific History* 38(2): 163–74.

Durkheim, Emile. 2014 [1893]. *The Division of Labor in Society*. Edited by Steven Lukes. Translated by W. D. Halls. New York: Free Press.

Dutton, Thomas. 1985. *Police Motu: Iena Sivarai (Its Story)*. Port Moresby: University of Papua New Guinea Press.

Dwyer, Peter, and Monica Minnegal. 2023. A Road, a Border, and Development in New Guinea. *The Asia Pacific Journal of Anthropology* 24(4): 251–71.

Edmundson, Anna. 2022. 'Preserving the Papuan': JHP Murray and Doomed Race Theory in Papua New Guinea. *History and Anthropology* 33(2): 243–62.

Edwards, Paul. 2003. Infrastructure and Modernity: Force, Time, and Social Organization in the History of Sociotechnical Systems. In *Modernity and Technology*, edited by Thomas J. Misa, Philip Brey, and Andrew Feenberg. Cambridge, MA: MIT Press.

Edwards, Terra. 2018. Re-channeling Language: The Mutual Restructuring of Language and Infrastructure among Deafblind People at Gallaudet University. *Journal of Linguistic Anthropology* 28(3): 273–92.

Errington, Joseph. 2003. *Linguistics in a Colonial World: A Story of Language, Meaning, and Power*. Oxford: Blackwell.

Feld, Steven. 1982. *Sound and Sentiment: Birds, Weeping, Poetics, and Song in Kaluli Expression*. Philadelphia: University of Pennsylvania Press.

Feldman, Ilana. 2008. *Governing Gaza: Bureaucracy, Authority, and the Work of Rule, 1917–1967*. Durham, NC: Duke University Press.

Firth, Stewart. 1976. The Transformation of the Labour Trade in German New Guinea, 1899–1914. *The Journal of Pacific History* 11(1): 51–65.

Fishman, Joshua. 1968. Nationality-Nationalism and Nation-Nationalism. In *Language Problems of Developing Nations*, edited by Joshua Fishman, Charles Ferguson, and Jyotirindra Das Gupta. New York: Wiley.

Fitzpatrick, Peter. 1980. Really Rather Like Slavery: Law and Labor in the Colonial Economy in Papua New Guinea. *Contemporary Crises* 4: 77–95.

Fitzpatrick, Philip. 2005. *Bamahuta: Leaving Papua*. Canberra, Australia: Pandanus Books.

Fleming, Luke. 2015. Taxonomy and Taboo: The (Meta) Pragmatic Sources of Semantic Abstraction in Avoidance Registers. *Journal of Linguistic Anthropology* 25(1): 43–65.

———. n.d. On Subalternating Sounds: The Whorfian Projection of 'Primitive Language' in 19th Century Anthropology. Unpublished manuscript.

Flierl, Johannes. 1936. *Is the New Guinea Primitive Race Destined to Perish at the Hands of European Civilization?* Tanunda, South Australia: Uaricht's Printing Office.

Foster, Robert J. 2023. Tenuous Connectivity: Time, Citizenship, and Infrastructure in a Papua New Guinea Telecommunications Network. *The Asia Pacific Journal of Anthropology* 24(2): 91–115.

———. 2024. *Uneven Connections: A Partial History of the Mobile Phone in Papua New Guinea*. Canberra: Australian National University Press.

Foster, Robert, and Heather A. Horst. 2018. Introduction. In *The Moral Economy of Mobile Phones: Pacific Islands Perspectives*, edited by Robert Foster and Heather A. Horst. Canberra: Australian National University Press. Pp. 1–17.

Franklin, Karl. 1972. A Ritual Pandanus Language of New Guinea. *Oceania* 43(1): 61–76.

Fricke, Theodore. 1947. *We Found Them Waiting*. Columbus, OH: Wartburg Press.

Fritzsche, Peter. 1992. *A Nation of Fliers: German Aviation and the Popular Imagination*. Cambridge, MA: Harvard University Press.

Gage, Justin. 2020. *We Do Not Want the Gates Closed between Us: Native Networks and the Spread of the Ghost Dance*. Norman: University of Oklahoma Press.

Gal, Susan. 2018. Registers in Circulation: The Social Organization of Interdiscursivity. *Signs and Society* 6(1): 1–24.

Gal, Susan, and Judith Irvine. 2019. *Signs of Difference: Language and Ideology in Social Life.* Cambridge: Cambridge University Press.

Gammage, Bill. 1975. The Rabaul Strike, 1929. *The Journal of Pacific History* 10(3): 3–29.

Gardner, Helen, and Christopher Waters. 2013. Decolonisation in Melanesia: Introduction. *The Journal of Pacific History* 48(2): 113–21.

Gershon, Ilana. 2010. Media Ideologies: An Introduction. *Journal of Linguistic Anthropology* 20(2): 283–93.

———. 2019. Porous Social Orders. *American Ethnologist* 46(4): 404–16.

Getachew, Adom. 2019. *Worldmaking after Empire: The Rise and Fall of Self-Determination.* Princeton, NJ: Princeton University Press.

Golub, Alex. 2024. Never a Colony? Rethinking the Colonisation of Enga Province, Papua New Guinea. *Oceania* 94(2): 103–17.

Golub, Alex, and Courtney Handman. 2024. Introduction to Special Issue "Rethinking Decolonisation in Papua New Guinea." *Oceania* 94(2): 44–54.

Graham, Laura R. 2002. How Should an Indian Speak? Amazonian Indians and the Symbolic Politics of Language in the Global Public Sphere. In *Indigenous Movements, Self-Representation, and the State in Latin America,* edited by Kay B. Warren and Jean E. Jackson. Austin: University of Texas Press. Pp. 181–228.

Guha, Ranajit. 1983. *Elementary Aspects of Peasant Insurgency in Colonial India.* Delhi: Oxford University Press.

———. 2003. *History at the Limit of World-History.* New York: Columbia University Press.

Guillory, John. 2010. Genesis of the Media Concept. *Critical Inquiry* 36(2): 321–62.

Habermas, Jürgen. 1989. *The Structural Transformation of the Public Sphere: An Inquiry into a Category of Bourgeois Society.* Translated by Thomas Burger with the assistance of Frederick Lawrence. Cambridge: Polity Press.

Hage, Hartley. 1986. Languages and Schools. In *The Lutheran Church of Papua New Guinea: The First Hundred Years, 1886–1986.* Adelaide, Australia: Lutheran Publishing House. Pp. 409–41.

Hall, Robert A., Jr. 1953. *Haitian Creole: Grammar, Texts, Vocabulary. American Anthropologist.* Memoir 74. Washington, DC: American Anthropological Association.

———. 1955. *Hands Off Pidgin English!* Sydney, Australia: Pacific Publications.

———. 1958. Creolized Languages and 'Genetic Relationships.' *Word* 14(2): 367–73.

———. 1962. The Life Cycle of Pidgin Languages. *Lingua* 11: 151–56.

Hallpike, Christopher R. 1977. *Bloodshed and Vengeance in the Papuan Mountains: The Generation of Conflict in Tauade Society.* Oxford: Clarendon Press.

Halvorson, Britt. 2018. *Conversionary Sites: Transforming Medical Aid and Global Christianity from Madagascar to Minnesota.* Chicago: University of Chicago Press.

Handman, Courtney. 2015. *Critical Christianity: Translation and Denominational Conflict in Papua New Guinea.* Oakland: University of California Press.

———. 2017a. Languages without Subjects: On the Interior(s) of Colonial New Guinea. *HAU: Journal of Ethnographic Theory* 7(1): 207–28.

———. 2017b. Walking Like a Christian: Roads, Translation, and Gendered Bodies as Religious Infrastructure in Papua New Guinea. *American Ethnologist* 44(2): 315–27.

———. 2019a. A Few Grass Huts: Denominational Ambivalence and Infrastructural Form in Colonial New Guinea. *Anthropological Quarterly* 92(4): 1015–38.

———. 2019b. The Spatiotemporal Transformations of Lutheran Airplanes. *Signs and Society* 7(1): 68–95.

———. 2024. Ritual, Media, and the Here-and-Now of Decolonization. In *The Oxford Handbook of Ritual Language*, edited by David Tavárez. Oxford: Oxford University Press. Pp. 207–27.

Harms, Erik, Shafqat Hussain, Sasha Newell, Charles Piot, Louisa Schein, Sara Shneiderman, Terence Turner, and Juan Zhang. 2014. Remote and Edgy: New Takes on Old Anthropological Themes. *HAU: Journal of Ethnographic Theory* 4(1): 361–81.

Harrison, Simon. 1993. The Commerce of Cultures in Melanesia. *Man* 28(1): 139–58.

Hau'ofa, Epeli. 1994. Our Sea of Islands. *The Contemporary Pacific* 6(1): 147–61.

Hayano, Dan. 1990. *Road through the Rain Forest: Living Anthropology in Highland Papua New Guinea*. Long Grove, IL: Waveland Press.

Hayek, F. A. 1945. The Use of Knowledge in Society. *The American Economic Review* 35(4): 519–30.

Hayes, Joy. 2000. *Radio Nation: Communication, Popular Culture, and Nationalism in Mexico, 1920–1950*. Tucson: University of Arizona Press.

Hayles, N. Katherine. 1999. *How We Became Posthuman: Virtual Bodies in Cybernetics, Literature, and Informatics*. Chicago: University of Chicago Press.

Healey, Christopher. 1990. *Maring Hunters and Traders: Production and Exchange in the Papua New Guinea Highlands*. Berkeley: University of California Press.

Heatherington, Kregg. 2012. *Guerrilla Auditors: The Politics of Transparency in Neoliberal Paraguay*. Durham, NC: Duke University Press.

Heller, Monica. 2006. *Linguistic Minorities and Modernity: A Sociolinguistic Ethnography*. Second edition. London: Continuum.

———. 2010. Language as Resource in the Globalized New Economy. *The Handbook of Language and Globalization*, edited by Nikolas Coupland. London: Wiley. Pp. 347–65.

Hess, Michael. 1983. "In the Long Run . . .": Australian Colonial Labour Policy in the Territory of Papua and New Guinea. *Journal of Industrial Relations* 25(1): 51–67.

Hoenigman, Darja. 2012. From Mountain Talk to Hidden Talk: Continuity and Change in Awiakay Registers. In *Melanesian Languages on the Edge of Asia: Challenges for the 21st Century*, edited by Nicholas Evans and Marian Klamer. Honolulu: University of Hawa'i Press. Pp. 191–218.

Huber, Mary Taylor. 1988. *The Bishop's Progress: A Historical Ethnography of Catholic Missionary Experience on the Sepik Frontier*. Washington, DC: Smithsonian Institution Press.

Hudson, W. J. 1966. Australia and the Colonial Question at the United Nations. PhD dissertation, Australia National University.

———. 1970. *Australia and the Colonial Question at the United Nations*. Sydney, Australia: Sydney University Press.

Hull, Matthew. 2012. *Government of Paper: The Materiality of Bureaucracy in Urban Pakistan*. Berkeley: University of California Press.

Imlay, Talbot C. 2013. International Socialism and Decolonization during the 1950s: Competing Rights and the Postcolonial Order. *The American Historical Review* 118(4): 1105–32.

Innis, Harold. 2007 [1950]. *Empire and Communication.* Lanham, MD: Rowman and Littlefield.

Jaffe, Alexandra. 1999. *Ideologies in Action: Language Politics in Corsica.* Berlin: Walter de Gruyter.

Jakobson, Roman. 1960. Closing Statement: Linguistics and Poetics. In *Style in Language,* edited by Thomas Sebeok. Cambridge, MA: MIT Press. Pp. 350–77.

Jebens, Holger, ed. 2004. *Cargo, Cult, and Culture Critique.* Honolulu: University of Hawai'i Press.

Jolly, Margaret. 1987. The Forgotten Women: A History of Migrant Labour and Gender Relations in Vanuatu. *Oceania* 58(2): 119–39.

Joseph, John E. 2000. *Limiting the Arbitrary: Linguistic Naturalism and Its Opposites in Plato's* Cratylus *and Modern Theories of Language.* Amsterdam: John Benjamins.

Keane, Webb. 2007. *Christian Moderns: Freedom and Fetish in the Mission Encounter.* Berkeley: University of California Press.

Keck, Margaret E., and Kathryn Sikkink. 2014. *Activists beyond Borders: Advocacy Networks in International Politics.* Cornell, NY: Cornell University Press.

Kelly, John D., and Martha Kaplan. 2001. *Represented Communities: Fiji and World Decolonization.* Chicago: University of Chicago Press.

Kik, Alfred, Martin Adamec, Alexandra Y. Aikhenvald, Jarmila Bajzekova, Nigel Baro, Claire Bowern, Robert K. Colwell . . . and Vojtech Novotny. 2021. Language and Ethnobiological Skills Decline Precipitously in Papua New Guinea, the World's Most Linguistically Diverse Nation. *Proceedings of the National Academy of Sciences USA* 118(22): e2100096118.

Kittler, Friedrich. 1999. *Gramophone, Film, Typewriter.* Translated by Geoffrey Winthrop-Young and Michael Wutz. Stanford, CA: Stanford University Press.

Kulick, Don. 1992. *Language Shift and Cultural Reproduction.* Cambridge: Cambridge University Press.

Kunreuther, Laura. 2014. *Voicing Subjects: Public Intimacy and Mediation in Kathmandu.* Oakland: University of California Press.

Laidlaw, Zoë. 2005. *Colonial Connections 1815–45: Patronage, the Information Revolution and Colonial Government.* Manchester, UK: Manchester University Press.

Landman, Jane. 2010. Visualising the Subject of Development: 1950s Government Film-Making in the Territories of Papua and New Guinea. *The Journal of Pacific History* 45(1): 71–88.

Larkin, Brian. 2008. *Signal and Noise: Media, Culture, and Urban Culture in Nigeria.* Durham, NC: Duke University Press.

Lawrence, Peter. 1964. *Road Belong Cargo: A Study of the Cargo Movement in Southern Madang District.* Melbourne, Australia: Melbourne University Press.

Laycock, Donald. 1982. Tok Pisin: A Melanesia Solution to the Problem of Melanesian Linguistic Diversity. In *Melanesia: Beyond Diversity,* edited by R. J. May and Hank Nelson. Canberra: Research School of Pacific Studies, Australia National University. Pp. 263–71.

Lee, Benjamin. 1995. Performing the People. *Pragmatics* 5(2): 263–80.

Lee, Benjamin, and Edward LiPuma. 2002. Cultures of Circulation: The Imaginations of Modernity. *Public Culture* 14(1): 191–213.

Lee, Christopher J., ed. 2010. *Making a World after Empire: The Bandung Moment and Its Political Afterlives.* Athens: Ohio University Press.

Lemberg, D. 2018. "The Universal Language of the Future": Decolonization, Development, and the American Embrace of Global English, 1945–1965. *Modern Intellectual History* 15(2): 561–92.

Lemon, Alaina. 2013. Touching the Gap: Social Qualia and Cold War Contact. *Anthropological Theory* 13(1–2): 67–88.

———. 2018. *Technologies for Intuition: Cold War Circles and Telepathic Rays*. Oakland: University of California Press.

Lerner, D. 1958. *The Passing of Traditional Society: Modernizing the Middle East*. Glencoe, IL: Free Press.

Lévi-Strauss, Claude. 2016 [1949]. *The Elementary Structures of Kinship*. Boston: Beacon Press.

Lipset, David. 2014. Living Canoes: Vehicles of Moral Imagination among the Murik of Papua New Guinea. In *Vehicles: Cars, Canoes, and Other Metaphors of Moral Imagination*, edited by David Lipset and Richard Handler. New York: Berghahn Books. Pp. 21–47.

Louis, William Roger. 1978. *Imperialism at Bay: The United States and the Decolonization of the British Empire, 1941–1945*. New York: Oxford University Press.

Luckhurst, Roger. 2002. *The Invention of Telepathy*. Oxford: Oxford University Press.

Luhrmann, T. M. 2020. Thinking about Thinking: The Mind's Porosity and the Presence of the Gods. *Journal of the Royal Anthropological Institute* 26(S1): 148–62.

Lutz, Catherine, and Jane Lou Collins. 1993. *Reading National Geographic*. Chicago: University of Chicago Press.

Mackay, Ian. 1976. *Broadcasting in Papua New Guinea*. Melbourne: Melbourne University Press.

Maier, H. M. J. 1993. From Heteroglossia to Polyglossia: The Creation of Malay and Dutch in the Indies. *Indonesia* 56 (October): 37–65.

Malinowski, Bronislaw. 2002 [1922]. *Argonauts of the Western Pacific*. London: Routledge.

Manning, Paul. 2018. Spiritualist Signal and Theosophical Noise. *Journal of Linguistic Anthropology* 28(1): 67–92.

———. 2021. Spectral Aphasia, Psychical Ghost Stories, and Spirit Post Offices: Three Modern Ghost Stories about Communication Infrastructures. *Signs and Society* 9(2): 204–33.

Martin, Keir. 2021a. Introduction: Dependence in Oceania. *Oceania* 91(2): 139–64.

———. 2021b. Wars of Dependence: Contested History among Tolai People of Papua New Guinea. *Oceania* 91(2): 296–309.

Mattelart, Armand. 2000. *Networking the World, 1794–2000*. Translated by Liz Carey-Libbrecht and James A. Cohen. Minneapolis: University of Minnesota Press.

Matthews, Andrew. 2008. State Making, Knowledge, and Ignorance: Translation and Concealment in Mexican Forestry Institutions. *American Anthropologist* 110(4): 484–94.

Mauss, Marcel. 1990 [1925]. *The Gift: Form and Reasons of Exchange in Archaic Societies*. Translated by W. D. Halls. London: Routledge.

May, R. J., ed. 1982. *Micronationalist Movements in Papua New Guinea*. Canberra: Australian National University Press.

Mazower, Mark. 2009. *No Enchanted Palace: The End of Empire and the Ideological Origins of the United Nations*. Princeton, NJ: Princeton University Press.

Mazrui, Ali. 2004. *English in Africa: After the Cold War*. Clevedon, UK: Multilingual Matters.

Mazzarella, William. 2017. *The Mana of Mass Society*. Chicago: University of Chicago Press.

McDonald, Robert, ed. 1976. *Language and National Development: The Public Debate, 1976*. Occasional Paper no. 11. Port Moresby: Department of Language, University of Papua New Guinea.

McElhanon, K. A., ed. 1975. *Tok Pisin I Go We? Proceedings of a Conference Held at the University of Papua New Guinea, Port Moreaby, P.N.G., 18–21 September, 1973*. Port Moresby: Linguistic Society of Papua New Guinea.

Mead, Margaret. 1931. Talk-Boy. *Asia: Journal of the American Asiatic Association* (March): 144–51.

Meiser, Leo. 1945. *Dictionary of Pidgin English*. Madang, Papua New Guinea: Bishop Noser Library, Divine Word University.

Melville, Herman. 2014 [1855]. *Benito Cereno: Short Story*. New York: HarperCollins [e-book].

Merry, Sally Engle. 2011. Measuring the World: Indicators, Human Rights, and Global Governance. *Current Anthropology* 52(S3): S83–95.

Midena, Daniel. 2014. The Wonders of Conversion: Objectivity and Disenchantment in the Neuendettelsau Mission Encounter in New Guinea, 1886–1930. PhD dissertation, Københavns Universitet, Det Humanistiske Fakultet.

Mihalic, Francis. 1968. *The Jacaranda Dictionary and Grammar of Neo-Melanesian*. Brisbane, Australia: Jacaranda Press.

Moulton, William G. 1961. Linguistics and Language Teaching in the United States 1940–1960. In *Trends in European and American Linguistics 1930–1960*, edited by Christine Mohrmann, Alf Sommerfelt, and Joshua Whatmough. Utrecht, The Netherlands: Spectrum. Pp. 82–109.

Mrazek, Rudolf. 2002. *Engineers of Happy Land: Technology and Nationalism in a Colony*. Princeton, NJ: Princeton University Press.

Mufwene, Salikoko. 2020. Creoles and Pidgins: Why the Latter Are Not the Ancestors of the Former. In *The Routledge Handbook of Language Contact*, edited by Evangelia Adamou and Yaron Matras. London: Routledge. Pp. 300–24.

Mühlhäusler, Peter. 1974. *Pidginization and Simplification of Language*. Canberra: Pacific Linguistics, Australian National University.

———. 1978. Samoan Plantation Tok Pisin English and the Origin of New Guinea Tok Pisin. *Pacific Linguistics* A-54: 67–120.

Munn, Nancy. 1977. The Spatiotemporal Transformations of Gawa Canoes. *Journal de la Société des Océanistes* 33(54): 39–53.

———. 1986. *The Fame of Gawa: A Symbolic Study of Value Transformation in a Massim (Papua New Guinea) Society*. Durham, NC: Duke University Press.

Nakassis, Constantine. 2016. Linguistic Anthropology in 2015: Not the Study of Language. *American Anthropologist* 118(2): 330–45.

Nelson, Hank. 2007. Kokoda: And Two National Histories. *The Journal of Pacific History* 42(1): 73–88.

Nelson, Michael. 1997. *War of the Black Heavens: The Battles of Western Broadcasting in the Cold War*. Syracuse, NY: Syracuse University Press.

Niezen, Ronald, and Maria Sapignoli. 2017. Introduction. *Palaces of Hope: The Anthropology of Global Organizations*. Cambridge: Cambridge University Press. Pp. 1–30.

Nozawa, Shunsuke. 2015. Phatic Traces: Sociality in Contemporary Japan. *Anthropological Quarterly* 88(2): 373–400.

Oberhaus, Daniel. 2019. *Extraterrestrial Languages*. Cambridge, MA: MIT Press.

Ogborn, Miles. 2007. *Indian Ink: Script and Print in the Making of the English East India Company*. Chicago: University of Chicago Press.

Palmer, Scott W. 2006. *Dictatorship of the Air: Aviation Culture and the Fate of Modern Russia*. Cambridge: Cambridge University Press.

Palmié, Stephan. 2006. Creolization and Its Discontents. *Annual Review of Anthropology* 35: 433–456.

Pennycook, A. 2009. English and Globalization. In *The Routledge Companion to English Language Studies*, edited by Janet Maybin and Joan Swann. New York: Routledge. Pp. 125–33.

Peters, John Durham. 1999. *Speaking into the Air: A History of the Idea of Communication*. Chicago: University of Chicago Press.

Pham, Quynh N., and Robbie Shilliam, eds. 2016. *Meanings of Bandung: Postcolonial Orders and Decolonial Visions*. London: Rowan and Littlefield.

Rabie, Deina. 2022. Linguistic Infrastructures: Language and Gendered Mobilities in an Imminent Post-Oil United Arab Emirates. PhD dissertation, University of Texas at Austin.

Raman, Bhavani. 2012. *Document Raj: Writing and Scribes in Early Colonial South India*. Chicago: University of Chicago Press.

Reddy, Michael. 1979. The Conduit Metaphor—A Case of Frame Conflict in Our Language about Language. In *Metaphor and Thought*, edited by Andrew Ortony. Cambridge: Cambridge University Press. Pp. 284–324.

Reinecke, John E. 1937. Marginal Languages: A Sociological Study of Creole Languages and Trade Jargons. PhD dissertation, Yale University.

Richards, Thomas. 1993. *The Imperial Archive: Knowledge and the Fantasy of Empire*. London: Verso Books.

Riles, Analise. 2000. *The Network Inside Out*. Ann Arbor: University of Michigan Press.

Robbins, Joel. 1998. On Reading 'World News': Apocalyptic Narrative, Negative Nationalism and Transnational Christianity in a Papua New Guinea Society. *Social Analysis: The International Journal of Social and Cultural Practice* 42(2): 103–30.

Roberts, Helen. 1961. *Champion of the Silent Billion: The Story of Frank C. Laubach, Apostle of Literacy*. Austin, MN: Macalester Park.

Romaine, Suzanne. 2013. The Status of Tok Pisin in Papua New Guinea: The Colonial Predicament. In *Status Change of Languages*, edited by Ulrich Ammon and Marlis Hellinger. Berlin: De Gruyter. Pp. 229–52.

Rosa, Jonathan. 2019. *Looking Like a Language, Sounding Like a Race: Raciolinguistic Ideologies and the Learning of Latinidad*. Oxford: Oxford University Press.

Royal Anthropological Institute. 1951. *Notes and Queries on Anthropology*. Sixth edition. London: Routledge and Kegan Paul.

Rutherford, Danilyn. 2018. *Living in the Stone Age: Reflections on the Origins of a Colonial Fantasy*. Chicago: University of Chicago Press.

Rutledge, Archibald. 1938. *It Will Be Daybreak Soon*. New York: Fleming H. Revell.

Sankoff, Gillian. 1977. Multilingualism in Papua New Guinea. In *New Guinea Area Languages and Language Study, vol. 3: Language, Culture, Society, and the Modern World*, edited by Stephan Wurm. Canberra: Pacific Linguistics, Australian National University. Pp. 265–310.

Schieffelin, Bambi B. 2002. Marking Time: The Dichotomizing Discourse of Multiple Temporalities. *Current Anthropology* 43(S4): S5–17.

———. 2008. Tok Bokis, Tok Piksa: Translating Parables in Papua New Guinea. In *Social Lives in Language—Sociolinguistics and Multilingual Speech Communities, Celebrating the Work of Gillian Sankoff*, edited by Miriam Meyerhoff and Naomi Nagy. Amsterdam: John Benjamins. Pp. 111–34.

Schivelbusch, Wolfgang. 1980. *The Railway Journey: The Industrialization of Space and Time in the Nineteenth Century*. Berkeley: University of California Press.

Schram, Ryan. 2022. Independent Declarations: Attributions of Peoplehood in News Narratives. *Signs and Society* 10(3): 287–313.

———. 2023. "Sanguma em i stap" (Sanguma Is Real): Sorcery Stories and the Ethnographic Citizenship of Tok Pisin Print Journalism. *Current Anthropology* 64(1): 49–71.

Schwarz, Theodore, and Michael French Smith. 2021. *Like Fire: The Paliau Movement and Millenarianism in Melanesia*. Canberra: Australian National University Press.

Scott, David. 2004. *Conscripts of Modernity: The Tragedy of Colonial Enlightenment*. Durham, NC: Duke University Press.

Scott, James. 2009. *The Art of Not Being Governed: An Anarchist History of Upland Southeast Asia*. New Haven, CT: Yale University Press.

Scott, Julius S. 2018. *The Common Wind: Afro-American Currents in the Age of the Haitian Revolution*. London: Verso.

Sears, Mason. 1980. *Years of High Purpose: From Trusteeship to Nationhood*. Washington, DC: University Press of America.

Selisker, Scott. 2016. *Human Programming: Brainwashing, Automatons, and American Unfreedom*. Minneapolis: University of Minnesota Press.

Shilliam, Robbie. 2015. *The Black Pacific: Anti-Colonial Struggles and Oceanic Connections*. London: Bloomsbury.

Shulist, Sarah. 2018. *Transforming Indigeneity: Urbanization and Language Revitalization in the Brazilian Amazon*. Toronto: University of Toronto Press.

Siegel, James. 1997. *Fetish, Recognition, Revolution*. Princeton, NJ: Princeton University Press.

Silverman, Eric. 2013. After Cannibal Tours: Cargoism and Marginality in a Post-touristic Sepik River Society. *The Contemporary Pacific* 25(2): 221–57.

Silverstein, Michael. 2000. Whorfianism and the Linguistic Imagination of Nationality. In *Regimes of Language: Ideologies, Polities, and Identities*, edited by Paul V. Kroskrity. Santa Fe, NM: SAR Press. Pp. 85–138.

———. 2005. Axes of Evals. *Journal of Linguistic Anthropology* 15(1): 6–22.

———. 2013. Discourse and the No-thing-ness of Culture. *Signs and Society* 1(2): 327–66.

Silverstein, Michael, and Greg Urban. 1996. The Natural History of Discourse. In *Natural Histories of Discourse*, edited by Michael Silverstein and Greg Urban. Chicago: University of Chicago Press. Pp. 1–19.

Simmel, Georg. 1997. The Sociology of Space. In *Simmel on Culture*. Edited by David Frisby and Mike Featherstone. London: Sage Press.

Sinclair, James. 1978. *Wings of Gold: How the Aeroplane Developed New Guinea*. Sydney, Australia: Pacific Publications.

———. 1984. *Uniting a Nation: The Postal and Telecommunication Services of Papua New Guinea*. Goolwa, Australia: Crawford House Press.

Slotta, James. 2015. Phatic Rituals of the Liberal Democratic Polity: Hearing Voices in the Hearings of the Royal Commission on Aboriginal Peoples. *Comparative Studies in Society and History* 57(1): 130–60.

Slotta, James, and Courtney Handman. 2024. Language and Communicative Inequality in the Last Place on Earth. In *Language and Social Justice: Global Perspectives*, edited by Katherine C. Riley, Bernard C. Perley, and Inmaculada M. García Sánchez. New York: Bloomsbury Academic.

Smalls, Krystal. 2018. Fighting Words: Antiblackness and Discursive Violence in an American High School. *Journal of Linguistic Anthropology* 28(3): 356–83.

Smith, Adam. 1970 [1776]. *The Wealth of Nations*. Edited by Andrew Skinner. New York: Penguin Books.

Smith, Rachel. 2021. Declarations of 'Self-Reliance': Alternative Visions of Dependency, Citizenship and Development in Vanuatu. *Oceania* 91(2): 236–56.

Standage, Tom. 1998. *The Victorian Internet: The Remarkable Story of the Telegraph and the Nineteenth Century's On-Line Pioneers*. New York: Bloomsbury.

Stasch, Rupert. 2009. *Society of Others: Kinship and Mourning in a West Papuan Place*. Berkeley: University of California Press.

———. 2015. From Primitive Other to Papuan Self: Korowai Engagement with Ideologies of Unequal Human Worth in Encounters with Tourists, State Officials and Education. In *From 'Stone-Age' to 'Real-Time': Exploring Papuan Temporalities, Mobilities and Religiosities*, edited by Martin Slama and Jenny Munro. Canberra: Australian National University Press. Pp. 59–94.

———. 2019. Primitivist Tourism and Anthropological Research: Awkward Relations. *Journal of the Royal Anthropological Institute* 25(3): 526–45.

Stead, Victoria. 2017. Violent Histories and the Ambivalences of Recognition in Postcolonial Papua New Guinea. *Postcolonial Studies* 20(1): 68–85.

———. 2019. Money Trees, Development Dreams and Colonial Legacies in Contemporary Pasifika Horticultural Labour. In *Labour Lines and Colonial Power: Indigenous and Pacific Islander Labour Mobility in Australia*, edited by Victoria Stead and Jon Altman. Canberra: Australian National University Press. Pp. 133–58.

Stead, Victoria, and Jon Altman. 2019. Labour Lines and Colonial Power. In *Labour Lines and Colonial Power: Indigenous and Pacific Islander Labour Mobility in Australia*, edited by Victoria Stead and Jon Altman. Canberra: Australian National University Press. Pp. 1–26.

Steffek, Jens. 2021. *International Organization as Technocratic Utopia*. Oxford: Oxford University Press.

Stella, Regis Tove. 2007. *Imagining the Other: The Representation of the Papua New Guinean Subject*. Honolulu: University of Hawai'i Press.

Stoker, Bram. 2018 [1897]. *Dracula*. New York: Simon & Schuster.

Strathern, Andrew. 1971. *The Rope of Moka: Big Men and Ceremonial Exchange in Mount Hagen, New Guinea*. Cambridge: Cambridge University Press.

———. 1975. Veiled Speech in Mt. Hagen. In *Political Language and Oratory in Traditional Society*, edited by Maurice Bloch. New York: Academic Press. Pp. 185–204.

Strathern, Marilyn. 1988. *The Gender of the Gift: Problems with Women and Problems with Society in Melanesia*. Berkeley: University of California Press.

Swadling, Pamela. 1996. *Plumes from Paradise: Trade Cycles in Outer Southeast Asia and their Impact on New Guinea and Nearby Islands until 1920*. Port Moresby: Papua New Guinea National Museum.

Swan, Quito. 2018. Blinded by Bandung? Illumining West Papua, Senegal, and the Black Pacific. *Radical History Review* 131: 58–81.

———. 2020. *Pauulu's Diaspora: Black Internationalism and Environmental Justice*. Tallahassee: University Press of Florida.

Taylor, Charles. 2007. *A Secular Age*. Cambridge, MA: Belknap Press of Harvard University Press.

Taylor, Rebe. 2016. The First Stone and the Last Tasmanian: The Colonial Correspondence of Edward Burnett Tylor and Henry Ling Roth. *Oceania* 86(3): 320–43.

Thompson, E. P. 1974. Patrician Society, Plebeian Culture. *Journal of Social History* 7(4): 382–405.

Tomasetti, W. E. 1970. *Australia and the United Nations: New Guinea Trusteeship Issues from 1946 to 1966*. Canberra and Boroko: New Guinea Research Unit.

Tomlinson, Matt. 2019. How to Speak Like a Spirit Medium: Voice and Evidence in Australian Spiritualism. *American Ethnologist* 46(4): 482–94.

———. 2024. *Speaking with the Dead: An Ethnography of Extrahuman Experience*. Santa Barbara, CA: Punctum Books.

Trentmann, Frank. 2007. After the Nation-State: Citizenship, Empire and Global Coordination in the New Internationalism, 1914–1930. In *Beyond Sovereignty: Britain, Empire and Transnationalism, c. 1880–1950*, edited by Kevin Grant, Philippa Levine, and Frank Trentmann. London: Palgrave Macmillan. Pp. 34–53.

Tuzin, Donald. 1997. *The Cassowary's Revenge: The Life and Death of Masculinity in a New Guinea Society*. Chicago: University of Chicago Press.

UNESCO. 1953. *The Use of Vernacular Languages in Education*. Paris: UNESCO.

United Nations. 1952. *The Story of Aman and the United Nations*. New York: United Nations.

Urry, John. 2007. *Mobilities*. Cambridge: Polity Press.

Velminski, Wladimir. 2017. *Homo Sovieticus: Brain Waves, Mind Control, and Telepathic Destiny*. Cambridge, MA: MIT Press.

Vicedom, George F. 1961. *Church and People in New Guinea*. London: United Society for Christian Literature.

wa Thiong'o, Ngũgĩ. 1986. *Decolonising the Mind: The Politics of Language in African Literature*. Nairobi, Kenya: James Curry.

Wagner, Herwig. 1986. Beginnings at Finschhafen. In *The Lutheran Church of Papua New Guinea: The First Hundred Years, 1886–1986*, edited by Herwig Wagner and Hermann Reiner. Adelaide, Australia: Lutheran Publishing House. Pp. 31–83.

Wagner, Herwig, and Hermann Reiner, eds. 1986. *The Lutheran Church in Papua New Guinea: The First Hundred Years, 1886–1986*. Adelaide, Australia: Lutheran Publishing House.

Waiko, John. 1993. *A Short History of Papua New Guinea*. Melbourne, Australia: Oxford University Press.

Wardlow, Holly. 2006. *Wayward Women: Sexuality and Agency in a New Guinea Society*. Berkeley: University of California Press.

Warner, Michael. 2022. Publics and Counterpublics. *Public Culture* 14(1): 49–90.

Warner, Tobias. 2019. *The Tongue-Tied Imagination: Decolonizing Literary Modernity in Senegal*. New York: Fordham University Press.

Waters, Christopher. 2013. 'Against the Tide': Australian Government Attitudes to Decolonisation in the South Pacific, 1962–1972. *The Journal of Pacific History* 48(2): 194–208.

———. 2016. The Last of Australian Imperial Dreams for the Southwest Pacific: Paul Hasluck, the Department of Territories and a Greater Melanesia in 1960. *The Journal of Pacific History* 51(2): 169–85.

Weber, Max. 1978. Bureaucracy. In *Economy and Society, vol. 2*. Edited by Guenther Roth and Claus Wittich. Berkeley: University of California Press. Pp. 956–1005.

Wedgwood, Camilla. 1953. The Problem of 'Pidgin' in the Trust Territory of New Guinea. In *The Use of Vernacular Languages in Education*. Paris: UNESCO. Pp. 103–15.

Whitaker, Mark. 2004. Tamilnet.com: Some Reflections on Popular Anthropology, Nationalism, and the Internet. *Anthropological Quarterly* 77(3): 469–98.

White, Luise. 2000. *Speaking with Vampires: Rumor and History in Colonial Africa*. Berkeley: University of California Press.

Wilder, Gary. 2009. Untimely Vision: Amié Césaire, Decolonisation, Utopia. *Public Culture* 21(1): 101–40.

Williams, Alan, ed. 2002. *Film and Nationalism*. New Brunswick, NJ: Rutgers University Press.

Williams, F. E. 1936. The Language Problem in Papuan Education. Mimeo paper prepared for the Seminar Conference on Education in Pacific Countries, Honolulu, Hawai'i.

Winter, Christine. 2012. *Looking after One's Own: The Rise of Nationalism and the Politics of the Neuendettelsauer Mission in Australia, New Guinea and Germany (1921–1933)*. Bern, Switzerland: Peter Lang.

Woolard, Kathryn. 1989. *Double Talk: Bilingualism and the Politics of Ethnicity in Catalonia*. Stanford, CA: Stanford University Press.

Worsley, Peter. 1957. *A Trumpet Shall Sound: A Study of "Cargo" Cults in Melanesia*. London: MacGibbon and Kee.

Wu, Ming-Jen. 2024. From Colonial Order to Decolonial Future: Colonial Neglect, Proximate Violence, and Mimesis among the Papua Besena Movement. *Oceania* 94(2): 88–102.

Wyndham, John. 2020 [1955]. *The Chrysalids*. New York: The New York Review of Books.

Yates, JoAnne. 1993. *Control through Communication: The Rise of System in American Management*. Baltimore: Johns Hopkins University Press.

Yeh, Rihan. 2017. La Racha: Speed and Violence in Tijuana. *Signs and Society* 5(S1): S53–76.

Zuckerman, Charles. 2016. Phatic Violence? Gambling and the Arts of Distraction in Laos. *Journal of Linguistic Anthropology* 26(3): 294–314.

INDEX

Founded in 1893,
UNIVERSITY OF CALIFORNIA PRESS
publishes bold, progressive books and journals
on topics in the arts, humanities, social sciences,
and natural sciences—with a focus on social
justice issues—that inspire thought and action
among readers worldwide.

The UC PRESS FOUNDATION
raises funds to uphold the press's vital role
as an independent, nonprofit publisher, and
receives philanthropic support from a wide
range of individuals and institutions—and from
committed readers like you. To learn more, visit
ucpress.edu/supportus.

9 780520 416000